Caribbean Passagemaking

Caribbean Passagemaking

A Cruiser's Guide

Second Edition

Les Weatheritt

SHERIDAN HOUSE

This book is dedicated to Gloria.

This edition published 2011 by
Sheridan House Inc.
145 Palisade Street
Dobbs Ferry, NY10522
www.sheridanhouse.com

First edition published 2004
Copyright © 2004, 2011 by Les Weatheritt
All photos have been provided by the author unless otherwise stated.

Library of Congress Cataloging-in-Publication Data

Weatheritt, Les.
 Caribbean passagemaking : a cruiser's guide / Les Weatheritt. — 2nd ed.
   p. cm.
 Includes index.
 ISBN 978-1-57409-308-7
 1. Sailing—Caribbean Area. 2. Caribbean Area—Description and travel. I. Title.
 GV817.C37W43 2011
 917.29—dc23
                                                          2011020048

Printed in the United States of America

Contents

CONTENTS

CONTENTS

Foreword

A lot has changed in the Caribbean since I wrote the first edition during 2004 and even more since I first sailed here as a schooner deckhand in 1969. Some things are for the better, improving life for the people of the islands and us sailors who visit here. Even old curmudgeons who don't always welcome change will admit that the essence of the Caribbean chain remains the same and the natural attraction for sailors remains as strong as ever.

> 'I would like to believe that nature had the sailor man in mind when she created the Lesser Antilles. She had decided to reserve one section of the seas that would be the perfect sailing ground . . . strong and steady breezes . . . plenty of sunshine . . . a line of islands not too far from one another.'
>
> Dennis Puleston, *Blue Water Vagabond*, 1939

The wonderful Trade Winds still provide the best sailing imaginable. The Caribbean Sea remains as turquoise blue to the eye and as silky soft to the swimmer's skin. The weather and the people remain as warm and welcoming. The islands are still places where you will find a multitude of stunning anchorages. None of this has changed and, to be sure, my prime harbors and sailing strategies remain as essential as ever to your cruising comfort and enjoyment.

This new edition points to three major changes in the region:

There has been much "progress" in yachting facilities, especially in the minds of those involved in the tourism industry. Even I, if I try hard enough, can see up-sides to progress. There are many more marinas, usually because of expanding charter fleets and an increase in mega yachts, making it easier for sailors to take on water, re-charge their batteries, run their shore-powered devices or just feel more relaxed about leaving the boat to go exploring for a day or two. Yacht tourism has greater official recognition for its contribution to the local economy and as a result we feel more welcome.

Customs and Immigration officials are under instructions to be more human and friendly. The traditional front line tourist services such as boat boys have greater recognition for the valuable service they provide, and go from strength to strength on our behalf. A more organized approach, such as in the Grenadines, brings greater income into these small deserving communities and a greater air of tidiness on the streets, both of which I like.

The weather is changing, especially outside the main sailing season as hurricanes seem both more frequent and potentially more devastating. This has the potential to be truly a life and death matter. I have provided more background on the forces underlying the weather and the sources of weather information. El Niño and La Niña should become everyday events in our sailing calendars. And I have expanded my critique of the facilities for yachts.

There is more crime and there is fear of rising crime. The Caribbean islands are not immune from this and I would be irresponsible not to discuss such a burning issue and try to put it in perspective. I have used this new edition to bring together more data and thoughts about crime across the region and crime on particular islands as well as piracy at sea. In February 2011 when we were last in Trinidad (headlines: Crime capital of the Caribbean) we heard lots of stories about the crime wave and we took great care not to be in the wrong places at the wrong time, but joggers still ran around the Savannah, people still strolled between down-town bars and restaurants at night, the crime seemed to focus on local youths and drug gangs rather than yachts and yachties, and I never met anyone I felt afraid of. So does my personal experience contradict common knowledge and what should I make of it? Go carefully, as you would wherever you go. Listen carefully to what people say. In the end decide for yourself if they are giving you good advice from personal experience or hyping up an already over-dramatized story.

There is no turning back the clock and nor should we want to. I wasn't blind to the faults of the region when I sailed here in 1969. And when I sailed here in my own yacht in the years after 1995 I could easily be provoked into massive (if witty) grumbles. Goodness me, I even thought I heard myself complaining this year in Trinidad. But I have never ever failed to recognize the superlative sailing of the Caribbean chain, especially when I'm sailing elsewhere, and I hope you will step up and unlock its many joys with the help of this book.

Of course it is already too late to experience the Caribbean of years ago. Life moves on, even in the slowest islands of the Grenadines. To experience the Caribbean as it is today, get down here now. Tomorrow is already on its way.

Fair winds,

Les Weatheritt
Trinidad, February 2011

Introduction

Pinch yourself

You wake up, but the dream continues. Fifteen knots of wind across the foredeck, and a cooling breeze over the cockpit. Deep blue seas and flying fish. Wispy lines of high cirrus to highlight the blue sky and brilliant sunlight. The hull lifts its shoulder to a sweet passing sea. Away ahead is the tall cloud-capped outline of the next island to visit while still clear behind you is the detailed landscape of the island you left earlier this morning. The sea, when it can be bothered to get off its waves, reaches you as a welcome warm spray. The wet weather gear is now firmly at the bottom of your locker. The crew sunbathing on the foredeck glances up. "Dolphin." Minutes later a school of fifty or more dash in on your starboard beam and begin to ride your bow-wave, taking the pole position in turns and rolling up to look at you looking down at them. Intelligent life, each in their element, the one studying the other. The dolphin, master of the water. The yacht gliding swiftly over the surface of the sea. Pinch yourself. Year after year, more sailors cruise in the Caribbean in just such conditions.

Columbus and me

Sailing lets you see the most wonderful places in the most fulfilling way. Of the seas I've sailed I rate the Caribbean as the most beautiful and fulfilling for a cruising yacht. In this respect I am in full agreement with Christopher Columbus, Admiral of the Seas, about how strange and beautiful the region is to those from the higher latitudes of Europe or America.

> "The small birds and the greeness of the fields make me want to stay forever. This country is so enchantingly beautiful that it surpasses all others in charm and beauty as much as the light of day surpasses night."
>
> Christopher Columbus, letter to the Spanish sovereigns Ferdinand and Isabella, on the first voyage of discovery 1492–93

Now, after eight years or so of spending each winter cruising the islands between Trinidad in the south and the Virgins in the north, I have visited every island in what I think of as the Caribbean Chain. Some I have visited many times. All were visited in the most recent of my cruises. No matter how often I have been there, each visit brings me something new. Every year always turns out to be different from any of the others.

Of the many lessons I have learned here one stands above all others: you can do your cruising the hard way by sticking to last year's plan or some other stubborn attitude that takes no account of the variations in the wind and currents here; or you can work with the grain of the conditions and have fun all the way. A second, less attractive lesson I have learned, is what can seem like an enduring strength of human nature: that so many experienced skippers are willing to hoist all sail and sheet right in to a straight repeat of their previous uncomfortable passages and still claim to enjoy sailing. The dominating characteristics of the Caribbean, the steady winds and currents and the allure of blue skies and warm seas, almost invite us to do just that. Almost, but not quite. This book will help you cruise the hard way or go more comfortably with the grain, but mainly the latter. I mean, I've got nothing against masochistic sailors as long as they don't expect me to come along willingly with them.

Hitting the harmonic beat

Tropical weather patterns are quite different from those in higher latitudes and there is much to gain from some understanding of how wind and current arise here and how they inter-relate.

Sailors fresh from temperate latitudes can find it hard to adjust to the regularity of the Trades and the predominantly one way flow of the current, and take a while to appreciate their strength, but sailing here is not such fun if you chose to sail against the conditions. Friends from Europe and North America come with glossy brochure expectations of gentle zephyrs and catspaws over azure seas. They are surprised by the steady strength of the Trade Winds and the punch of the never-ending rolling waves in the Leewards and Windwards. Of course, like any good skipper, I will always take the boat across or down wind to give my friends a magical, joyous sail but sometimes my plan misses the harmonic beat and we get very wet and bounced for twice as long as we all want. Sometimes we end up hove-to or standing off-and-on the end of an island waiting for dawn to light our way in. And if you think that sounds bad wait till the passage plan really hits bottom. When you don't get anywhere near your intended destination and struggle to make it back to your starting point, two days later. You don't have to suffer like this. No one should.

We were in Prickly Bay, Grenada, heading to Trinidad to haul-out. The strong southerly subsided and the seas outside looked flatter, we went. The wind was still southerly but forecast to shift to the east and give us the angle we wanted. At first we sailed slightly off the wind because

Protected from the sea and the swell but still catching a cooling breeze across her decks, *Petronella* is anchored behind the Fort Burt reef in Road Harbour, Tortola. *Photo: G. Jardine.*

we wanted an easy ride over the lumpy seas on Grenada's long shoaling tail. Then night fell and we continued slightly off the wind to reduce slamming and get some sleep. By morning, without the wind shift to the east, we had to sheet in hard but no matter how tight our sheets or how high we pointed, the magic carpet of the Equatorial Current had us in its west-running grip. We couldn't make Trinidad. Without a wind shift we would end up forty miles west, on the coast of Venezuela. Forty miles to motor dead against the wind and current to reach Trinidad. We turned back to Grenada to start again when the wind shifted. "Let's enjoy the night sail," G said. By the time we re-anchored in Prickly Bay we had taken two days to get nowhere, but the sailing was wonderful and so was the forecast for tomorrow. That's just the way it is sometimes.

The steady Trade Winds and the southeast Equatorial Current that prevail over the whole region are not without variation. They are not the same strength and direction from week to week, year to year or season to season. They are not the same throughout the region. The north, in the Virgins, is most susceptible to winter storms coming off the U.S. The south, in Trinidad, is less often hit by a summer hurricane. And then there are local effects, created by the islands themselves, disturbing the wind and the current. On top of all of this add the non-seasonal but recurring forces, such as El Niño (see Chapter 4), and the possible shifts in climate such as global warming, both of which probably produce their main effect in the hurricane season. Sailing conditions here, especially in the Virgin Islands, may not be hard when compared to winter gales in the north Atlantic or running down the Roaring Forties but they can put you and your vessel to the test. Taking the hard beat to windward does not mean that you will enjoy the experience any more than you did the last time. Working with these variations gives an all important, extra dimension to more comfortable sailing in the Caribbean Sea.

A dozen of us cleared out of Customs and Immigration that morning and shifted our anchorage from Chaguaramas to Scotland Bay, the first step in heading north out of Trinidad. We were all heading to Grenada. We had all heard the same forecast for a wind shift to the south. Over the next three days each boat chose its own time of leaving and over the next four to five weeks I met them all again to ask how good their trip had been. My curiosity was aroused. Eleven of the twelve got their timing wrong, including us. We all sailed with too much north in the wind or too much westerly current and we all, to varying degrees, got set to the west of Grenada. Some skippers accepted this and sailed on to Martinique or even Antigua. Some fought nature every inch and motorsailed the whole way. These journeys from Trinidad to Grenada varied from 15 to 36 hours. Only the German couple on *Water Music* got it exactly right. They waited till the forecaster said the wind was from the southeast and then they waited another 12 hours for the seas to turn with the new wind. Their beam reach took them east of their rhumb line to Prickly Bay, Grenada, and then as the Trade Wind shifted back to east-northeast their beam reach took them right into the anchorage. Fifteen wonderfully short hours with the wind and waves on the beam. It wasn't luck. Only this one boat in twelve had a clear, confident grasp of the weather.

You can leave the PhD in weather and climatology till later but to get the most fun from your sailing you must choose an appropriate strategy to cope with differences from the expected or hoped for conditions. What you should avoid is mental and planning inertia. The worst strategy, I can honestly tell you, is to plug on as though this year's wind is the same as last year's, even though your trip from Martinique to Guadeloupe has proved the opposite and you spent two days in port drying the bedding.

The enchanted chain

The great joy of the Caribbean is that the island chain seems to have been laid out to help rather than hinder the well-planned cruise.

First, these islands, like the backbone of a skeleton (as indeed they are, in a volcanic sense), lie close enough together to make most passages possible in daylight and, at worst, only one night at sea. Personally, I am much assured at seeing my destination before I have barely set off.

Second, they are all set in the same weather system, more or less. Sure, there are life-threatening weather events here which I will discuss later, but the point is that once you have understood how the relatively benign prevailing winds and current affect your sailing close to one island, and how an island generates local variations in these prevailing conditions, you have the basis to predict conditions for any other island. This, of course, is only true up to a point but it is a point that can be stretched a good way to help you approach a new island on your passagemaking. I love these short cuts to learning by experience.

Third, the prevailing winds and currents tend to go across the track of the islands rather than directly up or down. This gives the tricksy navigator a chance to minimize the time when the Force Six is dead on the nose. Sailing with the wind on the nose is hard work even where seas are warm. Boats travel fast in the typically strong Trade Wind breeze and when they rise up the two-meter swell to encounter the one-meter wave on top of it, the hit is hard. Spray flies back into the cockpit. Life below becomes noisy and uncomfortable. The curve of the island chain at Martinique means that on any passage up or down the islands there will be a period when sailing either north or south is hard work, followed by a period when the other arc of the curve makes sailing blissfully smooth and fast. The stuff that dreams are made of, when the sails set broad but full, the rush of water against hull soothes even the recalcitrant watch below, and the beam seas barely ruffle the rum in the punch.

And on the subject of the tricksy navigators, they just may be able to master sailing in the lee of some of these high islands. Most of us will resort to the engine on passages up the lee of an island but when exploring and day sailing for fun you can often find a sailing breeze right close in to the land.

> I learned a lesson as I bashed north into the seas off the leeside of Tobago. A little cutter was slipping along close in under sail so I headed in to see what they had found. A little breeze, coming and going but definitely there, let me sail north. The instant I went too far offshore the breeze died. I short tacked within its range. The view so close in was stunning.

Fourth, the tropics are good places to be when the alternative is a northern winter. G tells me she loves the four seasons of England and missed them after years of only the wet and dry of Trinidad. On the other hand, she hates the cold of an early English autumn and becomes quite churlish in the petrifying days of winter. The Caribbean sailing season is wonderfully arranged to correspond with the northern winter. The dangerous summer period of hurricanes can be spent somewhere else.

> Cruisers leaving Trinidad in the winter months of the dry season often get extra time to play Carnival as they wait for a wind shift to give them an easier ride to Grenada. This is the time when TV shows huge bad winter storms hammering North America, when freezing and unfreezing rivers across the Midwest and Eastern Seaboard flood thousands of homes with ice-cold muddy water. We had stayed a few more days. We were playing mas', as the local Trinis say. We chipped along at J'Ouvert, limein' with an American from a nearby mooring. She said she never intended to spend another winter in Massachusetts. Me neither.

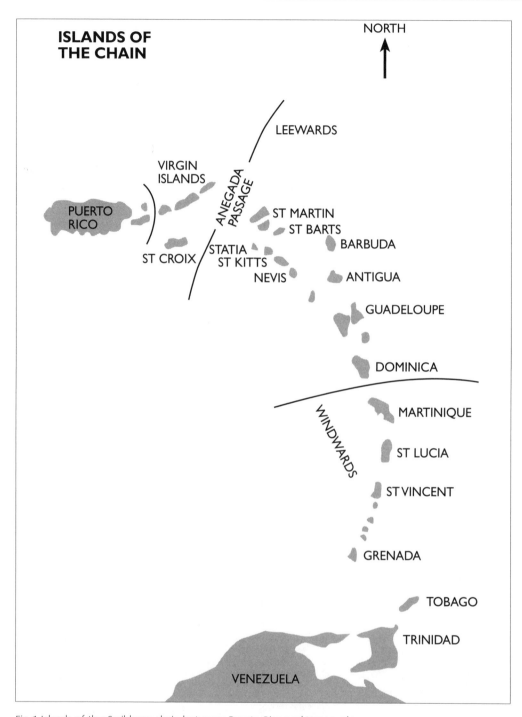

Fig 1 Islands of the Caribbean chain between Puerto Rico and Venezuela.

Fifth, if all this isn't enough to convince you, try sailing the Virgins. This is such a different experience from the Windwards and Leewards that it is almost not the Caribbean. It is a demonstration of how the Caribbean would be if the scale of the Windwards and Leewards were reduced by a factor of ten. You get a different pleasure here. You apply a completely different sailing logic.

Into the Virgins

In my mind's eye the Caribbean chain has two definite parts. The Virgins in the north and everything else to the south. This is because there are so many reasons for the Virgins to seem like a distinct sailing ground in their own right, breaking the logic of sailing in the Leewards and Windwards but still demanding a new simplifying logic of their own.

The United States Virgin Islands (USVI) and the British Virgin Islands (BVI) are a compact group of generally mountainous small islands interlaced with offshore rocks, islets and reefs all sitting on their own shallow shelf, the long underwater tail of Puerto Rico which extends about eighty miles eastwards. At their western end they are separated from the Spanish isles of Vieques and Culebra by the Virgin Passage. The USVI and BVI chain runs continuously east of this for about 45 miles, stopping at Anegada and the Horseshoe Reef where the depths rapidly drop away from the 20 to 30 fathoms typical of the Virgin Banks to the one thousand or so fathoms of the ocean.

The USVI and BVI are like a magical drowned country, where only hills and peaks still show above the water and sailing boats travel through sunken mountain valleys. On its eastern side the shallow Virgin Banks are guarded by reefs and banks where the seas may break heavily most of the year but on the other sides the bank is accessed by good wide channels. Swell from the ocean and the Caribbean Sea may run in these channels but once on the Bank a sailboat can usually travel in great comfort. The islands and reefs offer protection from the swell and the waves without doing much to slow down the breeze.

It was like entering an enchanted world, that first time we came to the Virgins after years cutting our teeth in the southern Caribbean. We had been three days and nights on passage from Martinique via Nevis with barely a handful of boats in sight at even the busiest times. Now we saw against the amphitheater of low hills a crowd of white sails beating and tacking in all directions, carrying on the social intercourse of the Virgins. We sailed slowly through Salt Island Channel and turned into Deadman's Bay on Peter Island. We tucked up close to the silvery beach. The incessant rolling of the Caribbean Sea stopped. We dropped anchor in five meters of crystal clear water. A cooling breeze came over the land. Surf beat on the rocks in the channel but it couldn't reach us here. As darkness fell and lights came on the islands seemed to merge into a single mass of land and we felt as though we had anchored in a land-locked lake.

North Americans have an advantage over Europeans in that they really don't have much choice about visiting the Virgins. It's part of their route down from the eastern seaboard. Europeans and others who come into the Caribbean somewhere down the island chain have to make a choice to come here, unless they are heading to the States. For them, the position of the Virgins to the west of the island chain means that a trip here may be followed by a hard beat back. But it would be a grave mistake on their part to make the choice not to visit the Virgins.

We nearly didn't come to the Virgins. It was always at the back end of our trips to the northern Leewards. What had the Virgins to offer to make the return journey worthwhile? We had heard about their greater levels of development, about the vast charter fleets, the huge marinas and the high cost of living.

When we finally made our first visit we realized that the Virgins can rejuvenate even the most jaded of sailors. We sailed everywhere in a kind of trance, loving so much of what we experienced, marvelling at what we had been missing from the rest of the Caribbean. If the Great Architect of Sailing were asked to nominate a Masterwork, this would be it. The glossy brochures that tell lies about most Paradises can be believed here. Here were bits of land arranged to protect us from the rolling Caribbean Sea, give us pleasant anchorages whatever the conditions and yet provide us with pilotage challenges to suit all levels of competence. After years of sailing the Leewards and Windwards the Virgins were like going on a sailing holiday.

We have only sailed in the Virgins in the low season, when we have been surprised by how empty much of the area is. In places such as The Baths on Virgin Gorda, and the very popular anchorages such as Hawknest Bay on St John, we had a glimpse of what the high season could be like. Busy. All my recommendations to go to the Virgins are contingent on you going out of the main charter season.

Leeward and Windward

American sailors will need to take a deep breath and gird up their loins before they can force themselves to quit this Virgin paradise and sail east and south into the bigger islands and longer passages of the southern Caribbean. But sail south you must. How sad it would be if a yacht entered the island chain at the Virgins and never experienced the thrill of real open-water voyages as the distance between islands increases. It would be nearly as bad as European sailors making their first landfall on St Lucia or Antigua and only sailing north from there as they scurried back home.

Not to sail south would be to miss out on the culturally distinct and more independent islands in the center of the chain, on the out-of-the-way anchorages still to be found there, and the stunning land and sea scenery of Tobago Cays and the Grenadines. Even worse, imagine a boat making it as far south as Grenada and then being put off going to Trinidad by the night sail or being put off Tobago by the up-current bash. Not to go south to Trinidad and Tobago is to do yourself out of some of the finest experiences of the Caribbean—sailing, cultural, scenic and yacht repairs (if the latter takes as much of your time as it does of mine!). Tobago—the true jewel of the Caribbean, with the best sailing and the friendliest people. Trinidad—most cosmopolitan, exciting and culturally innovative of the islands, the foremost party island of the whole region, not just at Carnival time but the whole year round. Both have some of the best natural walks and eco-tours of the whole Caribbean.

A sailor who has made it to any part of the Caribbean must take a trip all the way through the island chain.

Getting the best out of sailing in the Leewards and Windwards needs more planning than sailing in the Virgins. It's true that with luck even a rank amateur can get a good break on a badly planned journey, especially if the wind goes more into the east, and that in a bad year the crew of an experienced skipper can find themselves slamming to each island in turn and even then having to motor-sail the last ten miles into wind and current. In one year a cruising yacht sailing north might manage to make each island in turn spot on, close-hauled perhaps but without having to make a single tack. And in another year the only way to visit all the islands in comfort will be to sail all the way north in a single shot then island hop southwards in the kinder winds.

In my first season I had beginner's luck. I island-hopped north from Trinidad, even managing to get to windward of some of the islands so that I could make my approach with the wind free and the boat lifted by the perennial current. In my second season I tried to do the same and met stronger winds with more north in them, had to wear oilskins and suffer the ignominy of being miles to the west of my intended destinations. But the Caribbean is a forgiving sea and even skippers determined to misuse the elements get a second chance. It's the curve in the chain which makes the difference. Half way up the island chain the arc shifts. You move from the southern islands running northeast to southwest to the northern islands running northwest to southeast and this little bit more freedom on the wind makes life so much easier for boats sailing north that it comes like the most precious of gifts from the gods. Making use of this is an essential part of your sailing strategy.

Sail with a bad strategy and the local factors of island topography (and bottom-ography too) will make matters worse. The steady Equatorial Current changes considerably when it bumps against an island. At some point on the windward (Atlantic) side of the island the south east to north west flow divides at a sort of watershed to produce a north running stream and a south running stream. As a consequence, the currents off the ends of the islands are accelerated. A boat already being pushed to leeward on its passage between islands will meet one of these enhanced currents when making the last beat into land. The navigator should allow for this early in the day rather than watch in embarrassment as the boat falls massively off to the west at the end of what once looked to be a perfect landfall.

A boat sailing north with a lot of east in the Trade Wind may be lulled into attempting to sail up the windward side of the next island. I mean, why not keep the good sailing breeze rather than have to motor through the calms on the leeward side. Well, one reason is that watershed. The switch from the Equatorial Current to the local south-running current can almost stop you dead over the ground on a lee shore until you regain the northbound current after the watershed. A boat sailing south may come down the windward side with more equanimity. Their little problem will be that if they do not make allowance for the stronger push of current as they close the next island they will cover a lot of extra ground in a wide parabolic arc to hit the moving target of their landfall.

Greater cruising comfort (mental and physical) also comes from working with the local wind effects. There are diurnal changes in wind strengths, for example, and acceleration effects as wind meets land. Chapter 4 sets out the main ones affecting you.

An important consequence of these variations in wind and current is on the time passages take between islands in the Leewards and Windwards. I don't just mean an extra couple of hours which turns an eight-hour trip into ten. I mean whether you can make the journey in daylight or have to make a night passage or night arrival. Some anchorages are very much easier to approach in the dark than others but even the easy ones can catch you out if navigation lights aren't working or an offshore wind gets up or there is an invisible line of fishing floats to cross. Never rely on Caribbean navigation lights to be working. Remember that the best advice on entering a strange harbor at night is "Don't." Always stay out even if others, me included, have entered in the dark. The Caribbean is changing so rapidly that even last year's pilot may not show the new addition to a breakwater, or that the vital entry lights are still on the old bit of it.

> Coming north to Bequia from Carriacou or Union I always try for a full daylight passage. I've never managed it yet so I suppose that a night entry into Bequia is within the scope of most skippers cruising their own boat around the islands. I prefer daylight because the channel between Union and Palm Island and the navigation around Mayreau is (1) so pretty that I always want to see it and (2) too reef-infested to make for fun in the dark. The wind usually allows a boat to beat around Union Island's barrier reef then ghost to Mayreau close in to the southern bay. But then you must locate that insignificant little buoy marking the dangerous sunken reef off the northern headland of that bay. From here the breaking water off Catholic Island's low-lying rocks are visible. Take care. The current will push you west onto these rocks. Don't leave the tack too late. The current can sweep you into a *cul de sac*, leaving you with reef on either side and reef to leeward and short sloppy seas that kill the tack when you try to bring her head through the wind.

My first night approach to Bequia was also my first visit to the island. Admiralty Bay has a good wide entrance which helps a novice skipper but that evening I had a double helping of beginner's luck. First, I was north of West Cay, the outer end of the long rocky peninsular of Bequia's southern side, before dark and able to get a good sight and bearings on some landmarks through my binoculars. Second, as I closed the entrance to the bay another yacht motored up from the south and went in ahead of me, giving me his stern light to follow. Perhaps the next time I come to Bequia from the south I will plan a different route, coming round the west side of Union at night or starting from Chatham Bay, to leave the Catholic rocks and the Grenadine reefs well to the east and make Bequia in daylight. Just because I've done this entry in the dark doesn't mean I enjoyed the experience or would recommend it to anyone. The times I've entered Bequia in daylight have all been from the north and usually involved a night sail down the

The main charter marina's in Road Town, Tortola. *Photo: Courtesy of BVI Tourist Authority.*

coast of St Vincent. Since I have reservations about the anchorages of St Vincent, sailing by in the night is no great hardship for me.

A simple passage plan

This book is essentially about passage-planning and concerns itself with things that most directly affect sailing. However, it is also about bringing delight to your sailing here. And there is much to find delight in. I have found that the more I know about the land and culture the more I enjoy the bits between the sailing. What I know of the land is what sailors either most need to know or are most likely to learn, rather than the deep history of the islands, the full socio-economic accounts you might get from an academic textbook or even the hedonistic list of pleasures you might get from a good commercial tourist guide. Turn to these later, when the islands have taken their grip on you.

When exploring the Caribbean Sea you will enjoy the details and complexity, the cosmopolitan centers and the remote places of this group of islands. There is great history here, with cultural and architectural similarities and differences juxtaposed:

- There are eleven different national states in the 600 or so mile-long Caribbean chain with its twenty or so major islands
- There are countless number of rocks and reefs to be visited and used as anchorages

- There are more anchorages than I could name or shake a stick at
- There are three main European languages, probably three derived languages (Creole, Patois and Papiamento, the heavily African influenced versions of European languages) and several others surviving in immigrant communities
- There are four official currencies - two local, one European and the U.S. dollar

For passagemaking you can do away with these complexities and simplify to basics. I can travel the island chain using:
- one language
- one currency
- twenty prime harbors
- and a modicum of weather forecasting.

This passage planner starts at the northern end of the Caribbean chain and heads south. Don't take this to mean that I prefer the northern end of the chain. Quite the reverse, and it is one of my main aims in this book to encourage yachts to make the journey south and not miss a single one of these enchanted isles.

1

Coming to terms

What is this place they call the Caribbean?

Some terms will help you know where you are, geographically and culturally. The islands covered in this book are all in the Lesser Antilles, although not all the islands of the Lesser Antilles will be covered in this book. The Antilles are named from the legendary island of Antilia believed to lie between Europe and Asia. The Lesser Antilles—known prettily as the "Caribbee Islands" in the 17th century, after the Carib Indians found there—are simply those smaller islands not known as the Greater Antilles. The Greater Antilles are located around and include the very much larger islands, usually last ruled by Spain, at the northern end of the Caribbean Sea: Cuba, Jamaica, Hispaniola, Puerto Rico.

Columbus, in his four voyages from 1492 to 1504, and the Spanish Conquistadores touched on nearly all the islands in the Lesser Antilles, and Spain set up governments in most of them, but the Spanish were mainly interested in the bigger islands to the north. It was the other European powers of the time—Britain, France, The Netherlands and to a lesser extent Sweden and Denmark—who came to control the island chain in the last period of imperialism, before local control.

The United States was the covert Great Power of the region long before the 1890s and the Spanish American War in 1898, when it annexed Puerto Rico and made Cuba effectively a commercial dependency after years of owning most of its sugar production. The U.S. became more directly involved in the islands politically after World War I when it established a military protectorate over Haiti and the Dominican Republic. In 1917, the U.S. arrived in the Lesser Antilles when it bought the USVI from Denmark, after trying to purchase them for most of the preceding half century.

I am not sure whether Trinidad and Tobago are officially part of the Lesser Antilles. In some accounts they are; in others they are not. Trinidadians may even take offense at being thought a Lesser part of anything. Their island, while not as big as Cuba or Hispaniola or even Jamaica, is big enough for them to think of the people of the other islands in the chain as "small islanders."

The names of Caribbean islands reflect the different languages that have been used here. Some names have become anachronistic so that some islands are commonly known by a shortened version of their name, although still officially by their long

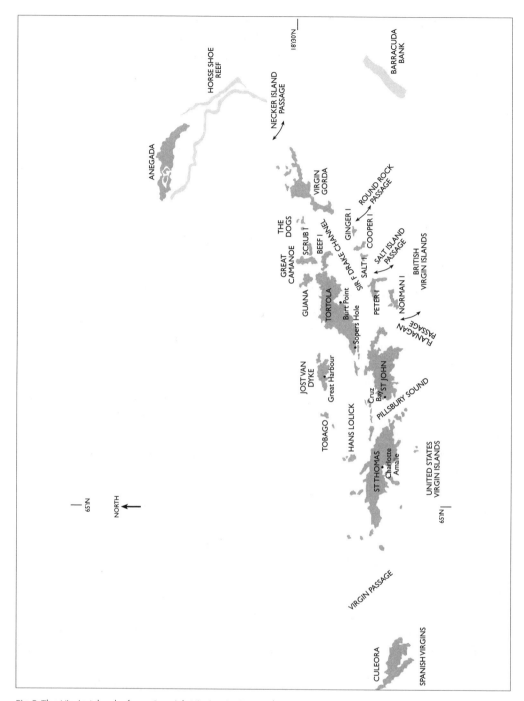

Fig 2 The Virgin Islands, from Spanish Virgins to Anegada.

version. Statia, the Dutch island of St Eustatius, is a good example. And as Caribbean English differs in pronunciation from British or American English, some of the names can catch visitors by surprise. Look at Chapter 8 for guidance on place names and local pronunciation.

The three regions of the Caribbean chain

This book covers three distinct island regions: the Virgins, the Leewards and the Windwards.

The Virgin Islands

The Virgin Islands lie to the north of the main island chain on the large shallow bank which extends eastwards from Puerto Rico, between the Virgin Passage to the west and Anegada to the east. There are very many small islands here but few are able to support habitation. Columbus named them after St Ursula and her 11,000 virgin martyrs.

The USVI has three main islands of St Thomas, St John and St Croix and some 60 or so uninhabited islands and cays. St Croix is an anomaly. It doesn't lie on the Virgin Bank but on its own platform about 35 miles south of the main group, surrounded by deep water. Since it's so far from the main group of Virgin Islands it's off this book's list of islands for passage planning.

The BVI lies to the east of the USVI, with U.S. St John and British Tortola barely separated by The Narrows. The main BVI islands are Tortola, Virgin Gorda, Jost Van Dyke and Anegada, with about 35 smaller islands. These and the main islands of the USVI all sit on the east or south side of the Virgin Bank. All, with the exception of Anegada, are volcanic in origin. Since Anegada is a dangerous island for anyone to approach at the end of a long passage, it too is off this book's list of islands for passage planning.

Visit St Croix and Anegada once you have established yourself in the main group of Virgin Islands or, in the case of St Croix, if it is a helpful stop on the way south. They are both within an easy sail of the main island group.

For most North Americans the Virgins are the gateway, the first islands to be visited in their trip to the Caribbean. By contrast, the Virgins are seldom going to be the first Caribbean landfall for European sailors, however navigationally challenged they are. This difference is important. North American sailors are gearing up for the Caribbean when they arrive in the Virgins. They are getting their first experience of the difference between home waters and the tropics. Europeans are gearing up to leave the Caribbean, possibly with an ocean crossing imminent. They deserve a holiday. The Virgins have a lot to offer both.

The season to visit the Virgins is roughly the same for both American and European cruisers, dictated by the same urge to avoid the cold and storms of northern winters and the tropical hurricanes of summer. North American cruisers, however, are likely to arrive earlier and stay later than Europeans. The North American migration south to the Virgins begins in October. The return trip north begins around April but late leavers may still be here in June. Europeans are probably not traveling north into the Virgins much before January and if they are heading back to Europe will be leaving no later than mid May. My advice is to come here either early or late, when you can avoid the high season of yacht chartering.

The relatively manageable distances for cruisers coming down from North America can tempt many into thinking of visiting the Virgins or the Caribbean for a single winter season, heading home when the spring comes. Europeans, too, may think the same about the Caribbean chain as a whole, but with less reason. Goodness me, I remember that my own plan was to pop across the ocean one Christmas for the fun of it and come back home in time for my birthday in May. I didn't of course. Instead I discovered that the Caribbean is not to be hurried. It repays you for the time you spend here.

If you are a North American with only a single winter for your tropical cruise, the Virgins are the ideal territory for you. They give you time to recover from your passage south; time to choose the conditions to explore those lovely islands, and time to prepare for your return north. Going further south into the island chain only adds to your burden of sailing. The heavy burden of having to sail to places like Nevis or Antigua or Bequia or even as far south as Grenada. The almost unbearable stress of having to make agonizing decisions about whether or not to visit all the little places in between.

Just as European sailors have the choice of cruising from Europe to the Caribbean on their own or in company, so do North Americans. Their American equivalent of the European ARC is the Caribbean 1500, organized since 1990 by West Marine as a rally of cruisers from Hampton, Virginia to the BVI, and setting off in early November. The idea was to allow sailors with little experience to sail down to the Caribbean in company with experienced offshore sailors. About 700 boats have sailed in this event and now between 50 to 60 boats a year take part. Although it is clear from the numbers that most North Americans come to the Caribbean under their own steam, it's always a comfort to have the choice of company. Then, in the following May, boats can cruise back to the States in company with West Marine's Atlantic Cup, rallying from Tortola to Bermuda and then to whatever your destination on the eastern seaboard.

Leewards and Windwards

The terms Leewards and Windwards are still in use today but without the old political meanings. The Dutch and the British colonists both used the terms Leeward and Windward but the Dutch put their Windward Islands in the region called Leeward by the British. The French, bless them, never used the terms.

There is no fixed agreement over where the Leewards end and the Windwards begin but for me, in this book, it is that the Leeward Islands run north from Dominica; the Windwards run south from Martinique. This, after all, is where the arc of the chain changes and the sailing northwards or southwards become harder or easier.

Trinidad and Tobago don't quite fit into the Windwards but, when it comes to inter-island cricket games, they play for the Windies.

The terms windward and leeward, of course, have a modern use. Each island has its own windward and leeward side and it would be a foolish sailor who did not know which was which. Regardless of the orientation of an island into the northeast Trade

Fig 3 Leewards to Windwards, the arc of the Caribbean chain.

Winds, this wind always hits the Atlantic side as the windward side. Only rarely, and temporarily, and usually only as an after-effect of tropical revolving storms, does the wind come from the west.

When the music of the empires stopped

You need some cultural landmarks as well as geographical ones to understand this region and its fascinating, polyglot societies. The original Amerindian settlers were probably the Cibony, nomadic hunter-gatherers coming into the islands from South America about 5,000 years ago. Little remains. They were followed by the Arawaks about 2,500 years ago, an apparently gentle farming people arriving by canoe, still surviving in Guyana. They were in turn largely displaced or exterminated by the warlike Caribs arriving about 700 years ago. The Caribs, who possibly came up from the Brazilian Amazon, had Mongolian features, light skin and straight black hair, probably like the North Asia peoples who colonized the Americas about 13,000 years ago. They had only been in the Caribbean for 100 to 200 years before Columbus' four voyages between 1492 and 1504 brought the Europeans.

At the time of Columbus the Caribbean islands had populations of both Arawaks and Caribs but it is the dominant Caribs we know most about. The Caribs seemed to prefer to remain based in the Lesser Antilles but they raided the Greater Antilles and terrorized the Arawaks living there. I'm not sure that the Caribs were any more of a problem to Columbus and the Spanish Conquistadors than the Arawaks but they were certainly given more damning reports in letters home. It may have been because the Caribs were not seen by the Spanish as good material to make into slaves, as the Arawaks were, or it could just have been that they had the temerity to chase Columbus and his men from a number of islands.

The Spanish found more to enrich themselves on the relatively Carib-free territory of the mainland and larger islands than they did in the Lesser Antilles and it was not until one hundred years later that the other European powers began to fill the void, slowly pushing out the Spanish presence and themselves settling these smaller islands. The Caribs did not give way willingly to this second wave of white imperialists. They resisted ferociously and were impossible to subdue.

In the long, slow struggle of one European nation against another, not only did European fight European for control of the islands but they fought Caribs too, in guerrilla skirmishes and massed battles.

The Caribs, as well as being fearsome fighters, were great boat builders, sailors and swimmers, fast enough to be able to attack sharks underwater and kill them with knives. They had an immensely strong sense and desire for liberty. Their society is thought to have had no inherited hierarchies of leadership. They jeered at the Europeans for their concern with rank and social standing. This, in part, made it impossible for the Caribs to co-exist with the Europeans, who in turn saw the only solution as extermination or exile. When the Europeans finally won they exiled large groups to the South American mainland, leaving only small pockets of Caribs surviving in the islands.

The Caribs were cannibals. Nothing unusual about that in the long history of mankind. Perhaps they ate the vanquished to place a military victory beyond doubt or question. A French writer of the 1650's reports that the Caribs considered the French to be the most delicious of the Europeans. Well, he would say that, *n'est-ce pas*? The English came second to the French. The Dutch were regarded as dull and rather tasteless. I doubt that much has changed.

By the end of the 18th century the only islands with large groups of surviving Caribs were Dominica and St Vincent, with the greater number on Dominica. One Carib legacy is local place names. St Vincent, for example, was known as Hairoun, land of the clouds. The island is no longer called Hairoun, but the local beer is. Trinidad's main local beer is called Carib. Perhaps this is fitting. The Caribs were reputed to enjoy serious drinking parties.

All islands here have a long historical association with one European country or another, usually with several at different periods as the pecking order of European nations changed, military strength changed and deals were done. You will be sailing among islands of the Netherlands Antilles, the French Antilles and the British West Indies, as well as independent states within the Commonwealth of Nations and islands which now form part of the U.S.

Although controlled by Europeans the plantation economy which operated on all these islands was based on African slave labor. Huge numbers of Africans were transported to the islands over several centuries and the modern populations of most islands are predominantly Black African. Later, after the abolition of slavery from the 1830s through to about the 1880s, some of the islands turned to India and brought in large numbers of indentured laborers, and populations in those islands are mixed. Only a few atypical islands have a large proportion of White Europeans.

Most islands in this chain had their most recent association with Britain. Federation had been an aim of the British from early in the 19th century and in the late 1950s, as island independence was coming closer, Britain tried again to combine most of the former British West Indies into an independent Federation of the West Indies. As in the past they failed to get local agreement over the structure of the Federation. Now a few islands remain British possessions but the majority are nations in their own right, having gained independence, or independence within The Commonwealth, during the 1960s to 1980s. They have British influences in their culture and styles of government, their legal and education systems, as well as using English as their official language and driving on the left-hand side of the road. For some the head of state is the British monarch.

The islands of the BVI are unusual in that much of their organization is influenced by their proximity to the USVI. The official currency of both USVI and BVI is the US dollar. Nowhere else but in the BVI does the Queen's head appear on postage stamps with U.S. dollar denominations. Or at least not yet. Most of the holidaymakers and charter crews in the BVI are from North America.

The USVI islands have gone through the usual swapping between European powers ever since Columbus first discovered them during his second voyage in 1493. The Netherlands, France, England and Spain all had a go at them but they finally settled with the Danes. This in itself makes them a little bit unusual. What is even more unusual is that when the Danes pulled out in 1917 they did so by selling to the U.S. The U.S. saw the strategic value of the islands in protecting the approaches to Panama, making the Virgins the only islands in the Caribbean chain ruled by the U.S. They have had various special, limited constitutional statuses over time, reflecting their essentially military role. Residents did not get U.S. citizenship until 1927. At present, residents do not have a vote in U.S. federal elections.

The French islands are fewer in number than the English-speaking islands. Guadeloupe and its dependencies of Marie-Galante, Iles des Saintes, La Desiderade, St Barts (Saint-Barthélemy) and St Martin are one *département d'outre-mer* or overseas department of France; Martinique is the other. The people of these *départements* are full citizens of France.

The Netherlands has the smallest share of this island chain: half the island of St Martin and the little island of Statia. From October 2010 these islands ceased to be part of the Netherlands Antilles. Sint Maarten became an independent state within the Dutch Kingdom and Statia became a municipality of the Netherlands with special status within the Dutch Kingdom. They can vote in Dutch national and European elections. Other Dutch islands—such as the ABC islands of Curaçao, Aruba and Bonaire—exist in the Caribbean but are beyond the boundaries of this book.

Most of the islands in the chain are part of the Eastern Caribbean collection of states. Apart from the French and Dutch islands, all islands from Grenada north to Antigua and St Kitts (St Christopher) are in the Eastern Caribbean. Although the islands of the Eastern Caribbean are separate nation states they share a common currency (the EC dollar, pegged in value to the U.S. dollar at EC$2.7 to US$1), a common language and a common telephone service. The first is very convenient since it cuts down on money changing; the last is not, since all the islands share the same and often unreliable service, despite some claims to having state-of-the-art fiberoptic digital systems.

These national boundaries, so modern, are yet so artificial. They violate the natural divisions of the region and are not really barriers as much as porous membranes through which individuals and groups constantly pass into Caribbeanness. Although each island does have a culture of its own, half the fun of the time you spend here will be in experiencing and unravelling the nature of Caribbeanness.

2
The secret to your simple passage plan

Knocking on Aries' door

I am not a salt-stained sailor dog in love with celestial navigation but there is one concept in that Byzantine discipline that I really like. This is the idea of using a single clear point in the heavens as the means to locating all those tricky stars that have to be found and brought down to the horizon before you can begin to know where you are on the surface of our planet. The single point in the heavens used for star sights in celestial navigation is called the First Point of Aries. Your almanacs give you the angle between each star and this First Point of Aries rather than the angle between each star and Earth. In practice this is a wonderful simplification. Think of this book as your own First Point of Aries as you navigate through the heavenly Caribbean islands.

This book aims to simplify your passage planning as you make open water passages from island to island, or those day-long or night-long jumps towards another harbor. It aims to give the cruising yacht comfort in ways that the comprehensive details of a pilot book do not. You will need pilot books as well as navigation charts to sail in safety here but pilot books are not the best tool for your strategy planning. Pilot books are busy documents, concerned with the full and accurate details of harbors and anchorages, and long may they be so. You will need the pilot and charts to get you into a harbor or anchorage, but before you do that you need the big picture of wind and sea and land to advise you where you should be aiming for in the first place as you cruise the island chain. For me, effective passagemaking must be comfortable and enjoyable, whatever my crew says about me to the contrary, and that is what I hope to help you achieve.

The Aries of my experiences, and central to this book, is that the most successful and comfortable passagemaking in the Caribbean chain need revolve around no more than a score of harbors. These, because of their ease of entry and predictable conditions, I classify as prime anchorages or pretty damn close.

Before reaching the paradise of the Caribbean Sea, even before I had sailed across an ocean, I had cut my sailing teeth in the treacherous tidal fog-bound and freezing waters of northern Europe, where careless or imaginative navigation is repaid by a night of extreme heel on a drying sandbank. But I am quick to adapt to new conditions. Here, in this sun-kissed sea with its necklace of diamond islands, I am a conservative and

Chaguaramas, Trinidad. Across the creek and into the trees. The view from our aft cabin while we were on the hard at Power Boats was across the creek to Hummingbird, where Trinidad's most famous round-the-world sailing family, the La Bordes, run a pretty little marina. *Photo: G Jardine.*

fearful sailor, lacking boldness. When I leave one island or anchorage I like to already have an idea of where the next safe haven will be and, for good measure, at least one accessible alternative. I recommend this approach as a way of keeping the crew on your side and your unbitten finger nails long enough to undo knots in the unforecast blow.

What I don't want to be doing on passage is wondering which of the half dozen anchorages mentioned in the pilot book for the up-coming island is the least worst. There are more pleasurable ways to get a raging headache. I just want to know the one anchorage which will be good for me whenever I happen to arrive, assuming the conditions to be more or less the same as when I started the journey. Getting this right makes for the most comfortable mental state when cruising between islands.

When making a day hop between islands I need to know when to leave in order to arrive at a safe haven before dark. I don't mind night passages when I have planned for them, but, equally, I don't like hanging off a harbor all night just because I got there an hour too late to enter in safety. Nor do I want to risk an entry at night just to give the crew a better night's sleep and a more affectionate attitude towards sailing.

Caribbean islands have so many tiny bays and out-of-the-way reefs to explore. The charts and pilot books are full of them. But for most of us making long passages the time for the *frisson* of excitement that the uncertainty of exploration brings is when the whole day and a certain bolthole lies ahead of you. I'll happily go exploring tomorrow but today I just want to be sure of a good landing at the end of my ten or twelve hour passage.

I know now that not all the islands have a convenient or comfortable harbor for boats on passage, even in normal conditions. When the winds and currents swing from the prevailing direction to somewhere else even the usually wonderful anchorage may be out of bounds.

There is a lot of good advice about islands to visit and anchorages to use to be had from experienced cruisers but often you need a little of your own to unlock it. The converse is also true. There is some pretty bad advice out there as half-truths and misconceptions get retold until they sound like received wisdom. The newly arrived sailor in this wonderful cruising area needs protection from these. This book is based on my experience during the last eight years of cruising the islands. I have a track record of very successful passagemaking to set before you. And as for the disasters? Well, let's all learn from those.

Prime is a small number

Prime harbors are the key to passagemaking in the Caribbean chain. They are your best ports of arrival and a good base for the exploring that comes later, once you have arrived. They may well also double as your departure point but by exploring an island you might find an anchorage you prefer for your departure. On many islands there are good departure points which I do not rate as prime, simply because they are not good enough for your arrival. In choosing your own jumping off point, bear in mind that a good night's sleep helps enormously in making the next ten-hour day enjoyable. The prime harbor will give you this, by being comfortable and secure. Saving two hours' journey time at the cost of being up half the night on anchor watch or lost sleep from worrying about getting your warp off the tree and wrestling the dinghy back on board at 6 am, adds nothing to the day that follows.

With the exception of the Virgins it is still the nature of the islands that prime harbors are usually bays where a boat can anchor and anchoring will be your most common way of coming in. Make sure you have the ground tackle for security and winches to make this easy for you. You may well find yourself re-anchoring a couple of times before you are happy. Don't feel like waiting if you doubt the security of your anchor. Get it up and put it somewhere else while the crew are still in the mood.

In some of the more popular bays it is increasingly the case that you can pick up a mooring buoy instead of anchoring. However, none of these prime harbors are places where you can tie up alongside or even expect a marina, although some are gateways to a marina. Marinas exist in the Caribbean, and are becoming more common year by year. They are more common in the Virgins and northern islands where yachting has been more a commercial product than in the southern end of the chain. But we yachties spoil ourselves with our own success. As yachting became an attractive source of revenue to entrepreneurs and island governments the charter fleets expanded and with them the need for marina bases. Then came mega yachts, needing bigger and deeper harbors and marinas that provided commercial developers with an opportunity to create huge luxury hotel, housing and retail agglomerations for land-based visitors.

There is a feeling among cruising yachties that island governments believe that mega yachts bring more business than cruising sailboats, and that these governments are wrong just as they were proven wrong to think that cruise ships brought more spending than yachties. The argument is the same: island governments once spent more on cruise ship facilities than on yachting, and now they are doing the same with mega yachts and not on us. Perhaps. What I think is more certain is that mega yachts appeal to property developers as the linchpin of a luxury hotel/residential scheme, and their private money talks loudly to public government. But there is another point that yachties should consider here as we complain that our economic role is undervalued in the path of development forced on the Caribbean as it finances the schools, roads, health care and much more, by its lack of economic alternatives to tourism. We complain, in effect, that we are invisible. We wish to be more visible. But we don't always like what island governments have in mind for us and we must take care not to wish for what we want in case we get it. Most of us want the free and undeveloped anchorages of yesteryear, with palm tree fringed beaches and smiling locals inviting us to a village jump-up. But the developers want us corralled as paying guests in marinas and government wants to tidy up our habits so that we fit more neatly into their policy files.

What began in the north has spread to the south. Sometimes change happens in a gradual way, as in Grenada where little marinas and mooring buoys came to the south coast to serve what is still essentially a cruising, live-aboard yacht population, and the development of a mega yacht facility at the island's capital is a logical step on from that. But it can also happen in a step-wise, leap-frogging way too, as in the little island of St Kitts which has gone from having nothing more than rolly anchorages to having a cruise-ship marina in its main town and a mega-yacht marina under development in an old salt pond. As yet we can't be sure that these new facilities will offer space to the itinerant cruising yacht, even if we want it. Let us welcome them as places where services such as hull or engine repairers can more conveniently reach you, places to take on water or complete entry formalities but let us also continue in the old way and assume that the first pilotage task in coming into any marina is just to enter the bay, where anchoring is usually possible anyway.

Those pretty little stone built harbors so common in New England and Europe, where yachts tie alongside with sturdy fenders and long springs, where crews climb up steel ladders to reach the dockside taverns and hot showers, are rarer than snowballs in the Caribbean. Timber or concrete jetties exist for local trading schooners and fishing boats but it would be a brave or careless yacht that risked its topsides on the ones that I know, where the swell never ceases. Where small harbors exist that a yacht might use they are usually deep inside a larger bay or an offshoot of a commercial port. Unless you already know them they are places you would check out after you have arrived at your initial anchorage.

I have designated 18 Windward and Leeward anchorages as prime harbors. Prime harbors are reliably easy to identify, easy to enter, and secure and comfortable when you are in them but they are not always the main harbors on an island and not all islands have one. Where I cannot bring myself to give an island a prime harbor (and it's true, some of these islands in this sailing paradise lack a good harbor) I give alternatives and under each island guide I give more details to help you with passage planning. Alternative anchorages allow scope for you to revise your plan according to how well the day has gone, or to fit better with tomorrow's plans to explore the island. Even these alternative anchorages, however, are chosen for their ease of access and comfort.

The relevant prime harbors on any particular passage are also listed at the head of each section on tips to passagemaking between the islands.

Prime harbors of the Windward and Leeward island chain

St Martin/Sint Maarten	Marigot & Simpson Bay
St Barts	Gustavia & Anse du Colombier
Antigua	St John's & English Harbour
Statia	None
St Kitts	None—use Nevis
Nevis	Pinney's Beach
Guadeloupe	Deshaies & The Saintes
The Saintes	Bourg des Saintes
Dominica	None—try Prince Rupert Bay
Martinique	Fort-de-France & St Anne/Le Marin
St Lucia	Rodney Bay
St Vincent	None—use Bequia
Bequia	Admiralty Bay
Union	Clifton
Carriacou	Tyrell Bay
Grenada	Prickly Bay
Tobago	Charlotteville
Trinidad	Chaguaramas

The passagemaking logic of the Virgins

Prime harbors for the Virgins have a different logic. Your focus after a long passage is all about getting up on to the Virgin Banks in the first place and while you will no doubt wish to choose an entry channel with a clearance port in mind, in reality you will not be short of good anchorages conveniently close together as you are in the island chain.

Consider the six ports of entry to the Virgins as a general target rather than your first or main anchorages. The main harbors are easily accessible but are usually best left to the big commercial ships except when you need to clear in or out or use the facilities there.

Though the BVI are British territories, Americans will feel at home here. The huge charter fleets cater mainly for American sailors and the islands' trade in goods is with the U.S. rather than Britain. And then, you can always visit the USVI later at a time of your own choosing.

USVI	Port
St Thomas	St Thomas Harbor/ Charlotte Amalie
St John	Cruz Bay
BVI	**Port**
Tortola	Road Harbour
Tortola	West End/ Sopers Hole
Jost Van Dyke	Great Harbour
Virgin Gorda	Spanish Town

Pilot books

Pilot books are absolutely essential to your sailing here. This is not one but don't worry, the region has become increasingly well provided with pilot books as it has become more popular with sailors. Looking back over the literature I get the impression that in the early days either side of World War II sailors here had to make do with monographs from writers who may not have visited all the islands they wrote about, or not long enough to support the lush detail they described. A few decades later more pilot books were available but with a tad too much about how they got the hook down and what they had for lunch. Today's crop of pilot books are serious and informative, well presented and, I hope, up to date and accurate.

My personal preference is for the Anglo-French pilot published by Imray, Laurie, Norie and Wilson for the Royal Cruising Club (RCC) Pilotage Foundation and Service Hydrographique et Oceanographique de la Marine (SHOM). I enjoy this pilot because I am familiar with others in the series. It is clear and to the point. With excellent photos and chartlets.

We also carry the British Hydrographic Office's *West Indies Pilot* Volumes 1 & 2. These are wonderfully dry but immensely detailed, largely written for captains of commercial ships but with masses of information for small yachts. These pilots seem to give many more anchorages than the specialized yacht pilots, perhaps because they expect their readers to be more competent at pilotage. Every serious cruiser should carry one, just as you also carry a sextant.

Reed's Nautical Almanacs, long used by European sailors and increasingly familiar to U.S. sailors since the publication of a U.S. version in 1974, now cover the Caribbean and is a serious nautical work. The information is very tightly organized and simple to use. It contains the essentials for pilotage from Bermuda to Mexico. The layout has been honed in the well-established European and U.S. almanacs. Since it is an annual publication improvements can rapidly be made in response to readers and to meet new topics.

In the Caribbean, however, the choice for many sailors is between those local sailors Donald M Street and Chris Doyle, a mixture of fact, anecdote and opinion with very different coverage and style. Doyle and Street have been writing guides for the last two or three decades. I carry out-of-date versions of both their pilots, partly because I get more comprehensive coverage of the region that way (and, after all, the rocks don't change that much!) and partly because I can see how much the region has changed since those pilots were written, but mainly because they came free with one of the boats I bought and I never ever throw books away. Check their latest editions on their websites: www.doyleguides.com and www.imray.com.

Separate volumes of *Street's Cruising Guide to the Eastern Caribbean* cover Anguilla to Dominica and Martinique to Trinidad.

Doyle's pilots are the *Sailors Guide to the Windward Islands*, the *Cruising Guide to the Leeward Islands*, and the *Cruising Guide to Trinidad, Tobago and Barbados*. Several are now jointly written with Jeff Fisher.

Street and Doyle are sailors steeped in the Caribbean and their books carry a wealth of information. I find Street particularly good on blow-by-blow sailing directions and all those amusing shortcuts between rocks and headlands that I lack the nerve to attempt. Chris Doyle excels at what you will find ashore and on whom to ask for where to fix what. They also write with wonderful anecdotes. You won't regret having them on board; but they are strong meat, men of character and idiosyncrasy. If you carry one, you must carry the other so that when you grow weary of the opinions of the first you can turn to the second.

Anyone planning to spend time sailing round a particular island should look out for a pilot or cruising guide specific to that island, often written by a local sailor. I know the ones for Martinique, St Martin and Trinidad and Tobago. Check with local chandlers.

A pilot book focused solely on the Virgins is *The Cruising Guide to the Virgin Islands* by Simon and Nancy Scott, published by Cruising Guide Publications, now in its 14th edition. Its chartlets are very thoughtfully produced.

This is a region of rapid and accelerating change in all respects, including those to do with sailing. In 1974, for example, Don Street described Gustavia, capital of St Barts, as a dirty harbor, and Le Marin in Martinique as infested. No doubt they were. You can see the historical scope for this when you visit them even now. But today Gustavia is the St Tropez of the Caribbean and Le Marin is a world-class marine leisure center. The point for today's sailors is that the region's facilities are expanding faster than a pilot book can be updated and that the deserted anchorages of yesteryear are buoyed now and have harbor masters to collect the dues.

The big force for change during recent years is simply the growing number of yachts. Demand creates supply, as an itinerant economist might say, and so the anchorages are fuller, the shore facilities improved, and yachting is becoming a bigger part of the local economy everywhere. There may be hiccups in the rate of growth, as war or terrorism or stock market fluctuations affect the willingness and ability of Americans and Europeans to go yachting, but my guess is that the number of yachts enjoying the region will continue to grow. No one can turn the clock back to the deserted anchorages and the days before yachting became a sector of visitor tourism, and not everyone would want to. But to catch the things I have enjoyed most here, you should come sooner rather than later.

Some of the changes are almost surreal. For example, I continue to be surprised that tiny Bequia, a long-time place of boat building and one of the great yacht anchorages of the region, should have good chandleries, which it does, yet I take it for granted that it and even smaller settlements will have a choice of Internet cafes. In my mind, good chandleries are only available in half a dozen major yacht centers but I expect to find Internet cafes wherever we can beach the dinghy to go ashore.

Sea charts—fine food for Joshua's goat

Charts are vital here as anywhere. Just because you can nearly always see to the island of your destination doesn't make charts less necessary. Dear old Joshua Slocum, patron of all who cruise in small yachts and occasional goat farmer, gave himself a serious fright when he thought he was being swept onto a reef off Tobago and didn't have a chart to reassure himself. I doubt that any of us can claim such a good reason for being without the right chart.

> "Running free along the coast of Tobago . . . I was startled by the flash of breakers . . . it was evidently a coral reef and a bad one at that. Worse still there might be other reefs forming a bight into which the current would sweep me . . . I had not sailed these waters since a lad and lamented the day I had allowed on board the goat that ate my charts . . . Almost aboard was that last breaker . . . when a wave greater than the rest threw her higher than before and behold, from the crest of it was revealed at once all there was of the reef . . . it was the great revolving light on the island of Trinidad, thirty miles away, throwing flashes over the waves."
> Joshua Slocum, *Sailing Alone Around the World*: still the classic must-read of blue water writing.

I use a range of charts, some bought secondhand and too old to boast about. Most of these are official British, American and French charts. Even now, in the 21st century, most of these charts are based on surveys done in the 19th century. The rocks don't change (much) but the coral heads, reefs and sandbars do, so take care when exploring new bays. Also, bear in mind that the survey methods and position fixing of a couple of centuries ago, and even a couple of decades ago, cannot match the accuracy of GPS. Your GPS plot will be exactly right in terms of the Earth's surface but may be badly out in terms of your position on the chart.

Commercially produced charts are available from two main sources:

- Imray-Iolaire by Imray, Laurie, Norie and Wilson in conjunction with Donald Street. They have Street's harbor guides and sailing directions on the back and are printed on waterproof paper. These are available in electronic media.
- MAPTECH Caribbean Yachting Charts which co-ordinate with the Chris Doyle guides to the islands and are available on CD.

Secondhand charts are available from other sailors and often still worth having. Too many charts are needed for the islands for any one person to buy and carry but you will never want to be without them. In places where VHF nets are run by yachts you will usually be able to contact a yacht leaving the islands or otherwise wanting to shed old charts which are now just ballast.

Three important points to remember when using charts of such mixed provenance and in an area where buoyage differs from your home waters:

- Check the depth measurements used on the chart. Feet, fathoms and meters are all possible.
- Check which way round the buoyage runs and then, when you are coming into a buoyed area, check that the actual buoyage is consistent with the charts. Islands in the Caribbean chain use the IALA B system of buoyage—red right returning.
- Buoyage is not extensive in this region but don't assume that where you expect to find buoys they will be in place. Buoys and navigation lights marked on your chart may be neither on station nor working.

A plot full of roses—those amazing pilot charts

Pilot charts are a planning tool and information source beyond the navigation charts. These mines of amazing information are published by the Hydrographic Center of the U.S. Defense Mapping Agency, and are similar to the Admiralty Routeing Charts familiar to British sailors. They are of just the right scale to allow you to plot the emerging weather patterns from the forecasts, although that is not their intended function.

Charts are published for each month. Wind roses and arrows show the strength, direction and probabilities of wind; curves show the speed and direction of ocean currents; lines show storm tracks and the seasonal limits of the Trade Winds; tables give expected barometric pressures. This last is probably also the least of what you want from the pilot charts because in the southern Caribbean part of the Central American waters pressure is remarkably consistent, with the same average expected level of 1012 millibars in each month compared to the range of 1012 to 1020 over the region.

The Central American charts cover a much greater area than the Caribbean island chain but that is just a bonus for you. You can see, for example, how the hurricane storm tracks of the region tend to miss the island chain. The detail given for the island chain is as much as most sailors can take on board anyway.

Navigation techniques—GPS is better than a hungry pig

Navigation here is relatively simple given that the typically mountainous islands show well above the horizon but you will, of course, be navigating by GPS. I know that some sailing purists argue against over-reliance on an electronic gizmo that can be rendered useless by battery failure, electrical storms, when the U.S. military declares a crisis, or even just coming too close to a U.S. warship, but such purists grow fewer year by year. Practice the hair-shirt alternatives after you've been hit by any of these crises, but meanwhile take care to balance out the wonderful accuracy of GPS with the inaccuracy of your charts.

The problem is that while GPS can be accurate to two meters the charts are not. Nor is their inaccuracy consistent. St Vincent, for example, seems to have been drawn with an error in its longitude while neighboring Bequia is just about spot on. Your stunningly clever electronic chart plotter could have you grinding your way uphill to Leroy's Rum Shop when you thought you were just about to drop anchor in the middle of Silver Sands Bay. Also, check the date and method of the soundings on the chart you are using. The coral head on which Jolly Jack Tar dropped his state-of-the-art lead line in 1839 will have come a few meters closer to the surface since then. And even last year's survey if it used a method other than side scan sonar could fail to report rocks as big as a house.

Beware of using a chart plotter linked to GPS for close quarters pilotage. The Caribbean is where the expression "eyeballing" was coined for navigation. Combine GPS with sensible eyeballing and chart-in-the-hand caution when approaching plotted dangers; use good practice log entry, so that the frequency of the position entries allows you to back-track on paper if the electronics fail; and remember the discrepancy between your satellite-derived lats and longs and those on your Caribbean charts could vary from a few meters to a mile.

1997. When Rm and I picked up the new boat in St Barts we were already late in getting to Trinidad. It lacked a fixed GPS but I had brought my emergency handheld. Just as well I brought some spare batteries too. As soon as we got offshore the little fellow told us his batteries were low and then said the same of the replacements. OK, so it was probably just his opening conversational gambit but I took it seriously and we only checked our position half a dozen times in the five-day non-stop passage down the length of the island chain. I knew if we sailed south the islands would come round to meet us. We checked our position in the Grenadines because the navigation got a bit tricky round the back of Kick-'em-Jenny in the dark and the next time I needed GPS was half way from Grenada to Trinidad, to check the currents. I know Rm switched it on a few times, but not after I warned him that this could prove disastrous for us later.

GPS is wonderful for three things. First, to point you at the right island. I mean, my goodness, with these short distances and the usually flawless visibility you can often see your intended destination before the crew has polished the mud off the anchor flukes. But sometimes you can see three or four other islands as well, and sometimes the island you want is somewhere under the heavy cloud on the horizon or blacked out by a stunning rain squall. Sometimes an island will go all shy on you. The horizon seems stunningly clear and yet some invisible haze has descended to stand like a curtain between you and your destination. Sometimes the red dust of the Sahara has blown over to cloud your vision. You need to get a bit closer before your chosen island takes shape. In that case you might like a bit of electronic help to save going to Redonda instead of Nevis.

Second, the last thing you want to do is just point the nose at the preferred island and sail down the line. The current will run you westward and the final track will be a huge curving course rather than an elegant straight line on the chart. Use the GPS to see what the current is doing to you, and believe it.

Third, you need the help of GPS to find the right bay as you close on the right island. Most islands have nearby alternatives to the bay of your choice, some of which would suffer damage to the reef-eco-system if you took your yacht and its keel into them.

Don't think you will need GPS and charts any the less in the Virgins, just because everything is closer together. This is precisely why you need more certain knowledge of where you are and what is around you.

If you don't want to use GPS then make sure you take good forward and back bearings or make use of known ranges to help cope with leeway and current in your pilotage and navigation. In the good old days of not-so-long-ago the little trading schooners and fishing boats sailing these seas developed local techniques of navigation, relying on the constancy of wind, current and visibility. I like to think of the old skippers knowing this sea from a mix of folklore and intuition, sailing by the shape and color of the sea, the constancy of the whirling stars, the hints in the flight line of sea birds that Columbus and the early Portuguese explorers followed; but it was probably more by luck and guesswork and a few local techniques of very Caribbean nature. I have heard of a few local techniques.

At night, wondering where they are, the skipper closes the land. When the dogs ashore begin to bark the crew on the foredeck calls out "What place this?" When a voice answers the skipper stands out to sea again. I can just about believe this one. Why not, I've done it myself.

The second is less believable, calling as it does for considerable advanced planning. It needs a long floating line, an energetic pig, and a boat sailing to Barbados. Barbados is a particularly difficult island for the eyeball navigator. It is upwind and up-current from most starting points, a long way from anywhere and low lying. Traders from

Light cloud on the peak. St Vincent is a high, green island and its leeward coast is stunningly beautiful. *Photo: Courtesy of the author.*

islands like St Vincent carried a pig on board so they could throw it over when they thought they were close. The pig, tied to the ship on a long line (because no one wants to lose their pig) and smelling the sweet molasses of Barbados, swam hungrily for the island and the ship followed.

Noah would have been envious. Modern sailing purists are less likely to be impressed. The point is, modern technology doesn't have to do much for you to do better than this.

Color coded reefs

One thing doesn't change though. Eyeball navigation is essential when closing on reefs. Don't sail among reefs on cloudy days or in bad visibility. You need the sun to be high but not in your eyes, probably sailing between 09.00 and 16.00 hours, and you need to practice a little to get the hang of the color changes that warn you of danger. Polaroid glasses help. These are some useful general rules, but remember they are only general and an approximation:

- Dark blue water is deep
- Lighter blue is shoaling
- Green is four to five meters deep, and time to take great care
- White, clear water is two meters and under
- Brown is a coral head
- Dark patches on the bottom are weed and grass but some reefs also show as black.

Use your echo sounder, of course. It is a great help in working out how much anchor chain or line to let out. But beware when on the move. Reefs, isolated rocks and the rocky ledges off many of the islands shoal so rapidly that it won't be the echo sounder which tells you when you have hit bottom.

Taking comfort from others—those daring bareboat charterers

I always like to see board sailors out in winds and waves that are just beginning to bother me. If they are coping on their tippy little boards then surely our heavy displacement, round-the-world sailing classic should cope too. Here in the Caribbean it isn't board sailors I take most comfort from but the charter yachts. I mean, there are so many of them that some, at least, must be skippered by rank incompetents and yet there they are, miles offshore but still afloat in a boat whose condition they neither know nor care about, and not yet dismasted as they hobbyhorse wildly in the short seas or infuriatingly overtake us hard on the wind.

The growth of the Caribbean charter fleets is a wonderful encouragement to the fearful like me. Take comfort from this and, if you are sailing your own boat, temper your temper when the next bareboat backs down on your anchor or stays up partying noisily all night. The people running charter fleets here see the Caribbean as the prime charter region of the world, the first place people think of when they want 20 knots of wind, warm clear water, languid nights and romantic anchorages with air links as good as anywhere else in the world. And they think it safe to put boats worth several hundred thousand dollars into the hands of strangers. That's how easy it is to go sailing here.

The charter business here, like yachting itself, has grown exponentially. It has moved from family businesses in the 1970s to a big industry now. Nothing in the island chain compares to the scale of chartering in the Virgins although probably the most visible growth in the last few years has been in the huge French fleets which now dominate the center of the island chain, and the use of much faster monohulls and large catamarans.

One of the joys of chartering here is that the conditions seldom stop you sailing, especially in the Virgins. The same is not true for passagemakers but then they have more scope to sit around the harbor honey spots waiting for their weather window. Charterers, though, can always put up with one whole day bashing to windward in the knowledge that they won't need to repeat this. They can then cruise in short hops and long protected lees till it's time to take the easy run back to base. If you are wondering about cruising here you can get an easy taster of the life by chartering first. Charter boats are good designs and G and I envy how well they are equipped. There are plenty of them and they are available from most sections of the island chain.

Surprise, surprise—sunset, sunrise

Some little things matter a lot. The sun here goes up and down with a rush. There is none of that lingering dawn and dusk of higher latitudes. This is usually of little consequence at dawn but you can get badly caught out at dusk unless you make a conscious effort to be ready for the dark.

The sun drops rapidly in its last half hour. The daylight remains almost blindingly brilliant until the sun is at the horizon. This is what catches out the unwary. Within the next half hour the light goes from brilliant to pitch black. Black as the deepest night. And nights here are more intensely black than you may be used to. Sailors from the U.S. and Europe expect summer twilight to last for hours. Back home, shore marks can be recognized long after sunset and walks along country paths remain manageable. Not so here. If you go walking in the countryside make sure you don't leave yourself with forest or rough tracks to do after dark. If you are sailing into an anchorage that requires sighting on marks, get there early.

> We came up from the south and made St Lucia close by the Pitons in mid afternoon. The wind held almost till we made the coast and then it shifted to blow directly down the north east leeward side of the island. We reckoned we could make Marigot Bay before dark but if we missed we would have to motor for at least two hours into the wind to make the more accessible Rodney Bay. We searched the charts and pilots for a nearer alternative. We looked wistfully at the Pitons but I wanted somewhere that didn't involve tricks with coconut trees. This was our first serious visit to St Lucia and we didn't know the coast. The little indented bays held no charm for us. We wanted out of the rolling north easterly swell. We were half an hour from sun down when we came up on Anse la Raye.

The tropical sunset takes a little getting used to. Its timing changes relatively little over the year, unlike sunsets further north. On Martinique, for example, roughly in the center of the island chain, sunset is 17.55 in mid January and 18.35 in mid June. (This is local time. All islands are on Atlantic standard time, UTZ-4, and there is no daylight saving). From my own observation I can tell you:

- within 20 minutes of the sun going down it is too dark to make out features on a headland half a mile away;
- in 35 minutes all the light has gone from the sky except for the wonderfully bright points of starlight. Neighboring boats in an anchorage are barely visible.

If you plan to enter an anchorage at night, plan to enter one that is wide-mouthed and free of dangers and has some shore lights. If you have a full or near full moon, wait for it to light your way. Never rely on navigation lights being where they should. Never feel you have to enter anywhere in the dark, just because you have arrived.

I wasn't happy with a first-timer into Marigot Bay in the dark so the choice was this little bay at Anse la Raye right now or Rodney Bay after two hours of motoring. No contest. We headed in, reading the pilot and checking the wonderfully detailed 1887 chart. Still a mile to go. I pushed the throttle to maximum. We were late. Behind me I sensed the sun going down like a ball of molten lead. As the sun hit the horizon we were drifting up to some pirogues. By the time we had bedded in the anchor and turned off the engine we could no longer see the two headlands a few hundred yards away, although we could hear the surf breaking on the nearer one to our north. We had only just made it in. When the waning moon came up three hours later we had some light to see the shore.

Staying put is no fluke—good ground tackle

You will spend more time at anchor in the island chain than you may be used to when sailing at home. You will need strong ground tackle even for everyday anchorages but the time will come when you will also need to put out two or more anchors, whether to hold you to the swell, to cope with a night squall or because you have remained in paradise too long and Hurricane Hooray is on his way.

As you read this book you will find that we have dragged anchor many, many times, and you may begin to think that we have dragged on many other occasions we are too shy to even mention. I regard dragging as the norm. If your boat isn't dragging then another one will be. The solution to better anchoring is to choose your spot carefully and lay your anchor tenderly. I have thought long and hard about anchor dragging, as befits a skipper of a boat with such a tendency, and I don't feel bashful about offering advice. After all, if I write it down now I might stand a better chance of remembering it in the future.

We have more anchors than I can remember on our boat but the one we mainly use is a CQR, a sort of plough anchor which, like all ploughs, needs to wriggle and worm its way underground, mainly through the action of the sea and chain. CQR stands for SECURE, and that is what we hope to be when we deploy this fine example of traditional engineering. We use an all chain rode, in common with most European sailors, of reassuringly heavy chain. The CQR also likes to be on a long scope and I like to sleep easy thinking of the deep catenary doing much of the work, and certainly not jerking me or Mr Secure upright in the gusts of the night, so we usually lie on a scope closer to 5:1 than 3:1. Despite being generous with our weight and length of chain, and the holding power claimed for the CQR, the anchor has dragged so many times that we now lay it down like a rare piece of porcelain. We do not drop our anchor. That is too careless a description of what we do.

Ploughs need time to settle. Just about the worst thing you can do is drop the anchor and a bundle of chain then motor back to set it. You will achieve nothing more than a shallow furrow with your plough tastefully lying on top of it. When you have selected your anchoring spot, overshoot by a boat length. Let the boat drop back slowly, using forward power if needed to control speed against the playful Trade Winds, as you lay the anchor on the bottom and feed out the chain or rode bit by bit until you have enough out for the depth of water. Then take five minutes or more to tidy up the deck, put on sail covers, debate the meaning of life and sit up on the bow admiring the scenery in general but some stable transit in particular. From time to time lay your bare hand on the anchor rode as it comes taut. You can almost always feel if the anchor is dragging and, if it is, re-anchor now rather than after the rest of the palaver. When you have waited twice as long as you first thought of, and your transits are steady, you may now use the engine to test the anchor. But remember, the point is not to see how many horse powers it takes to drag the thing back to the surface. Your anchor just needs a little encouragement from you to dig in deeper, and the rest is up to its designer.

I would argue that any plough anchor needs to be laid with care but I haven't given up on Mr Secure yet. We have a Danforth but they don't re-set as well. We encourage our CQR to stay set by two little tricks:

- A snubber of nylon line to take up snatch. This needs to be 20 or 30 feet long to work in really snatchy conditions. In tight anchorages we run this from our bob-stay-eye at water level;
- A weight on the anchor chain to increase the catenary effect. Weights which run down the chain are called "angels" or "chums" but we don't bother with such things. I consider them too troublesome to recover in the many crises my imagination conjures up, so we just run out a big loop of anchor chain behind the rope snubber. We wind this up on the winch like any other anchor chain.

Europeans usually use all chain on their anchor. Americans use rope. I had sat up for several hours after dark to work out if we were dragging. We seemed steady on two of our neighbors but closer than I remembered on the third. I watched the GPS and echo sounder. Neither confirmed that we were dragging but then neither confirmed that we weren't. I got up three times in the night to check our position. All became clear next morning as we were almost nudging this neighbor's stern. I had started winching in our chain to re-anchor when I realized they were moving. Not us. Up wind. Even I knew this was odd. "We're an ultra-light boat in 50 feet with 200 feet of line out," my American neighbor cheerfully told me. "In a two knot wind we sail all round the anchorage." I stopped winching. Neither of us were dragging. I didn't bother to tell him that we were a heavy boat in 30 feet with 90 feet of very heavy chain out. In two knots of wind we don't even straighten the catenary. Whatever that is. It was breakfast time but I went back to bed. Two cultures barely separated by their anchoring techniques.

You may need to learn new techniques to cope with anchorages in deep water or potentially deep water. Talking about anchorages is a good way to make new sailing friends. Here are some points to help you open the conversation. Some anchorages, such as St Pierre on Martinique, have a narrow shelf. You come out of the deep water of 30 meters or so and onto the shelf of about ten meters and drop anchor here, before the depths get too shallow as you approach the beach. Other anchorages are both deep and subject to inshore swell, such as the Pitons on St Lucia. Here you might try hanging your anchor on about 30 meters of chain until it catches the rising bank of land as you come close in to shore. Then run out a long and strong stern line to a palm tree, if there is still one standing.

The moment will come when you will wonder about putting out a second anchor. My feeling is only to do this when you have to. A second anchor adds a dimension of complication that you may regret later. Apart from times of approaching storms I would only put out a second anchor in four circumstances:
- To hold the boat into a swell
- Where a wind switch is expected
- Where the current reverses and there is little swinging room
- Where others are lying to two anchors.

I would never lie to a second anchor if everyone else is on one anchor. With a stern anchor out I would always have ready a long line and suitable float for when I have to get out in a hurry leaving the stern anchor behind for collection later. The hardest thing is not the practical ways of temporarily jettisoning an anchor, but the mental one of sailing off in the hope that the precious thing will still be there a day or two later when the conditions allow you to pick it up. I learned my techniques while in the Canaries, those sun-kissed Atlantic isles where the wind always seems to come onshore into your anchorage when you are least wanting it. Coming back for an anchor only seems hard to do when you have never left an anchor behind before. Believe me: when the time comes, do it.

Sailing text books advise you to run a trip line on the crown of your anchor if you suspect the bottom to be fouled and your anchor liable to snag down there. I have snagged anchors and I have used trip lines. My preference is to cope with a snagged anchor rather than the mess a trip line can get you in. A trip line round the propeller can be terminal in a crisis, which is what I consider the natural condition of much of my sailing. Think long and hard before you add this complication and source of danger to your anchor.

The other aspect of frequent anchoring is recovering all that weight. Many boats, and especially the charter fleet, have power winches often on remote control. We don't, but even so we have a powerful enough manual winch for visitors to try to just power up the chain without further thought. On our own, G and I work more circumspectly. We let the boat do most of the work. We think it is kinder to the boat as well as to us, keeps things more under control and by keeping us more in touch with the boat avoids some of the dramatic mishaps we have seen.

> Our friends M & J were doing nothing very much in the cockpit when the French charter yacht came in and the man on the helm gave the order to let go the anchor. He had not thought to tell the foredeck crew to make sure it was attached first and they hadn't. M & J heard the splash and understood the conversation. M got out his diving gear and went over to recover the anchor for them. The boat came back in to the chosen spot. The anchor, this time with rode attached, went over on the command, and all watched in horror as the untied bitter end of the rode flicked out across the foredeck and flashed over the side. Two nil to the anchor. M went below to put away his diving gear. They hadn't thanked him the first time so he felt they should learn some lessons for themselves.

Wait till you have some slack in the chain and recover that. The boat will slide forward and more slack will come available. Even when using the engine to help create slack, we never haul beyond the catenary. When the chain is straight up and down we take a good look around before the next step of breaking out the anchor, then we haul the anchor clear of the water and cat it on our bow roller before picking up speed.

One final word about anchoring: beware the charter yachts. Often you have no choice, if you are already anchored and a charter boat or six come in to your bit of paradise. But be aware that charter skippers often have little anchoring experience or lots of experience but no good judgement. They also like to get to where the action is, and assume that you are part of it. They will often come in or end up closer than you'd like with a huge amount of warp to swing on. Some of the more daring cat skippers will weave through the parked boats to get to the shallows at the front of the anchorage, using only their maximum engine revs and top boat speed to keep clear of other vessels. And unlike us, they don't have to break sweat to raise an anchor, thanks to their electric windlasses. That little bit of sweat involved in raising the anchor helps concentrates the mind when it comes to choosing a good place to drop the beast in the first place.

With charter yachts, the danger isn't just when they come in to anchor but when they are leaving. G and I usually let heavy old *Petronella* drift while we raise the last 20 feet or so of chain and stow the anchor at the bowsprit before casually strolling back to the cockpit. *Petronella* seldom goes far. Usually she manages to swing herself through the wind so that she is almost pointing out of the anchorage. It takes only a little blast on the throttle to finish the turn and get underway. Charter yachts, by contrast, like to be in gear and under way, possibly on full throttle, from the moment the foredeck signals that the anchor has broken out. This means they come racing back up through the anchorage until they have no choice but to heave the helm hard over to avoid the beach and go in the direction they first thought of.

I may have committed worse anchoring sins myself, but I like to think I knew it at the time (or shortly thereafter).

Your best strategy is to find more remote places to anchor. Oddly enough, this is often easiest in the most densely chartered locations. In the Virgins, for example, you can ask a charter company for the chart they give to their customers. This red-lines the anchorages off-limits to the charter boats. Some of these are not so hazardous to frighten me, so I doubt that many other cruisers would avoid them. Also, the pilot books in the Virgins are keen on telling you which anchorages are for lunch time only. We have spent many a happy night alone and apparently secure at a lunch time anchorage, wondering what the others knew about the dangers there that we didn't.

3

The sea that flows

The Caribbean islands lie across one of the great flows of water around the Atlantic basin. The sea, that great smoother-out of world weather extremes, moves huge volumes of salt, heat, carbon dioxide and all the other miscellanies collected by sea water, around the world in great temperature movements of currents from equator to poles, from surface layers to deep ocean. These ocean currents can be enormous. One of the five great currents, the Atlantic Gulf Stream, is 50 times greater than all the Earth's freshwater rivers put together. Winds at the ocean surface are one of the great influences on currents. The difference in solar heating between the tropics and the poles drives atmospheric winds such as the Trade Winds and these drive the surface ocean currents. The spinning of the Earth itself affects the oceans. This, the Coriolis Force, gives a sideways kick to the ocean currents just as it so importantly does to winds or, for that matter, to any other object in motion. For us in the northern hemisphere the Coriolis Force deflects ocean currents and winds to the right.

Virgin Gorda—plenty of room to go sailing. *Photo: Courtesy of BVI Tourist Authority.*

The Caribbean island chain is close to the margin of what oceanographers call The Subtropical Gyre. That is to say, the islands lie in one of the enclosed flow patterns of the ocean occurring between latitudes 10° and 40° North. Because the Coriolis Force changes by latitude, increasing in strength from the equator to the poles, gyres have an asymmetrical shape. At the western margins of ocean basins they run strong, narrow and fast. This means that the boundary currents further west in the Caribbean Sea can run at speeds up to four knots compared to the broader, weaker eastern boundary flowing off, say, the coast of Europe running at under a quarter of a knot.

The subtropical gyre that you will be sailing in is part of a circular system of flows that run from Africa to the Caribbean as the Northern Equatorial Current, through and up the Caribbean then back across to the mouth of the Mediterranean and down towards Africa, and so on forever. The South Equatorial System on the south side of the equator feeds a current up the coast of Brazil and into this gyre. The effect is the powerful and constant Caribbean current.

The Caribbean current

The Caribbean current generally travels from southeast to northwest and can be expected to flow at up to two knots in open water and at an accelerated four knots in the inter-island channels. It has seasonal variations, running harder in the summer than the winter and tending more to the northwest in summer, but always running much stronger in the southern part of the chain, between Trinidad and Grenada. In some summer months it runs between Trinidad and Tobago and later in the year runs much stronger round the north of Tobago following the 200 meter depth contour.

The strength of the current further north in the island chain seems to vary less than in the south. Perhaps as the ocean current strengthens from winter to summer part of it gets deflected round the northern end of the chain as a whole rather than increasing its speed through the inter-island channels.

Selected current flows in the island chain

Month	Speed in two locations	
	Trinidad to Grenada	St Vincent to Guadeloupe
December	1 knot	< 0.5 knot
February	1.2 knots	0.5—0.8 knot
April	1.5—2 knots	0.5 knot
June	1.5 knots	1 knot
August	1.5 knots	0.8 knot
October	1 knot	0.6 knot

We are always troubled by the strength of the current on passages where the wind direction forces us to have the sails sheeted tight, but some locations seem to have a stronger current than others. Strong currents of up to four knots are likely to be found through the narrow channels of the Grenadines to the north of Grenada, including the channel between Bequia and St Vincent. Further north, in the St Lucia channel between that island and Martinique and on the northern end of Martinique in the channel to Dominica, the current can run at three knots.

The west-going current along the coast of Trinidad makes the passage to Tobago difficult. The current is accelerated by having to squeeze through the 30-mile gap between the two islands. Most yachts from Trinidad heading for Tobago motor along the north coast at night when the winds drop, staying about a mile off to avoid the current or catch a back eddy. In the morning they hope to be in a position to beat north across the current for the southern end of Tobago.

All sailing passages between islands need to take account of the prevailing Equatorial Current but the flows are harder to predict as you close the ends of the islands and local factors come into play.

When I look at the pilot charts with their wind arrows and current flows and try to relate the direction of the two I find something is odd. The oddity is that wind-driven currents don't follow the wind. This is something Norwegian explorer Fridtjof Nansen noticed while he had time on his hands during his three-year exploration of the Arctic in the 1890s. He passed his observations to fellow explorer Vang Walfrid Ekman who had the mathematics to develop a theory to explain this. At the heart of Nansen's observations and Ekman's theory is that the two external forces creating the current—the wind and the Coriolis Effect—have to be in balance. In the northern hemisphere the Coriolis Force, which only acts on moving objects, pushes moving ocean water to the right of its direction of motion. The faster the water moves, the more strongly it is pushed. To balance the two forces the ocean current has to move a mass of water 90° to the right of the wind. This mass is actually a column of water reaching from the surface to a depth of about 500 feet. The deflection to the right varies with depth. Overall this 500-foot column of water turns at 90° to the wind but on the surface the movement is only some 20°.

You don't have to try to visualize all of this and the mathematical formulae as well. Just make a note that a current is turning to the right, and in the Caribbean this means that a west-going current is swinging north of west.

What a swell ocean this is

Of course, the wind isn't always the benign 15 knots promised in the brochures. Sometimes it is a pleasant 20 knots and sometimes an over-robust 25, with gusts of 30 not unknown. Most cruising yachts can cope with such winds easily enough. More of a problem may be the waves and the swell, especially if they are coming from a different direction to the wind.

Swell in the Caribbean is continuous. It is always with you whether you are sailing or anchored. The only variable is how high it is and the direction it is coming from.

Winds produce waves in the most delicate way. The new wind across a flat sea deforms the surface of the water and this in turn perturbs the flow of air. The first ripple becomes a fledgling wave, shaped by the wind's pressure, so that the face is to leeward, the back to windward and a convex curve sits between them. Just like wind across your sails, the air pressure on the front face is weaker than that on the rear face. The wind transfers its energy to the water and the water takes the line of least resistance, climbing upwards between these different pressures of air. The strength of the wind, the distance or fetch over which it blows and the depth of water combine to produce the natural periodicity of the waves. The organized parallel lines of waves are, when seen from the height of your deck, a confusion of different heights and sudden spouts of collapsing energy.

As you make a passage between islands you are sailing with two components that make up today's waves: the local waves produced recently by local winds and the older waves of swell resulting from distant winds. The strong winds in the Atlantic which generate swell in the Caribbean are not always the Trade Winds.

Two points come out of this:

- The islands in the north of the Caribbean feel the strongest swell. This is mitigated for those sailing in the Virgin Islands by the shallow Virgin Bank and the dense line of land along the southern edge of the bank. The islands in the chain from St Martin to Dominica will have stronger swell as a result of winter storms in the Atlantic than the islands south of there.

- Swell generated far out in the Atlantic may come from north or south of the wind you are sailing in. Swell, combined with the waves from today's wind, can make for wet, slamming sailing with water running on the deck even when on a beam reach. The normal strength of the Trade Winds can result in three-meter swells as well as driving most boats at full hull speed or pretty close. The inevitable effect of the one meeting the other is that the boat will sooner or later slam hard or plunge deeply, throwing spray the length of the boat and running white water down the decks. This is exhilarating sailing on a short hop between islands but hard work for a full day or night, and even harder work during a passage of several days.

Log, May 2001.

The southeast winds of the last week have made our journey south fast but wet. The north ends of islands seem more uncomfortable than the south. The swell seems to follow us round as we come out of the passage between islands and into the lee of the land, not letting go its grip on our journey. If anything, it rises even higher just before we get the lee from the land, as though to remind us who is boss out here. Strange, but the usually bumpy channel between St Vincent and Bequia was much drier than the channels between Guadeloupe and Dominica and between Martinique to St Vincent. Coming south of Bequia we had magnificent sailing as the reefs and islands of Mustique and the others along that outer arc took the brunt of the ocean swell without depriving us of the honest ocean wind. We flew along in flattish seas until some strange effect was generated by Canouan and Mayreau. Instead of even flatter seas as we came along Tobago Cays we had mountainous swell that ran around the north of Canouan and again off Mayreau. This was nothing compared to the tide rip we went through off Kick-'em-Jenny as we passed from Carriacou to Grenada. We bore off to take the seas at a better angle. A couple of yachts heading north were having a hard time, full sail and slamming. We had two reefs in the main and half the genoa rolled away, plus staysail and mizzen. We were making full hull speed and not straining the sheets, skipping over the swells like a little tropical bird.

The southeasterly is a strange wind. We sailed down the leesides of St Lucia, St Vincent and Grenada. Unheard of.

The seas when sailing in open waters are often more of a problem than the wind strength. Caribbean seas are more boisterous than you might expect for the wind strength compared to your home waters. This is only to be expected. The Trade Winds have a fetch of 3,000 ocean miles before they hit the underwater mountains of the Caribbean. Waves can build quickly on the back of swells when a Force Three suddenly jumps up to a Force Five, as will often happen along the leeside of the islands.

Frustratingly, when the breeze is light the perennial swell from the Trades or an Atlantic storm can roll your boom and rob your sails of drive.

Swell is one of those mysteries of the sea that bothers you most, not when you are busy sailing but when you are quietly moored up somewhere with the time and inclination to be plagued by it. One of the major snags to the Caribbean is that swell refracts around the headlands to find its way into most anchorages, even those which seem to offer hope of a lee. In those lovely little sandy islets facing into the wind you might even find waves refracted round both ends to produce totally chaotic and potentially dangerous waves right where the best shelter should be.

My tip is that your best bet is to assume that anchorages most subject to swell will have it when you get there, and you should therefore have a fallback position. There are three fallbacks to consider:
- stay the one night and just curse your bad luck;
- move straight on even if this means an overnight sail;
- set the crew on anchor watch and take a quick-acting sleeping pill.

I find I can cope with a few hours of miserable rolling and then, even with mizzen sail set and flopper stopper deployed and my head a-lolling with fatigue, I'd really rather go to sea. The only thing worse than a rolly anchorage is a rolly night on a swelly, windless sea—but you rarely get a flat calm in these Trade Wind seas.

I had Prince Rupert Bay marked down as untenable and warned the crew as we came up the coast of Dominica. "Oh yeah," they clearly thought as we dropped anchor in a mill-pond, "the old Jeremiah is wrong again." I couldn't help but dig a deeper hole for myself by repeating my gypsy warnings on their deaf ears. By morning we were rolling our scuppers under. No one had been able to sleep since midnight. I didn't want to say "told you so" but on the other hand I couldn't stop myself. Odd then, that a year later when we put back into Prince Rupert Bay for an overnight stop, we didn't roll at all. Yet Bequia, Chatham and Prickly Bay had all been rolling merrily.

The mystery of tides

Tides are just a mystery. That's how it is for many of us.

I have spent many a happy Caribbean passage in ignorance of the tides here. I mean, why not? They are not the rip-roaring 40-footers of southern Brittany or the 55-footers in the Bay of Fundy, the whirlpooling horrors of New York's Hell's Gate or the murderous boils and 16-knot rips of Alaska's inside passage. These are bathtub events that rarely rise and fall more than half a meter and surely cannot work up much pace in such a height. Surely these are as nothing compared to the effects of wind-generated surface flows and the steady push of the Equatorial Current.

Or perhaps not. I have wondered at the accuracy of the GPS as we appear to be sliding east of our heading when I have yet again been telling all who will listen that we will be set west by the current. No navigator of my uncertain skill likes to be made to question the accuracy of GPS. Rather than do that, or resort to more traditional navigation techniques such as sextants, compasses, log entries and chicken innards, I prefer to think that tides do have a noticeable effect on a sailing boat and should be taken into account. The question is: how to do that?

Working with tides in the Caribbean is no easy matter. Few people here bother much with them. I mean, they are never going to prevent you getting over a harbor bar, or make you take the ground, and all that inconvenient stuff they impose on your sailing back home. Sailing off Britain or Brittany, where the tides can range from 12 feet to 40 feet, I would never ever make a coastal trip without first filling in my tidal atlas and studying the tidal diamonds on the charts. Here, I have almost forgotten what a tidal atlas is. No one I have met carries tide tables. Almost no one I have met even knows if such things exist. *The British Admiralty Annual Tide Tables* cover the whole of the Caribbean chain but the limited number of standard ports used, and the different tidal patterns of these standard ports, makes it difficult to work out local times. As a result, most people tune into the local weather forecasts and pick up the times of high and low waters that way. Of course, what they can then do with that information is often limited to a few pieces of received wisdom.

Reed's Almanac claims more comprehensive information on tides than other pilots. Their data allows readers to calculate times and heights at different locations but is less complete and accurate for the Caribbean chain than, say, for North America:

* The time and height are calculated on constants that may fail to reflect actual daily variations, not least because of the distance between the secondary locations and their reference port.
* Local phenomena can have major effects, especially hurricanes with their massive surges.

This tabulated information doesn't allow you to calculate the all-important flows. Local navigators generally work on the assumption that in the channels between the islands the flood tide moves water from west to east and an ebb tide moves water from east to west. This runs counter to what you might casually deduce and is worth remembering.

It means that the flood tide helps stem the prevailing current through the channels while the ebb tide adds to it.

A lunar solution

Tides follow the moon, more or less. If you relate the time of tides to the rise and fall of the moon you will find some evidence that tides start to flood at a time close to moon rise and ebb at a time close to when the moon is at full height. Using this information you can reckon that the tide is flowing eastwards from moon rise to moon zenith and ebbing westwards from zenith to moon set. You can get these tide times from local tables and moon rise from an almanac; often you can get both from a local newspaper, but you can also make your own observations of moon rise and zenith.

By observation you will see how the time of moon rise and moon zenith changes with the state of the moon. The new moon rises in the east at about dawn, so as night falls you will see the new moon already well over to the west. The closer the waxing moon is to being full, the closer it comes to rising in the east at sunset. In the wonderfully clear and dark nights of the Caribbean you can watch how moon rise and moon zenith jump in time each evening. What you see of the moon is only part of the story of its rise and fall. By extrapolation you can work out the moon's apogee for the hidden half of the lunar day and so arrive at the tide times for the two highs and lows in each day.

Your visual celestial indicator of the direction of tidal flow (the moon, as we usually call it) also helps you deduce the strength and height of the tide. Over the 15 or so days of the lunar cycle between new moon and full moon tides are at their highest and therefore strongest about three days after a new moon and again about three days after the full moon.

A twist in the tale

The tide behaves slightly differently along the length of an island. The obstacle of an island forces the tidal flow to run northward or southward. On the flood, the obstacle is the whole west side of the island; on the ebb, the obstacle is the east side of the island. In both cases, the tidal stream must go north or south. As with the Equatorial Current, the tidal stream will find some watershed point of neutrality part way along the coast of the island at which it splits into its north and south flows. A skilled (or pernickety) navigator who listens to the radio could usefully time a passage to carry a fair tide all the way along the coast of a larger island.

The foot to foot-and-a-half rise and fall of tides may be slight but they are moving a huge mass of water. As a result, they can work up to a noticeable speed in particular pinch-points. I have concluded that my studied ignorance of tides is too cavalier and runs against the grain of my hard-won philosophy that passagemaking here should be as comfortable as possible. I now consider it foolish to knowingly set off on an up-current passage with the tide against me, when I could so easily have arranged matters to go when the tide is helpful. To make such a passage in ignorance is, of course, still forgivable.

A good rule of thumb is that in the places where the Equatorial Current runs hardest the tidal effect will be greatest. This means that you should give greatest thought to the tide in the channels between islands and at the tips of the islands.

Where you may be advised to take tidal flows into account I have mentioned this for particular passages.

It is ironic, given the way the glossy brochures *almost* claim that even an unskilled child of five could manage a 40-foot charter yacht in the Virgins, that the Virgins are one of the areas where you should take greatest care with your tides. They are, of course, an area with lots of passages between islands and lots of ends of islands for water to accelerate round. They also, unlike the rest of the Caribbean chain, lie along the line of the Equatorial Current rather than across it. This means that many of your trips are made directly with or against the current, and therefore the tide. This makes working with a helpful tide even more important to your comfort.

The Virgins, too, are an area of great tidal mystery. What tides are likely to be doing in the main passages is clear enough but as for the rest, the water flows are much more likely to be a result of wind and other meteorological conditions. Watch the moon but keep those tea leaves and chicken innards close by you.

A simple guide to tidal flows through the Caribbean chain:
- Tides flood from west to east
- Tides run from west to east shortly after moon rise
- Tides ebb from east to west
- Tides run east to west shortly after moon zenith
- Tides then run eastwards again after moon set and westwards again after moon apogee
- The fuller the moon, the closer it is to rising in the east at sunset
- Tides are strongest just after full moon and new moon

4

The wind that blows

"In the Indies ships only sail with a following wind. The strong currents that flow and the winds together make ships lose in a day as much way as they gained in seven. Ships only sail with a regular breeze and sometimes lie in port waiting for six or eight months."

Christopher Columbus, letter to the Spanish sovereigns Ferdinand and Isabella, on the fourth voyage of discovery 1502– 1504

Columbus was a great navigator and seaman and discovered a great truth about this region, but you and I in our weatherly yachts with reliable diesel engines and the magic of weather faxes can do better than the old Admiral of the sea, can't we?

I'm trying to lose my anti-social disregard for weather forecasts before I lose all my sailing companions. I used to take the view that I would just take what nature offered, on the flimsy grounds that I could cope with any of the usual stuff except hurricanes. And I felt I showed how responsible this approach was by telling all who'd listen that at least I didn't plan to be around when hurricanes were on offer. For a year or more out here I didn't even know about the local weather forecasts. I used to claim that none existed, and for all I know I might have been right that year. For a while my companions put up with my assertions that (a) the weather was always manageable if not always favorable and (b) tomorrow would be like today or better, so why worry. I used to tell my friends that sailors who complained about rough seas in the Caribbean had no experience of "proper sailing." What I meant was I had spent years being battered by wind and waves in the North Sea and Biscay and, look, it hasn't done me any harm.

Well, my attitudes have changed now even if my practices are still a little lazy. Since sailing in the hurricane season I've learned where the good weather stations are and when to listen to them. Since picking a really bad period of strong adverse winds to sail north through the island chain one winter, I'd rather not repeat those awful days of wet clothes, sleep deprivation and lack of interest in *haute cuisine*. Then, having invited more and more friends to visit us in the Caribbean I have had more and more opportunity to listen to myself explaining how normal it is to have such a strong sailing breeze and lumpy sea.

Of course it's only the pussy cat sailors who wait for a good forecast instead of taking it on the nose, but we pussy cats stay drier that way.

My laxity of weather forecasting was, of course, brought about by two things:

- Local conditions. The northeasterly Trade Wind is the most remarkably constant of the world's great wind belts. The Trades originate in the high pressure belts of the Atlantic and work their way across the Atlantic on their way to the equator.

- Ignorance of the subtle weather patterns that bring about cyclic shifts in the prevailing conditions. Weather patterns here are not the ones I had learnt from sailing in non-tropical latitudes. In the higher latitudes of home, the weather is dominated by high and low pressure systems moving from west to east, but here in the tropical northern hemisphere the weather comes from pressure systems moving north to south and being modified by the Coriolis Effect of the Earth's rotation. My growing realization that I could and should identify and work with these patterns has enormously increased my personal comfort and standing in the eyes of my crew.

> We have discovered how to get weather forecasts over the SSB radio. It's very amusing listening to people who seem determined to speak through goldfish bowls or with their head in a clamp. I suppose you have to learn the technique before you get your ham radio license. I was mastering the accents and vernacular nicely until Rb complained and I stopped practicing aloud as a gesture of goodwill. We listen attentively each morning. G hears all the stuff about changes bringing bad weather tomorrow; all I hear is "no significant change" to the wonderful stuff we had yesterday. Truth, as Aristotle said, is somewhere in between.

Constant like the Trade Winds

The atmosphere enveloping the globe is in reality a fluid in constant motion. The prime forces accounting for this motion are:

- The variations in temperature between poles and equator. Hence, now that you are close to the equator, its importance to you.

- The rotation of the Earth, deflecting all moving things (including air or water) to the right in the northern hemisphere. This Coriolis Effect is of vital importance to your weather now that you are in the tropics.

The northeast Trade Winds which cover the island chain the whole year are one of the most persistent of the Earth's great air movements and it is fair to call them prevailing. They are typified by blue skies with high, scattered, rainless, fleecy clouds but the weather here can also be disturbed and it must always be remembered that this is the breeding and hunting ground of the hurricane.

The true direction of these winds is east northeast and they blow between 10 to 25 knots. From December to April they are at their strongest, averaging something like 18 to 23 knots and with more east in them. Calms are rare but at times the wind and rain will come with intense squalls when gusts may be up to 40 knots. These squalls can usually be seen a long way off. When approached by a squall at sea we used to shorten sail and bear up to sail through it, until someone told me they preferred to run off, sheeting in hard to keep the speed down. That's what we do now and it works, as long as the extra 10 or 15 knots of wind passes in the usual few minutes.

The main difference between a gust and a squall is the time they take to pass. The gust is short lived. You will have a few minutes' warning of it from the disturbance on the surface of the sea to windward, and when it comes it will bring a stronger wind, probably up to half as much again as the preceding wind, and a veer of about 30° clockwise.

Beware the gust associated with cumulus clouds. More frequent and stronger, as the colder higher air rushes to the ground in exchange for air warmed by the surface heating.

But beware even more the gusts from cumulonimbus clouds, those giant versions of cumulus that at the equator might rise as columns 18,000 feet high and have a base of 10 or more miles. These are the most dramatic of all cloud types and the ones to produce thunderstorms and hailstones. These are the "anvil" shaped clouds. Squalls are the prolonged, monstrous gusts from their downdrafts.

Ahead of the cumulonimbus cloud your surface wind will be innocently blowing gently towards the storm raging at the foot of the cloud. Within a mile or so of the cloud the surface wind will fall light as it rises to enter the cloud. Then you will see the "coldnose" of dark, rolling or clearly turbulent air running ahead of the cumulonimbus cloud column. The wind comes when this reaches you, rising from nearly nothing to 40 knots or more in a matter of seconds, rain coming soon after and then, in minutes, the wind drops to half its speed and later, as the rain eases, the wind falls light.

This cloud and its "coldnose" are traveling at up to 25 knots. When you see the black arch of cloud at its base and the whipping up of the sea you will be able to judge how severe it will be and whether you need reduce sail or even drop sail. At half a mile distance you have about a minute to make your sailorly decision.

The northeasterly Trade Winds do not always blow from the northeast but you can usually expect a lot of easterly winds. Over a representative selection of areas for the island chain the winds come from northeast and east for more than 80% of the time and for some months, in some sections of the chain, they will blow from these directions for up to 96% of the time.

It is the summer months when you are most likely to find southerly winds but G and I have sat with the pack in Trinidad at Christmas, where and when the winds have the most degree of north in them, waiting for a forecast shift to the south to give us an easy ride to Grenada.

Winds are likely to be strongest in the winter months, when you can expect the Trades to be blowing up to a Beaufort Force Five. In the summer this steadies to a more regular Force Four. Calms are very rare, but so too are winds of sustained gale force. This does not take into account the seasonal factors, when short-lived squalls can be expected, or the local factor of acceleration round headlands or off the high mountains. These important elements of your weather windows, the cyclical fronts in winter and the tropical waves of summer, are discussed later.

In some years strange and unaccountable effects disturb the prevailing patterns for long periods of time. In 1997, for example, unusually strong winds and frequent showers persisted over the northern half of the chain for weeks. High pressure systems rolling in and sitting over the islands were not dissipated by winter cold fronts, as they usually are.

Though the Trades are remarkably persistent you should look for shifts in the weather system because the consequent shifts in wind strength and direction make your sailing life easier. I have learnt to call these breaks "weather windows" as everyone else does. The vital thing is to anticipate and use these breaks when you are planning a passage, especially against the prevailing ocean currents. Look for a disturbance in Trade Wind weather if the forecast is for a true northeast or southeast or unusually strong or weak winds. Winter wind shifts may come about as a big weather system sweeps down from the U.S. or as some local tropical variation comes into play. I don't mean anything as dramatic as the hurricanes of the summer months. Key to these wind shifts is the Intertropical Convergence Zone (the ITCZ), long known to us sailors as the Doldrums.

The Intertropical Convergence Zone—the Doldrums

The rotation of the Earth produces the northeast Trade Winds in the northern hemisphere and the southeast Trade Winds in the southern hemisphere and a boundary area between them, a narrow band of unstable weather called the Doldrums or, more formally, the Intertropical Convergence Zone (ITCZ). The Trade Winds form a belt of high pressure running along the low pressure area of the ITCZ. Being over the equator and subject to the greatest heating from the sun the zone is an area of relatively strong convection and moist air. The air movements here are mainly vertical rather than horizontal, hence the ITCZ mainly brings frustratingly light sailing winds but can contain storm cells of high wind, heavy cloud, intense rain and thunder.

Be aware of the shifting location of the convergence zone because of its important influences on the weather in the Caribbean. The zone travels north and south across the equator in line with the seasonal movement of the sun but not at quite the same time or speed. The ITCZ lags the sun by a couple of months. The sun is at its northern maximum in June but the ITCZ is not at its maximum until August to September, hurricane season, when it is usually between 9°N and 12°N. The sun reaches as far south as it is going in December, the ITCZ in February.

When the ITCZ starts its spasmodic movement north from below the equator some time in May it can bring squalls of wind capable of gusting at 50 knots, usually from the south and southeast. These are usually short lived but a really bad squall can last up to two hours. The warning signs are an increase in the upper level cloud and thunderstorms in the early evening. Make sure your ground tackle is able to cope.

In 2002 the ITCZ never got much beyond 10°N and this was one reason why the hurricane activity did not live up to forecasts. In May 2003 the ITCZ suddenly went from 2° or 3° north one day to being off Trinidad the next, well ahead of its usual timetable. Members of the Antilles emergency and weather net set to discussing how to get their training sessions in earlier than usual.

The northward movement of the ITCZ means the end of the dry season and the beginning of the wet. With the ITCZ close to the equator in the winter there is less convection and therefore less rain in the islands. The dry season is usually reckoned to run from January to June and the wet season from July to the end of December but the length and timing of these seasons varies across the island chain as well as from year to year. Sometimes this simplification into two seasons instead of the four we have in the higher latitudes is a poor description of reality. It rains ferociously in each. The locals do not exaggerate when they say "a bucket a drop."

During the rainy season you can usually expect a short period of dry weather like an Indian summer bringing that short hot spell in October before Autumn settles in for real. When we get that in Britain it's because the weather gods just want to remind us of what was missing during May, June, July and August. This dry interlude is called a *Petit Carême* in most islands.

In the dry season you may go for weeks without any rain at all. In Spring 2001 between Antigua and St Martin we had no rain for four weeks. Hatches wide open at night. No night squalls. We forgot what rain was. The land, however, everywhere looked parched and burnt and the smoke of fires rose from the deep forest.

Santa's clause—the Christmas winds

G tells me often enough that no one from Trinidad would sail north in December or January, so I suppose the good people of that island have yet another reason to doubt the sanity of people who like messing about on yachts. The Christmas Winds or, as the French call it, "Vents Noel," are a recognized part of this season. Christmas is when the Trade Winds typically strengthen and they continue strong till mid April.

As the ITCZ moves south in the Autumn and heralds the start of the main Caribbean sailing season it pulls the axis of the American weather systems south with it. A pattern of frequently repeated highs and lows invades the Caribbean. The northern Caribbean catches the worst of this in the form of the Norther, a north wind behind a cold front coming out of the Gulf of Mexico. The front will often be hard to see, being weak and usually cloudless, but as it passes, the wind will rise suddenly in a bitterly cold squall from the north that may persist for several days at gale force in the Gulf itself. These winds reach down into the Virgin Islands and even as far as the northern Leeward Islands, weakening the northeast Trade Winds. They seldom come with much force into the southern Caribbean because of the sheltering effect of the high islands and the warmth of the Caribbean Sea. Beware when sailing in the Virgins. The north facing coasts in the Virgins become exposed and the anchorages on those coasts can be untenable, even dangerous in the northerlies.

The expected effects are:

- As the front comes down the wind veers east or even southeast and weakens, even going to the south and southwest immediately ahead of the cold front.
- After the front passes the wind strengthens, blowing from northwest at 20 to 30 knots with stronger gusts.
- As the front stalls the wind veers to north and northeast, the high pressure rebuilds and the Trade Winds resume.

Given the regularity and frequency of the cycle, which can be as rapid as three to four days, this is where to look for the break in the prevailing Trades, allowing you an easy passage to wherever you have planned. But remember that these strong winds blowing at 35 to 40 knots for several days, even as long as a week at a time, can make for wet weather sailing if you try to head north across one of the inter-island channels where seas might be up to 12 feet or more.

The visible signs of changing weather are:

- High cumulus replaces the clear Trade Wind sky. Light rain replaces the usual fine weather.
- Behind the front the weather is stormy, with heavy showers and even thunder storms.
- Cloud clears as the Trades return.

Your best warning of impending change is the radio forecast. The barometer gives very little indication of change. Rising barometric pressure here (in contrast with temperate latitudes, where rising pressure usually means more settled weather) means stronger winds and higher seas but the rise is often so small compared to what you see in temperate latitudes that you may miss it completely. What adds to the problem of spotting barometric change is a regular diurnal effect peculiar to the Tropics, as a wave of pressure sweeps around the world, a bit like an ocean tide. The pressure changes by three to four millibars, with the lowest pressures of the day expected at about 4am and 4pm and the highest at 10am and 10pm. You need an accurate barometer and a series of readings twice daily to get a feel for this diurnal variation, otherwise barometric pressure appears so steady that it is of little help in weather forecasting except when a hurricane is developing. We have a little electronic barometer which is capable of measuring and remembering these variations.

The effects of these winter wind shifts are also important for boats at anchor. Swell that would not bother a boat at sea can plague anchorages. Since most anchorages are on the lee side of the islands, the westerly winds following the cold front can make some usually good anchorages uncomfortable, even untenable. Roadstead anchorages like Canouan, which are subject to strong gusts off the hills, can become very uncomfortable when the accelerated wind whistles down at speeds of up to 60 knots and pretty little waterspouts go whizzing around the harbor. Remember why you came sailing here. You don't have to go anywhere today if the conditions don't suit you. Why put yourself or your crew off the pleasures of sailing.

Winds from the north are often strong but so far in my sailing here I have found that the Trades and their variations, though boisterous, are nothing that a well equipped yacht with a skipper quick to reef need fear.

Summer waves

In the non-hurricane months of winter the main interest in the weather is in the systems coming from the north and west of the Caribbean region, but in the hurricane season of summer the main interest is in the weather systems coming from the east and the southern part of the Atlantic.

In early summer, when the ITCZ starts to move north, the first tropical wave will be reported coming off the coast of Africa. This wave is an area of low pressure, not yet revolving. In the main part of the hurricane season tropical waves will be forming every few days. Some will make it all the way across the Atlantic, moving at about 10 to 15 knots and bringing strong winds and rain. As the wave approaches the Caribbean winds will increase and move back to north of east. Line squalls bring the rain and the wind, possibly gusting up to 45 knots. The tropical wave may last one or two days. As the wave passes the wind goes south of east and slackens, to be replaced by the usual Trade Winds of 15 to 20 knots.

The greater the convection, the stronger the tropical wave and the greater the chance that it will develop into a hurricane. Thunderstorms are associated with strong convection and may even be accompanied by waterspouts. Avoid these, no matter how bored you are that day.

The relationship between the ITCZ and the tropical wave may be important in helping to trigger or to establish the shift in gear from tropical wave to hurricane. The ITCZ can impart spin to this non-circulating area of low pressure and when that happens the tropical wave is redefined as a tropical depression, one step closer to a hurricane.

Out through a window

The winter fronts and the summer waves are the key to the breaks you need in the prevailing Trade Winds when facing the Equatorial Current, but are only part of what constitutes a favorable weather window. Take account too of the height and direction of swell.

The relationship between wind, current and sea state is vital to your passagemaking. The Trade Wind generates waves across a whole ocean, although after about 400 miles it probably doesn't matter how far the rest of the fetch is. Add to this the effect of distant storms in the Atlantic, local winds and chop induced by the current, and you have a mix which makes for more uncomfortable windward sailing than back home. An adverse swell may take a day or two to subside if the wrong wind has been blowing for several days. Allow for this in your passage timing when looking for a favorable weather window.

I can put up with having to make small tacks to sail the last five or 10 miles when we have been pushed too far west but I no longer assume that we can make a long

Peter Island, BVI—looking down from the hillside walk into the popular anchorage. The little islet of Deadman's Chest and the hills of Salt Island form the backdrop. *Photo: G Jardine.*

passage without a favorable wind and win. A good rule of thumb is that sailing with a Force Five or more forward of the beam will be too wet and hard to be comfortable for long. Food will be hard to prepare and harder to hold down. Sleep will be a pleasure postponed. Neither you nor your crew will be a joy to behold in the Customs office.

Try to make sure the favorable conditions will last for at least a day longer than your passage. Then seize the window but don't feel obliged to jump. Weather windows, like weather forecasts, are like well run buses: another one will be along in a while.

Most passages between islands run northerly or southerly and you need a wind which lets you sail a little free. Most cruising yachts lack the windward performance of racing yachts or even, I hate to say, modern charter yachts. Cruisers carry too much weight and many are of conservative design. Also, most cruising crews won't put up with living on their ears so they choose their wind accordingly. You should know what course your boat can sail on the wind. Windward sailing is a large part of passagemaking out here.

> Log, Spring 2001.
>
> Sailing down from Grenada to Trinidad we got the perfect chance to measure our performance against wind and current.
>
> Under ideal conditions we can make good speed when 45° off the wind but in the usual lumpy seas between islands we need to sail 70° off the wind to make decent progress. Sailing to Trinidad at that angle we were making five to five and a half knots compared to six or seven knots when broad reaching.

So, with the wind from the east the best we could sail south was 160° true ie 20° better than our required course. The effect of the one knot of Equatorial Current on our speed of five knots was to push us 20° to the west ie taking all our contingency. Our leeway was now critical to where we would arrive. Leeway, combined with the wind and current, was a trap. If we came harder on the wind we increased the leeway and, at the same time, lost boat speed relative to current speed. We might be pointing at the Bocas but the magic carpet of the Equatorial Current was sweeping us sideways to a destination 40 miles along the coast of Venezuela. If we freed sheets to gain boat speed and reduce leeway we would arrive in Venezuela sooner. Big deal.

Halfway to Trinidad we decided to turn round. Now we found we couldn't even make Grenada. We turned the GPS off and on and gave it a good shaking but the same answer came up. In these conditions when sailing northwards the best we could point was 20° true. The relative wind had dropped on this course so we were making less speed through the water and became more affected by the one knot of Equatorial Current. Despite leeway we seemed to have a good chance of returning to the bottom end of Grenada, until local conditions kicked in. To avoid the nasty Reindeer Shoal southwest of Grenada we had to deliberately sag off to the west. This improved boat speed but as we came round the Reindeer and level with the southern end of Grenada we met the locally enhanced Equatorial Current. Even though we tightened sheets we were being pushed further up to the northwest.

According to academic calculations, no sailing boat can sail closer on the wind than 37° to 38°. I'm not sure I would want to be on a boat that could manage that, even academically. Cruisers like us on a sturdy, comfortably heavy boat probably hope for 50° and five knots. Let us assume that you can manage that. Now plot a few vectors with a one to three knot current across or against you. The current is everything so far as your passagemaking goes. Now try a few vectors with extra leeway to represent getting knocked off course by boisterous waves. The current is even more of everything than before. That's why you need a window.

Local factors affecting winds

As day follows night

During the winter there is a tendency for winds to increase from sometime in mid-morning through to the afternoon and for this increase to last into the night, possibly till near dawn before it calms down. This diurnal variation is important not only in itself but because it can reinforce the prevailing winds or other local effects. The increase can be from 5 knots to 10 knots. As a rule of thumb, the stronger the Trade Winds blow the greater the diurnal effect.

Foot on the gas pedal

Land effects can make for much stronger winds than you might have been led to expect from the offshore forecast. You should bear these two factors in mind:

- As the true ocean wind meets an island it tries to follow the coastline and as a result can be accelerated by anything from 5 to 10 knots. The wind, like most of us, likes to take the path of least resistance. It prefers the smooth surface of the sea to the roughness of the land, and holds off turning over the land for as long as possible. The effect is that a wind blowing obliquely onto the land will deflect at the shore to run in the direction of the land and so will be speeded up. The angle of many Caribbean islands puts the Trade Winds obliquely onto them.
- As the land heats up faster than the sea and cools faster at night, land and sea breezes affect the strength of the wind striking the coast. The strong sunshine of the Caribbean produces strong land and sea effects, often making sea breezes (the flow of air from sea to land) felt many miles offshore. Look for the sea breeze setting in during late morning, strengthening to Force Three to Four and then even rising to Force Five or Six in the afternoon. Initially it will blow straight onto the land but the Coriolis Effect will cause it to veer, possibly by as much as 40° by late afternoon.

The sea breeze usually dies away around sunset when the land and sea temperatures become more equal, and the land breeze sets in during the evening. Weaker than the sea breeze, this usually dies away at sunrise.

Sometimes, of course, the conditions are just right for land and sea breezes and yet they do not develop. Often this is due to the local topography. The high land of many islands will make the sea breeze run parallel to the coast and possibly accelerate it. As with the diurnal effects, the stronger the Trade Winds, the greater the acceleration effects. These can reach up to five miles offshore and at the start of a trip can be offputting. You may be inclined to turn back to wait for gentler breezes, not realizing that the gentler breeze lies ahead of you in the form of the true ocean wind.

I have felt noticeable acceleration effects off the high volcanoes and headlands of:
- Statia
- Southern Montserrat
- Northwest Guadeloupe and between Guadeloupe and The Saintes
- Southwest Dominica
- Northwest Martinique, Diamond Rock and St Anne
- Northwest St Lucia and the Pitons
- Northwest St Vincent and in the Bequia Channel
- Northwest and southwest Grenada.

What's katabatic about that?
The high hills can also make for strong gusts on the leeside of an island, just when you would expect to be in calm waters. When a fast moving down-draft of air creates low pressure, the wind can be sucked into shore and give you a westerly breeze close in to land. Some anchorages are uncomfortable because of this. I'm told that these can be so bad that one or two charter cats usually get flipped each year by these sudden gusts. That's nature for you. Always trying to entertain us cruisers.

A fright full of rain

The high and massive islands are rainmaking machines. The northeasterly Trade Winds carry considerable moisture across the ocean and are forced to drop it as they rise to meet the high mountains of the Caribbean. The islands have high humidity, usually between 65% and 80% and rising to 90% or more in the wet season, but this does not always make itself felt. The constant Trade Winds turn humid air into balmy breezes. The low lying older volcanic islands do not generate the same amount of rainfall as the newer, higher volcanic islands, their tendency to drought now exacerbated by high-impact tourism.

The heavy cloud that usually sits over the high islands streams off to leeward. With northeast winds you will catch this cloud off the southern ends of these islands and with southeast winds you will catch it off the northern ends. As you sail towards these swirling cloud masses your heart may sink and you may be reaching for the oilskins. The chances are that none of this threat will reach you. The rain and cloud often cannot be sustained once they fly clear of the land. You will learn to distinguish between island-generated weather and ocean weather until, of course, your panache gets a good soaking when a real ocean squall hides itself in the cloud off the end of an island and catches you.

> Log, May 2001.
> We watched in horror. A black band of rain swept in to the south end of Dominica and the high rugged land disappeared. We were right in its track. Should we drop the mainsail now or NOW!? My heart beat suddenly hit a rate of 200 or more as a screaming wind blast came at me from the other side of the boat. The wrong side. What inversion of the natural order was I about to suffer? A light aircraft flashed by just above mast height, throttle open and banking hard. The pilot must just have seen the rain band as he came round the end of the island. The worsening rain band blacked out even more of the island. It never managed to reach us. We were a mile offshore. One mile was enough. But why he was flying at mast height I have no idea.

Tropical squalls

You need to know when to hide and when to use the wind that comes with one of these often severe local storms that we call squalls. You will meet more of them in the tropics than in the temperate latitudes so a few clues are needed to tell you when you have a bad one coming. The bigger the cloud mass, and the taller it is, the greater chance of unwelcome strong winds. If you get wind before rain then the additional wind that comes with the squall will probably not be as great as when you get rain before wind. Find a little rhyme to remind you of this. Also, look out for a sudden drop in temperature. The greater the drop, the more wind you should expect. And of course, you will see the wind on the water before it hits your sails.

Beware the midnight hour. One little glitch in squall watching is that most squall activity takes place at night. At night the cloud tops can radiate heat back into the upper atmosphere and this enhances their ability to grow. In daytime the cloud tops absorb energy from the sun and so don't suck up as much warm moist air from sea level.

In the Caribbean squalls move at the speed of the local Trade Winds but because of the Coriolis Force they are moving slightly to the right of the direction of the Trades. A black cloud down to the south of you may well be coming your way and if it does you will get a clockwise wind shift of about 5 to 20 degrees from the surface winds you were enjoying. The squall brings less wind on its windward side, sometimes you will even be left in a flat calm for an hour or two when a squall passes over you and before the Trades find their way back. If you were running and saw a not-to-worrisome squall on its way you might chose to alter course to stay in front of it in the enhanced winds. If you were beating you might chose to go to windward to keep out of the stronger winds.

Well, just listen to that—weather forecasts

The reason for your interest in the developing weather is simple: you can't sail any distance to windward in a Force Five. You will become a follower of forecasts and forecasters.

A good source of weather forecasts for the Caribbean chain is the American National Weather Service through its NMN station. This station gives its forecasts in a standard format familiar to most American sailors and with a little practice is easily mastered by Europeans used to BBC and similar national forecasts. The main problem is with the electronically generated speech, which puts pauses in the wrong places or leaves them out altogether and compounds the "goldfish bowl" problems of SSB reception.

The area you need to listen for now is the Eastern Caribbean Zone and, for good measure, the southwest North Atlantic. You should, of course, know your own latitude and longitude but I find it helps to listen with a chart of latitudes and longitudes in front of me so that I can locate the developing features. The forecast begins with the ruling time and a synopsis of conditions then gives weather in three 12 hour bands of time—the next 12 hours, 12 to 24 hours and 24 to 36 hours—before ending with an outlook for the next few days. Probabilities apply to the accuracy of the forecast: about 90% for the first 12 hours and then 75%, 66% and 33% respectively for the subsequent time periods.

When we use this forecast G tries to make us listen to it at the same time each day and not miss any days, and to record the significant features for later reference. The point is:
- you are looking for changes between forecasts;
- you are looking for the unusual.

These American National Weather Service forecasts are just a little too formal to be theatrical entertainment so when we first discovered SSB weather nets as we sailed south to Trinidad at the start of the hurricane season G made me listen to them all. Now we had theater and information. We put so many hours into concentrated radio listening that we had no time left to go sailing. The gaps and differences between the reports and forecasts made a huge void of confusion, in which we sat, petrified by our lack of comprehension. We were ready to go with George and Alex had us untying our sail covers but Eric sent us huddling below until George came on again. We never managed a regular spot with the much respected Herb. A new word crept out of the SSB reports and into our sense of ourselves. We had a new possession, a "window," which we had not realized we even needed till now. In this new, better informed life of ours we often sat so long waiting for "our window" that we finally just had to revert to our old ways and go and live with the consequences.

The U.S. Coast Guard also transmit complete offshore information on SSB for areas from New England to the Caribbean but their times are subject to change. U.S. sailors should check with USCG before leaving.

SSB Weather Stations

Station	Time	Frequency	Notes
Eric Mackie (Antilles emergency and ham weather net)	06.30	7162/3 LSB	Based in Trinidad. Bias towards southern Caribbean
George (on Lou's Caribbean maritime mobile net)	07.15	7241 LSB	Based in US Virgins. Covers Bahamas to Colombia. Very detailed assessment of factors affecting weather and SSB propagation
George	07.30	7086 LSB	More details than above
Alex on *Albatross*	07.30	8155 USB	
Marine Weather Center	08.30	8104 USB	Based in Florida. Client based reports. General synopsis and then details for areas around individual clients. Email on: info@mwxc.com
Marine Weather Center	09.00	12359 USB	For Trinidad, Venezuela, Panama and the Bahamas, Miami and Atlantic
Marine Weather Center	09.30	16528 USB	As above
Herb Hilgenberg *Southbound II*	16.00	12359 USB	Now based in Canada. A long-time source for specific advice to Atlantic sailors. Herb trades his forecast for your observations of your local weather
George	16.45	7086 LSB	The "cocktail hour" forecast
Eric Makie (Antilles emergency and ham weather net)	18.35	1815 LSB	As above

VHF weather repeats

VHF Net	Time	Channel	Notes
Trinidad net	08.00	68	Run by long-stay foreign yachts. Weather report from yachts able to receive SSB or weatherfax
St Maarten net	07.30	14	Run by Pastor Tom from a shore station. Mainly based on Marine Weather Center

George's forecast comes on as part of Lou's SSB maritime mobile radio net and is continued in its own right and in greater detail when George receives detailed verbal reports from his yacht stations and also sends out weatherfaxes.

The Marine Weather Center is nicely timed to let you hear George first. "Sponsoring vessels" pay a fee to get specific advice on their chosen routes. This means the service covers boats trundling up and down the Caribbean, boats heading through Panama, boats heading up to the U.S. and boats positioning themselves to cross the Atlantic. These sponsors not only receive localized forecasts but some also report details of the weather at their current position. David Jones, a fine character who started the Caribbean weather net in 1993 and became known as "the weatherman" died in November 2003 but his service lives on through Chris Parker, a live-aboard weather specialist. Chris, chief forecaster for the Caribbean net after David's death, set up his own Marine Weather Center in Florida in 2010. Chris follows on from David's Caribbean Weather Center in providing sailors with customized weather reports for the Caribbean, Bahamas and Eastern Atlantic Ocean. You can get a personal service through email, SSB or by phone. Find them on www.mwxc.com.

The Marine Weather Center gives each sponsor a forecast of weather in their area for the next few days and advice on when to make their next intended passage. The old Caribbean Weather Center claimed 7,000 boats a year as "sponsors" and I assume the new service is similar in size. Boats with a serious voyage in mind will find this service of great value, particularly since it will suggest latitude and longitude waypoints to get the best weather for the trip. You could make a lot of new friends, bumping into them as you all reach the same specified turning point between Bermuda and the Azores.

We found the old Caribbean weather net potentially the most useful forecast because some of its sponsors were near neighbors of ours or planning to sail the same route, and what was relevant to them was also relevant to us.

Boats able to pick up Pastor Tom's St Martin VHF net at 07.30 on Channel 12 will hear a summary of the Marine Weather Center synopsis for the region.

No forecast will get it right and for us it was always interesting to contrast George with the Caribbean weather net. The Caribbean weather net was the more pragmatic. They didn't reveal their hand in the opening general synopsis. When they heard the actual weather from their sponsor boats they responded to it, fitting their highly specific observations into their more general analysis. George can never tell us the weather for where we are; the Caribbean weather net could, by reference to their sponsors.

George is actually a bit of a star. He not only does weather on the Earth but the Sun and Galaxy too. Although I sometimes grumble at him I suspect it is only because this high flier isn't often as interested in our part of the Caribbean as we are, or as we would like him to be. I suppose that until hurricanes start to develop there just isn't enough in the way of weather to interest a man like George. George is also based in the Virgin Islands and that means that his natural meteorological focus is to the north. The Mona Passage between the Dominican Republic and Puerto Rico and the Anegada Passage between the BVI and St Martin are frequently used by boats from the U.S. and can be rough places with large swell and confused seas.

Listening to George it usually sounds as though the Virgins have more weather than the Leewards and Windwards. This isn't necessarily a thing to worry about given the degree of protection on the banks but it does mean you should keep more of an ear open for weather when sailing to and from the Virgins. Also, beware the big storms to the north which can make the north coasts of the islands untenable. These northerlies can last quite late into the winter. One May while in St Martin we listened to reports of big winds and rain over the Virgins as they caught the outlying winds from a big storm in the Atlantic. Then in April 2003 the Virgins got hit the other way. An almost unprecedentedly early tropical storm over Bermuda brought five days of such heavy rain and wind to the Virgins that the boats in the spring regatta complained they were getting British weather. And in between these events we have listened many times as George tells us about weather changes in the Virgins while the Leewards and Wind-wards go through their predictable cycles.

For us, with the southern Caribbean in our sights, George seems a tad focused on the Virgins. As we lie at anchor somewhere from St Martin to Grenada wondering about tomorrow's weather it seems that George skims over our part of the Caribbean chain.

Of course George doesn't wholly ignore the southern end of the chain. He often in-cludes Trinidad, perhaps because there is more remarkable weather here at the receiving end of the Trades. And even more often he includes the mainland of southern America, such as Colombia, since they too have distinct and sometimes satisfyingly extreme (and therefore eminently reportable) weather. But for us, wondering whether it will blow 17 or 22 knots and from a variant of southeast or a variant of northeast, we just don't count that much.

The personality of each forecaster comes through in a refreshing way that adds to the entertainment and enjoyment of the forecast. Perhaps because we spend so much time there, and perhaps because we knew him when he ran the mini-mart grocery in Peakes' yard, Chaguaramas, we get particular pleasure in listening to Eric Mackie of Trinidad, now a popular TV weather forecaster. We are not alone in this. Members of the local land-based (as distinct from maritime-based) Caribbean emergency and weather net are generous in their praise of Eric. Like us, these radio hams appreciate Eric's love of what he is now doing and the way his enthusiasm comes through. Those tuned in to Eric's net are the old boys from every island in the chain. They know one another. They are comfortable swapping "ole talk" and commenting on life around them, especially politics. This is a good station to listen to for a view of life and culture in the southern Caribbean.

These old boys probably also like Eric for his naturalness. Eric loves to drop in observations of what the sea was like as he drove along the north coast of Trinidad that morning, or of the power of his new computer in handling satellite images. Eric also communicates a sense of what this weather may mean for those receiving it. After days of low pressure in Venezuela and Colombia when massive rainfall generated huge mud slides, road closures, loss of power and polluted drinking water, Eric was the only forecaster to express explicit sympathy for people there. Eric from Trinidad knows these things from personal experience and puts this into his weather report for us.

Eric, being in Trinidad, also gives more weight to the weather in the southern Caribbean. This is what we usually want, since we spend much more time listening to weather at the end of our sailing season when we are hurrying back south than we do at the beginning when we are dawdling north.

Learning when to worry

As we spent time listening to forecasts in the early months of the hurricane season G impressed on me that I needed some better understanding of the terms used, so that she could get a better sense of when to start worrying. My lax and contradictory explanations of weather features was not giving her any comfort and I got snappy when she said it was her turn to read the weather book. Some of the forecasters' terms were really not so difficult to follow as long as they were written in the right order in my crib sheet:

- Tropical disturbance, tropical wave and upper level troughs will be mentioned frequently in the broadcast forecasts. They are nothing in themselves to worry about. They are just poorly organized weather systems interrupting the Trades with rain of varying intensity.
- Tropical depressions, the next rung up, bring rain and strong winds but are highly variable. The winds can be 35 knots or can be no more than the normal Trades. Take shelter if you think a depression is on its way.
- Tropical storm is trouble. This brings intense rain and winds up to gale force. If the storm worsens it will turn into a hurricane.

A window is a pain, not a door

You might conclude that waiting for weather windows in the usually benign eastern Caribbean is not a good use of your time. Certainly, you can be put off going to sea by those weather advisors and fellow sailors who think that yachts should stay tucked up in port when winds blow at over 20 knots. In the end, whatever the forecast, you have to make your own judgements to sail or stay. No forecast absolves you from your duty to keep a close watch on the three vital elements that tell you what weather is approaching: pressure, wind and sky.

April 2001. The English yacht in Anguilla wanted to head south. Everyday the skipper came on the morning net to see if he had "his window." We listened in. At first we listened because we were in St Martin and wanted the same window. Later we listened for the pure theater of it. We loved the perfectly captured pitch of disappointment in his voice when David said there was no window, and the hint that this skipper held David personally responsible for making him cruise to Anguilla in the first place. In the end we left St Martin without a window. We had already missed two and so had Mr Anguilla, and it looked as though we'd miss another if we hung around up north. Mr Anguilla was still asking for his window a couple of days later, after we had sailed one hundred miles south. The wind had been less than perfect but not impossible. The swell was more on the nose than the wind and we had water running on deck all day long. But we had got far enough south to widen our choices for day or night passages. We never heard when Mr Anguilla left and whether he had his window. We became too busy sailing to listen to the weather.

Our experience is that the niceties of wind speed and direction are too subtle for forecasters to get right even within a 24-hour period. If the wind speed is under 20 knots and the wind direction is good for you, then sail. If you're finding it too uncomfortable when you get out there, change your strategy. Stay in harbor for a few days or weeks until something changes; or choose to make a different passage. Don't island hop if the wind is on the nose and waves are slamming into you. Use the curve in the island chain to go with freer sheets and more comfortable motion.

These things seem like self-evident truths, commonplace even, when read in the cold, calm light that shines on the page. But they are less evident when you are trapped in a sailing plan and it doesn't occur to you that plans are for your convenience not *vice versa*. The cardinal rule of Caribbean sailing is something the great military strategist Clausewitz very nearly said: no plan survives its first encounter with the elements. Dump the plan. Make another one.

Of course, in hurricane season the weather forecaster is king. Now you really must listen if you are sailing, even if you are south of Grenada and out of the official hurricane zone. In Grenada and Trinidad and Tobago you can still get swiped by a tropical wave or the feeder bands; and even here hurricanes are not unknown. When Flora hit Tobago in September 1963 almost 80% of the rainforest was destroyed; and if the British and French navies hadn't paused briefly from firing cannon at each other, and sheltered together in St David's Harbor, Grenada, in the 1800s, both might have been destroyed by a hurricane.

Hurricanes—something significant in the weather

If every paradise has to have its bad side, hurricanes are it for the Caribbean. (Hurricane, typhoon and cyclone—same beast, different names. All are tropical revolving storms). The Caribs knew their wrath. The name of their god of wind—Huracan—was not to be spoken in case summoned. Hardly had the Europeans discovered the Caribbean than their map makers were noting the fury of hurricanes.

> The Caribbee Iles in or near the month of Auguft are dreadfully afflicted with furious storms called Hurricanes which as it were are peculiar to them.
>
> Notes on *A Map of the World* by John Senex and John Maxwell, 1711

Readers of a nervous disposition, or prone to bad luck, should look away at this point.

Hurricanes are not like a gale. Not even like a bad winter gale in the mid Atlantic. They are a quantum leap above what most sailing boats can survive. A bad sailing season in the U.S. or Europe may see wave after wave of summer gales sweeping over, spoiling your cruising and wreaking havoc with racing schedules. Boats will limp into harbor with torn mains and blown-out jibs. After your third or fourth gale at sea you might wonder about swapping sailing for gardening but by then you may well have the hang of that summer's weather and be sailing in the lulls, sheltering in the gales. Hurricanes aren't like any of that. They are wild storms of intense wind around a low pressure center, commonly able to generate 120 mph winds by centrifugal force, and sometimes 200 mph. They bring thunder, lightning, monstrous seas and torrential rain.

> "For more than nine days I was lost without hope. Eyes never saw the seas so rough, so ugly or seething with foam. The wind did not allow us to go ahead or run or shelter under any headland. I was held on those seas turned to blood, boiling like a cauldron on a mighty fire. For a day and a night the skies blazed like a furnace . . . lightning burnt in such flashes and fury that we believed the ships would be utterly destroyed. All this time water fell unceasingly from the sky. Not rain, but like a repetition of the Deluge."
>
> Christopher Columbus, letter to the Spanish sovereigns Ferdinand and Isabella, on the fourth voyage of discovery 1502–1504

Hurricanes are truly dangerous storms, one of the most intense weather events on Earth. The U.S. hurricane center estimates that the total energy released through cloud and rain by an average hurricane is equivalent to 200 times the electrical generating capacity of the whole world. I cannot begin to imagine how they know either of those two facts but whether they are close to the truth or out by a factor of 200, I know that this is more energy than I ever want hitting my little yacht.

U.S. sailors will have more awareness of hurricanes than Europeans because their Caribbean coast and Atlantic coast all the way up to Long Island is routinely hit by these storms. In Britain, hurricanes and great storms of hurricane magnitude are very rare events but remembered long after for their devastations.

We've had some unusually bad weather in Britain these last few years but the most recent great storm passed over the U.K. in late October 2002. Falling trees killed six people before the storm went over to mainland Europe where another 24 people were killed. The winds and rain are still fresh in my mind as I write this, but I remember just as vividly the impact of what was a greater storm of 1987 when huge trees in the streets of London smashed down on cars and houses. This wasn't a hurricane in the technical sense since it didn't originate in the Tropics. It was a weather bomb from a deep depression originating in the Bay of Biscay, moving through the western English Channel and rapidly northeast to reach the Humber estuary on the east coast of England five hours later.

This remarkably ferocious storm came with gust speeds and mean wind speeds as great as those expected to recur, on average, no more than once in 200 years. It killed 18 people in Britain and four in France. The death toll would have been worse if it had struck in daytime. Some 15 million trees were destroyed, roads and railways blocked, cars crushed.

Greater yet was the great storm of December 1703, still remembered in Britain after three hundred years. Much of what we know of that storm comes from "Robinson Crusoe," author Daniel Defoe's 1704 account of all the evidence he could find on the storm. This "hurricane" (although there is nothing now to tell us whether it was tropical in origin) which rampaged across southern England with extreme effect was probably a fast moving intense secondary low with a central barometric pressure of less than 950 millibars. The strongest winds were on the southern flank, which meant the English Channel and the southern North Sea. The prolonged windy weather which preceded the intense storm had forced much of Britain's shipping to seek shelter and turned them into targets for the new storm. About 700 ships on the river Thames near Greenwich were driven together into a hopeless tangle. Over the whole country nearly 8,000 lives, a third of the merchant fleet and most of the Royal Navy's ships were lost. That is how memorable these massive storms are.

The very specific way in which tropical hurricanes are propagated means that they can be recognized in their early stages and their progress to maturity monitored. Hurricanes develop from the widespread accumulation of thunderstorm cells found over tropical seas. Moist air rises up in the cloud masses of such cells to condense in the cooler air of the higher atmosphere, and release the heat drawn from the evaporating water. The air column becomes warmer and lighter, barometric pressure at the surface of the Earth falls and more moist air is sucked into the thunderstorm system. The system feedbacks positively, fuelling itself. The accumulation of low pressure thunderstorm areas builds up into a tropical depression which, in this region where full gales are rare, is classified as a tropical storm when winds reach Beaufort Force Eight to Eleven, from 35 knots upwards.

In any one year about 80 to 100 tropical depressions develop but only about 10 will become tropical storms, which is when they are given names. Many of these tropical storms won't develop into full hurricanes, but they can still produce extensive damage ashore with rainfall produced flooding. For a small yacht facing a Force Eleven storm the difference between a tropical storm and hurricane may be academic. Tropical storms become classified as a hurricane when they rise above being a violent storm to reach Force Twelve with winds of 64 knots and over—"that which no canvas could withstand," as Admiral Beaufort said, describing his highest category of wind strength. After that hurricanes are graded from one to five. Categories 3 to 5 hurricanes are collectively known as major or intense hurricanes (see Appendix 2).

Most hurricanes do not blow harder than 90 knots, but even this is greater than a very bad Atlantic winter storm. Changes in wind speed don't really tell the story. Remember, wind pressure is the square of wind speed. The damage produced increases exponentially with the winds, so that a Category 4 hurricane on the Saffir-Simpson Scale may produce on average up to 250 times the damage of a Category 1 hurricane.

Caribbean hurricanes, tropical storms and tropical depressions start life off the coast of West Africa but only when the weather conditions enable them to seed and grow. Weather forecasters monitor conditions to see if these will allow the hurricane to propagate. If conditions don't, you can relax. Even if they do, it doesn't mean that the hurricane will develop or that it will come your way, but you need to be alert and stay tuned. You need all the preparation time you can get whether you decide to run out of the way or dig into a hurricane hole.

I think of hurricanes as a bit like the low pressure depressions which bring gales to the temperate regions of the north Atlantic, but more extreme. They form in a similar way to a depression. A depression begins at the edge of two air flows, the tropical air moving east and the polar air moving west along the polar front. The key to their formation is the great temperature difference between the two air masses. Perhaps because of friction between the two air flows a wave-type distortion appears on the polar front with a local fall of pressure at the tip of the wave. This can then turn into the vigorous depression common to us northern European sailors in our home waters, when the warm and cold fronts march across the sea and across our weather forecasts.

Hurricanes need four main conditions to propagate:

- They must start more than 5° off the equator. Any closer than this and the Coriolis Force from the Earth's rotation would be too weak to divert winds from a straight path into the eddies found in higher latitudes.
- Surface sea water must be at least 27° C. Warm ocean water is the main energy fueling the hurricane. Warm water from the equatorial belt is moving north with the ITCZ, and pushing up into the vital region where the Coriolis Effect can be felt.
- Wind speeds at different altitudes must be similar, so that weak ventilation prevents the airing of thunderstorm cells. The concentration of moisture and the rising temperature reduce barometric pressure at the surface. Propagation is only possible from about June onwards, when jet streams in the upper atmosphere are weak. The jet stream is thought to inhibit convection.

- They need a trough-like disturbance in the upper air to give the wave-type distortion that appears in a conventional low pressure depression. For the hurricane, this comes from an "easterly wave," an occasional disturbance in the deep easterly flow of air in the Trades.

This vital easterly wave is, in effect, the local trigger for the hurricane given that the other three factors are already in place. Perhaps it too comes about through friction between two airflows moving in different ways: the east moving Trade Winds and the stationary Doldrums. In the Doldrums the air moves vertically, rising because of heat convection, but not horizontally. It is therefore stationary relative to the Trades. The easterly wave pushing into the Trades is an injection of Doldrum air—moisture laden and with vigorous convection. This releases huge amounts of latent heat which turns into kinetic energy and is then turned into a cyclonic rotation by the Coriolis Force. Here begins the hurricane.

Hurricanes have tendencies but they follow no rules. They are all the more dangerous because of their unpredictable timing and paths. Most are born on the east side of the ocean and blow across at 10 knots or so with the ocean winds. As they reach the Atlantic's western boundary they turn northwards towards the pole in a path usually called parabolic. Hurricanes early in the season have a tendency to head north and most head to the northwest at some point. The problem is to know when. They can stall, curve the wrong way or loop their own loop, and even pick on the same island twice. One of the few predictable things about hurricanes is that they only occur in the summer months, between late May and early December and seldom strike the Caribbean chain south of Grenada. But don't rely on this. In the last few years there have been more late-season hurricanes in November and in 2001 the last hurricane of the year was in December. And, then, in 2003 the first tropical storm came through six weeks before it was officially scheduled. The official hurricane season is June to November and the official zone is north of Grenada but nature is getting less bound by what officials tell it.

Long run hurricane frequency

June	5%
July	7%
August	29%
September	36%
October	9%
November	3%

Source: Pilot Charts of the Central American waters

You can remind yourself of the hurricane season with a little local rhyme. The original isn't as up-to-date as it should be. It leaves out both November and December. Late season hurricanes may be on the increase but they are not new. The hurricane that hit Christopher Columbus during his 1502–04 voyage was late in the season. I have added a new last line to help us all.

June too soon;

July stand by;

August—come she must;

September—remember;

October—all over;

November/December—still flames in the embers.

Hurricanes are too powerful for any of us to risk meeting a rogue which doesn't fit the official timetable and routeing chart.

Hurricanes are fascinating for meteorologists and sailors alike. (You can get information and satellite pictures of hurricane systems on www.mwxc.com). Anyone visiting the Caribbean will soon become aware of the hold they have on island life. They touch the experiences of all sailors here, whether you encounter one directly or not. When I returned to Trinidad in November 1995 after leaving *Petronella* there at the end of my first sailing season I encountered the aftermath of Hurricane Luis. Trinidad was too far south to feel the full blast of Luis. Even so, Trinidad caught some feeder bands that raised waves up to the second floors of homes down the islands to the west of Trinidad, but it was the boats sheltering in the Lagoon at St Martin that were hammered. Over 100 boats sank in that respected hurricane hole. Now, some of these were down in the Trinidad yards for repair. Beautiful 40-footers and 60-footers. Immaculate on one side and stove in on the other, where they had been driven ashore or rammed by other yachts. A friend has a copy of a video taken on a yacht in the Lagoon during the hurricane. Black shapes appear out of driving rain and slip by barely recognizable. Yachts dragging. Finally a shape drives down directly towards the camera and as the outline of a yacht comes clear the film ends.

Better to be hit by a simulation

Not surprisingly, meteorologists study hurricanes intensively and have developed sophisticated computer simulations to track their development and movement. Earlier forecasts relied on mean sea level pressures or low altitude wind speeds but now wind speed and pressure data is collected from different parts of the hurricane system by small radio devices parachuted from aeroplanes specially developed to fly into the eye of the storm. Roughly speaking, computer simulation then predicts the position of the eye up to 120 hours in advance and compares this with satellite images of the actual position. If the predicted and the actual positions are within about 40 nautical miles, the prediction is reckoned to be good and more forecasts are attempted for 24, 48, 72, 96 and 120 hours in advance. The practical point for those of us on the water is that this type of very advanced prediction of hurricane track by computer simulation is only able to forecast the center of a hurricane four to five days in advance, with an error limit of about 440 nautical miles. After the first 24-hour forecast the several tracks predicted at each time period begin to diverge increasingly widely.

Because hurricanes move with the general air flow in the medium level atmosphere they first travel eastwards with the Trade Winds before gradually bending off into the higher latitudes and finally reaching the prevailing westerlies and more moderate climate which takes them east and back out into the Atlantic. During the 1990s the path of most hurricanes and tropical storms was north of Barbados and St Lucia. The main routes cluster over the islands from Guadeloupe to the Virgins. Despite the number of hurricanes in this period the islands are often lucky and escape a direct hit.

Hurricanes have a long reach. The eye of the hurricane, the vortex of the storm, can reach from 10 to 100 miles in diameter. The eye is an area of thin cloud and light winds with monstrous chaotic seas being swept in from all sides. The worst winds, cloud cover, rain and seas are around the eye but the still vicious winds further out can support feeder bands reaching out hundreds of miles. The Virgins and islands like St Martin in the northern part of the island chain have the most hurricane scars but massive damage was done just by swell from the 1999 Hurricane Lenny in the Grenadines and Grenada.

We knew Jean-Louis and Mari from Trinidad, near neighbors off and on for the year or so it took them to fit out their 30-foot racing boat for cruising. They and the dog were sailing around Venezuela, and anchored off Los Testigos. They felt the unusual swell coming in and immediately decided to get out of the anchorage. The engine wouldn't start so they had to hoist sails. There was no wind. Or at least, no horizontal wind. There was plenty of up and down wind as the swell came in at 30 to 40 feet high and was threatening to hurl them at the cliffs. They got clear but it shook them. It was the speed at which the swell came in, without warning. The sky never stopped being clearest blue.

The safe advice is to not go sailing in the Caribbean hurricane zone during the season but this isn't always possible. You, like me, will find yourself one summer north of Grenada and playing the odds of when and where a hurricane might strike. The time you have to prepare for a hurricane depends on how fast it is traveling. Despite the great advances in forecasts you get remarkably little preparation time when a hurricane is traveling at up to 30 knots. The only benefit of a fast moving hurricane is that it clears quickly and is reputedly easier to forecast.

It isn't just ferocious wind speeds which do the damage. Hurricanes carry huge amounts of water vapor and release this as torrential rain. Up to two meters of rain can fall over two days.

Catastrophic floods and mud slides bring immediate damage but also loss of life later from the disruption to water and food supplies. Failures of medical care can cause epidemics.

More damage ashore is usually done by the storm surges of water forced against coasts by the wind and by the dome of water in the vortex of the hurricane, raised by the low barometric pressure at the eye of the storm. The sea can remain rough for days and the waves and currents cause disastrous erosion. Hurricanes can disturb wind patterns across wide areas so that an open roadstead anchorage hundreds of miles away from the storm center becomes a dangerous lee shore and the swell batters the coast on even the sheltered side. In 1995 when hurricane Iris went north up the island chain without any major hit, anchorages on the south side of the eye were untenable because of the southwest winds and high seas. Lenny in 1999 was more dramatic.

When Lenny came to Bequia the crew on the American trimaran *Pistachio* were grateful for help from one of the sons of Daffodil Harris, of Daffodil Marine Services. Bequia was beginning to feel unusual west winds and the young man had paddled out on a surfboard to help *Pistachio* raise anchor and run out to sea. It was already late when he started his return journey. The swell was running in huge waves up the beach. The young man was tipped by a wave, lost his board and had to swim to shore. He timed the surf, clambered up on to the stone jetty and ran for his life. A wave reared up to block the view from *Pistachio*. When the crest subsided the young man was safe on higher ground. The stone jetty no longer existed.

Thank you, Buys Ballot

When a tropical storm or hurricane threatens the Caribbean a storm watch is included in the Marine Advisory issued every six hours from 03.00 by the Tropical Prediction Center in Miami. The Advisory reckons to give 36 hours' notice. When the storm watch is upgraded to a storm warning the Advisory gives 24 hours' notice. As well as this you can get some advance warning of a hurricane from natural signs.

A fall in barometric pressure, normally remarkably steady down the island chain, is a good indication. If pressure falls five millibars, taking into account the usual diurnal drop of three or four millibars, a hurricane is almost certainly on its way. A long, low swell can usually be observed in advance of the storm. Wind strength will increase markedly or switch direction, accompanied by the unusual but classic cloud formation of an advancing depression. From out of an unusually clear sky come cirrus, alto stratus and broken cumulus. When the dark line of cloud bears down on you the winds will increase to hurricane force.

"As the bar of the storm approaches, the seas which have been gradually mounting become tempestuous. Squall lines sweep past in ever increasing intensity. With the arrival of the bar the day becomes very dark, squalls become virtually continuous and the barometer falls precipitously, with a rapid increase in wind speed. The center of the storm may still be 100 to 200 miles away. As the center comes closer the wind shrieks through the rigging, rain falls in torrents, the wind fury increases, seas become mountainous, the tops of huge waves are blown off to mingle with the rain and fill the air with water. Even the largest vessels become virtually unmanageable and may sustain heavy damage. Less sturdy vessels do not survive. The awesome fury can only be experienced. Words are inadequate to describe it.

"In the eye of the storm the wind drops to a breeze, the rain stops, skies clear enough to permit sun to shine through holes in the thin cloud, visibility improves. Mountainous seas approach from all sides, apparently in complete confusion."

From a photocopy marked *Tropical Cyclones* which I have carried for years. The source has been washed away.

To understand these changes, carry a good barometer and one of those informative picture books on weather systems. But above all carry a good radio and listen to the SSB nets. *In extremis*, seek help from Buys Ballot.

The 19th century Buys Ballot's Law is one of the few invariable laws in meteorology. It raises your immediate chances of survival by helping you forecast the location of the storm. An observer in the northern hemisphere facing the wind will have the center of low pressure approximately 100° to the right, which is just a little behind you. Point your left hand into the wind palm down and extend your thumb as far as you can. Your thumb will be pointing towards the center of the storm. Now you can predict the direction of the expected wind and your position relative to the worst parts of the storm and decide to hide or run.

Hurricanes, like other northern hemisphere depressions, spiral anti-clockwise, with winds drawn in to the eye or vortex, and normally travel to the north or northwest. Because of this movement adding swirl to the front side the dangerous half of the storm is its right hand or northern semicircle and its most dangerous quadrant is the northwest. The southern half is, possibly just out of hope, known as the navigable semicircle. Winds in the dangerous semicircle are up to 50% stronger than in the navigable semicircle. Also, the direction of the wind in the dangerous semicircle will force a boat towards the storm whereas the wind in the navigable sector pushes a boat away from the center.

To take avoiding action you need to know the direction of track. The best general advice is for a yacht in the track of a hurricane to go on port tack and maintain a broad reach as the wind shifts. However, hurricanes can travel faster than you can prepare for them at the last moment and the final track they take is unpredictable. You don't want to be playing Buys Ballot's Law close to the eye of the storm but if you are out at sea or out of reach of a hurricane hole it gives you some idea of which way to run to survive. That is exactly what it is: a survival tactic.

Little is known of the currents produced by the ferocious winds of a hurricane, presumably because the vessels out there at the time have other things on their minds. The currents, like the wind waves, are probably less than they might otherwise be because the effect of the high winds is moderated by their relatively short time on any given track and therefore the fetch is reduced. A slow moving hurricane will produce the strongest current. Beware of the possible strong and abnormal currents in working out your escape route. One ship reported being set southeast 50 miles when they expected a southwest current.

I know of very few small yacht accounts of surviving hurricanes at sea. John Caldwell, the developer of Palm Island in the Grenadines, writes of his experience in a 29-foot wooden cutter in *Desperate Voyage*. He describes the early signs of the storm's approach, the violence of the dangerous sector, being in the eye itself and then the damage done by the still immense seas of the navigable sector. Surviving a mature hurricane is rare.

In a hurricane hole and digging

Hurricane holes are fine in theory but there is a certain *frisson* of fear in sitting in a hole as a target for the ultimate storm that cowards like me would rather avoid. No hole will be safe in a bad hurricane. Also, the rise in the number of yachts sailing the Caribbean works against the safety of hurricane holes. Safety in a hurricane hole is not measured in large numbers of likeminded others. The ideal hole probably has one other yacht in it, round some corner and out of your way. The more yachts in a hole, the greater the chance of a boat dragging. If just one skipper flings a puny anchor over and books into the nearest hotel then the domino effect applies when the wind tears loose that boat's grip on the bottom.

> The crazy old god Huracan seems to rub his hands with glee at the chance to punish the hubris of us yachties and the commercial developers who follow us around the islands where they never followed us before. Whenever yachts feel safe enough to congregate in large numbers that crazy old Huracan ups and teaches us a lesson. The Lagoon of St Martin. The south coast of Grenada. Port Zante on St Kitts. And how do we respond? New mega yacht marinas in St Martin, Grenada and tiny St Kitts. Perhaps the lesson for cruisers is to leave those big targets to Huracan and hope he will leave us to our older strategies.

The well equipped cruising yacht should have heavy storm anchors and long warps to look after itself in a bad storm, but few charter yachts carry heavy gear and nor do their staff have the time to moor up a whole bareboat fleet.

Hurricane holes need organization. There are not that many holes in the region. None at all in the Grenadines, Dominica, Montserrat, St Kitts, Nevis, Statia or Saba and none that I would trust in the Virgins, given the number of charter boats that will be trying to get there too. And don't just go by the label. St John has a bay called Hurricane Hole but a lot of boats were lost there during Hugo and Marilyn. The hurricane hole qualities of Simpson Bay Lagoon in St Maarten must have gone down since the increase in mega yachts. A 100-foot mega yacht on the run can do a lot of damage.

It's true that the huge charter fleets in the Virgins face hurricanes but they have no choice but to be in the Virgins and you do. Also, some charter fleets have their own strategy and it isn't one you can adopt. Skippered boats converge on a selected, protected anchorage and raft up, using all their ground tackle to create a massive holding power. I asked a skipper who had been in the Virgins during Lenny what it felt like to be on this raft in a hurricane. "No idea," he said. "We were all booked into a nearby hotel." If you were in the firing line when that raft broke loose it would be best if you had done the same.

You only need to look at the shells of beached ships on the coast of Dominica to realize there is little shelter there. Some of these may even date back to Hurricane David in 1979.

If you were quick enough to get there before the locals you could try the Rivière Salée on Guadeloupe. I might once have tried Le Marin in the south of Martinique but I would have to hope for space in one of the little side coves. Much of the mangrove protection at the top of Le Marin Bay has been lost to marina pontoons and there are fleets of charter boats up there.

Grenada is on the cusp, so to speak, but a lesson for us all. Most yacht insurers drew their line for the hurricane zone as south of 12°30 N or 12°50 N which meant that as Grenada invested in new facilities along its southern coast more boats were attracted to this "safe zone" as an alternative to Trinidad, because they were covered against damage by named storms. Why not? There hadn't been a hurricane hit since Hazel and Janet in the mid 1950s and Flora in 1963. Things might have been different if Joyce had hit the island in 2000 as forecast but she tracked further south as a tropical depression. If Joyce, then Ivan in 2004 might not have been such a surprise.

Ivan hit Granada in September 2004 as a Category 3 but was re-classified as an intense Category 5 the same day. Ivan's eye passed over the south coast of Grenada bringing the added problem of a wind reversal and making normally safe bays and anchorages open to surge as the eye passed. About 800 boats were on the island. Ironically, some yachts had come to Grenada from the north having been warned that Ivan would strike St Lucia. Sadly, some had come from the south, from Trinidad, including friends of ours. Nearly all the yachts ashore were blown over or seriously damaged. More would have been lost if staff and sailors hadn't re-chocked boats during the lull when the eye went over. That sort of bravery isn't something any one can expect twice.

There were tales of yachts being blown out to sea and then back when the wind went round, only to be wrecked on the shore. Five of the 28 yachts anchored in Prickly Bay drifted out to sea with crew on board, never to be heard of again. Only four of the 90 or so boats in Mount Hartman Bay escaped serious damage. The final reckoning was that 400 of the 800 yachts were damaged to the value of U.S. $40 million. Many insurance underwriters moved their southern boundary of the hurricane zone to 12° North, potentially ending Grenada's future as a place to store boats in hurricane season. Some, however, will still give cover to boats if properly stored ashore.

Of course the damage to yachts was a tiny fraction of the disaster that struck Grenada as a whole: 40 people died; 90% of homes were destroyed; two thirds of the population were homeless; the nutmeg and spice crops were ruined. The island suffered U.S. $900 million damages. In such unimaginable circumstances law and order breaks down, as the world was to see again a year later when Katrina hit New Orleans. A state of emergency was declared in Grenada, a curfew imposed, looters shot dead. Yachts were looted at first for their valuable equipment then later simply for the basics of food and water. Yachties grouped together in the boatyards to defend themselves against mobs armed with cutlasses.

The 2004 hurricane season was the nightmare of that decade. We were on the other side of the Atlantic, crossing from the Azores to northwest Spain and working south to the Portuguese Algarve. The weather was dry and sunny though the persistent southerly winds were unusual. Also unusual were the fierce late summer winds and torrential rains from the tail ends of Caribbean hurricanes. One after another they came charging across the ocean, still full of venom. We cowered below, only forced on deck when we had to raise the dragging anchor. We watched the synoptic weather charts as Ivan left Africa and made its way across the ocean to replace Lenny as the hurricane to talk about and remind the Caribbean not to be complacent about who and what is in the hurricane belt. Somehow we all seemed to know that Ivan would be a bad one.

Ivan was trouble. He struck further south than the official hurricane belt. He increased in force as he moved north and became a Category 5. He slammed the populous islands of the Greater Antilles and then land-fell on the U.S. Ivan eclipsed all the other hurricanes between Lenny in 1999 and Tomas in 2010.

In the aftermath of Ivan it seemed all too easy to blame the insurers for luring yachts to places like Grenada by offering cover. One insurer said after Ivan that there never really were any "safe latitudes" in the Caribbean. Don't think of it as their fault. The decision to be anywhere is yours.

Ivan was a reminder that no one in the Caribbean can be complacent about where hurricanes may strike. A year later hurricane Emily hit Grenada as a Category 2 and also caused widespread damage to Carriacou and Petite Martinique in the Grenadines.

We had a personal interest in Ivan. G's eldest son was working in the Caymans at the time. As Category 3 Charlie had passed the Greater Antilles and was hitting the U.S. eastern seaboard a week before Ivan entered the southern Caribbean, he told us, "Charlie nothing, but Ivan looking real bad." When Ivan's storm surge hit Grand Cayman it was nearly as high as the island itself. 95% of buildings were damaged or destroyed. G's son was trapped in rising water that only just leveled out in time. In the end he survived but his car and his apartment and his belongings were washed away. It wasn't the flood water that wrecked his apartment but the damage after the storm blew the roof off.

The old timers are probably right when they say there is no longer a safe hurricane hole in the Eastern Caribbean, because of the danger from other boats. But if you are here in the hurricane season you must always have a hole in mind. Keep no further than a 12-hour downwind-sail and get to it while there is still a good vacant spot, preferably deep in the mangroves and under a good lee. When the warnings come the local boats get there quickest and may not leave much room for you. Then you need at least two days to strip off the sails and running rigging, lay out anchors and run stout lines ashore, making sure that you wrap them with leather or rubber or cloth to prevent chafe. Do the work before the weather worsens. The rain before the hurricane will be so heavy you won't be able to see your bow, never mind the neighbors. In 60-knot winds you will have to turn your back to breathe. Long before the 130 mph winds arrive you will need facemask and snorkel if you have to go outside. If you do have to go on deck keep low and never let go of a secure hand hold.

When your preparations are complete hope that others in the hurricane hole are equally well organized and haven't left their boat as a bomb to come floating down on you at the height of the storm. You either act fast when you get the three-day warning or you spend half your hurricane season at anchor in a good hole. If the latter you might be better off out of the zone altogether. Bear in mind that after the few days of storm come several weeks or months of confusion as the island struggles to recover.

The experience of others, who have faced hurricanes so that you and I don't need to, suggests the following:

- Find a place in the mangroves where you can nose right in and get shelter on three sides. The system of mangrove roots gives you the best soft landing. Try to go somewhere other than a marina. Get out of the vicinity of charter fleets.
- Come in bows first. This keeps the rudder from pounding and bursting the hull.
- Try not to be downwind of danger or buildings, especially corrugated iron roofing. Caribbean buildings are prone to shredding in 100 mph winds. Coconuts are like cannonballs in 135-knot winds.
- Dog down the hatches, protect the windows and block up your hawse hole. When the waves are running green on your deck your bilge pumps may not cope with the water coming down your hawse hole.
- Keep lines from chafing. Lines ashore need several turns around tree trunks. Anti-chafe plastic tubing must be loose and not too flexible. Tube gripping the line will cause it to overheat and weaken. We carry old fire hose.
- Get anti-chafe on early and in the right position. When the lines are under tension it is difficult to adjust the protection.
- Use long, strong snubbers to prevent coming up hard on your chain. Even with a short fetch you will be rising eight feet to the waves. Some 20 feet of snubber might be fine in a gale, 50 feet in a hurricane.
- Have a back up storm snubber on your main anchor lines to give you time to renew the primary snubber if it goes.
- Build in redundancy. Have lines to spare anchor points in case, for example, one of the trees you have tied to is not well rooted enough to hold your strain. The intense rain can soften the ground.
- Use all you have. Anchors in lockers won't save you. When the big winds come you won't be able to dinghy them out.
- Carry hurricane lines. You need at least three ¾ inch nylon warps of about 300 feet. A single line of this length is stronger and more convenient than knotting one up from short lengths.

- Carry long feeder lines. Main warps are heavy, especially when wet, and difficult to lay out. Use ultra light and ultra strong line like Spectra, conveniently wound on a spool, to position your boat. Then lay out the main warps.
- If you are anywhere on the track of a hurricane act as though you will get its full force. Tracks are unpredictable. When the feeder band winds are blowing at 40 knots and the panic hits is not the time to start taking off your 800 square foot fully battened main.
- Don't assume you can use your engine to help hold you up to your anchor. Debris will soon block the water intake or wrap the propeller.

Prepare for the worst. Don't think that something unimaginable won't happen. In the immense violence of a hurricane the word "impossible" will have lost its meaning.

Names to remember

We are lucky that the island chain is more likely to be hit by tropical storms and depressions than hurricanes. As a tropical depression develops into a tropical storm it is given a name. The list is prepared years in advance and alternates in alphabetical order between male and female names. There have only been six hurricanes in the island chain in the decade up to the 2010 but some of these names, and some from earlier decades, are whispered with respect and fear for years after.

I have heard some influential people in the so called "yachting sector" say that the Caribbean suffers from the fallacy of being exposed to hurricanes. I don't think it's a fallacy. Quite the reverse. The worst storms are those that damage our hopes or certainties, such as Ivan in 2004 which proved that the south coast of Grenada was still within the hurricane zone, Lenny in 1999, known as "the great destroyer" for coming in on the leeward or less protected side of the islands, and Luis in 1995 which sank over 100 yachts in the Lagoon to show that St Martin was not as safe a hurricane hole as we all supposed. Where does the fallacy lie in that lot?

Tomas. 2010. A Category 1 when it hit Barbados in late October, Tomas went on to just miss Grenada before hitting St Vincent and St Lucia as a Category 2. Hit and miss seems the right description. Tomas must be one of the most unpredictable storms, changing up and down in intensity and making nonsense of the predicted tracks. But it was dangerous, doing intensive damage to Barbados, St Lucia and St Vincent. Barbados appeared to suffer the biggest economic loss but at least 14 people were killed in St Lucia; many roads disappeared under landslides; the main towns of Soufrière and Vieux Fort were cut-off; and the banana crop vital to the island was wiped out. And then Tomas strengthened and went on to hit the sad country of Haiti, still suffering from the massive earthquake damage at the beginning of 2010 and the lethal damage from a succession of four hurricanes in 2008.

Earl. 2010. In August Earl intensified into a hurricane as it passed just north of the Leewards to become a major hurricane when it hit the northern Virgin Islands. Storm alerts were issued from Montserrat to St Martin all through Antigua and Barbuda but thankfully no major damage was reported.

Omar. 2008. A major hurricane in the north of the chain damaging Antigua more that the other islands. Omar was unusual in that it came out of the Caribbean Sea traveling northeast as it crossed the island chain.

Dean. 2007. The Caribbean was lucky. Dean, one of the most destructive of recent hurricanes, killing 45 people overall, slipped through the St Lucia channel between St Lucia and Martinique while only a Category 2. It caused about U.S. $400 million damage to Martinique and Guadeloupe and about $8 million to St Lucia, although its surge and storm winds affected every island in the chain. Damage could have been worse. The island governments had advanced warning of Dean and activated the hurricane emergency response groups throughout the region in anticipation of great damage given his intensity.

Emily. 2005. The first intense hurricane of the record breaking 2005 season. Outside the island chain, in the U.S. mainland, 2005 will always be remembered as the year of Katrina. Emily was classified as a hurricane as she passed Tobago. She was Category 2 when she hit Grenada on July 4 intensifying the next day to Category 3 and then to 4 and 5 as she ran northwestward to Mexico. Emily is the earliest Category 5 hurricane recorded for the Atlantic basin. Emily hit Grenada while the island was still trying to recover from Ivan's immense destruction.

Ivan. 2004. Proof that Grenada is in the hurricane zone. Ivan, another intense hurricane in another busy hurricane season, arrived over Grenada as a Category 3 hurricane four days after he had left the vicinity of the Cape Verde islands. Later that day he was upgraded to catastrophic Category 5, with 150 mph winds. Ivan blasted the yachts in the main harbors and along the south coast of Grenada but he also brought devastation to the whole island. Ivan was the 10th most intense Atlantic hurricane ever recorded.

Isabel. 2003. The first Category 5 hurricane in the Atlantic basin since Mitch in 1998. Isabel reached winds of 140 knots in the open ocean but weakened as it neared the shores of the U.S. and met cooler sea temperatures. She made landfall on the North Carolina coast as a Category 2 blowing at 85 knots. Isabel tracked northwest across the eastern U.S. producing vast amounts of rainfall and causing damage estimated at $1 billion. 30 people died.

Olga. 2001. An unusual hurricane in an unusual year. One of the very few to survive into December.

Michelle. 2001. Another late season hurricane. Hit Cuba in early November and only failed to cause mayhem because half a million Cubans had been evacuated from the path of the hurricane.

Iris. 2001. A Category 4 and the deadliest hurricane of 2001. More than 30 people were killed. The banana crop of Belize was wiped out and there was extensive flooding and infrastructure damage just one year after Belize was slammed by Keith.

Lenny. 1999. The great destroyer. Events in the region are still defined as "before Lenny" or "after Lenny." Lenny broke the rules. It was one of the most errant and destructive storms to hit the Caribbean. At least ten people died. Lenny was only the fifth major November storm on record. Storms as late as this seldom make it to a full hurricane. What made Lenny even more unusual was that it came in on the leeward, less protected side of the islands. Most people thought the season was over until Lenny arrived. Lenny followed an unusually varied path, like the stochastic walk of a dog meeting lamp posts. As a consequence, forecasters were getting the track wrong even just hours in advance.

On 17 November 1999 Lenny was declared a Category 4 storm. It hit St Croix with 150 mph winds and 15-foot storm surge, washing away homes, roads, boats and part of a cruise ship dock. The following day Lenny stalled over St Martin dropping about 30 inches of rain and sinking or grounding about 130 boats, mainly in the Lagoon. Three days later Lenny headed out to sea and storm warnings were lifted. By then the main town of Anguilla had been flooded, 400 people in Martinique and 450 in Guadeloupe were homeless, houses in St Lucia were swept into the sea and as far away as Grenada U.S. $5 million of damage was done to coastal roads. Beaches and jetties were washed away, palm trees felled and massive damage done to coral reefs on the leeward side of islands from Grenada to the Virgins. In Soufrière, St Lucia, streets were buried under three feet of gravel from 30 feet surf. Even the north coast of Trinidad reported the worst seas in 50 years.

Georges. 1998. Considered to be as bad as David in 1979, Georges came close to damaging Dominica but instead headed north. Its hurricane force winds extended 150 miles from the center and hit Antigua and Barbuda, St Kitts and Nevis. It came close to damaging Dominica. All the Leewards felt its extensive tropical storm winds.

Luis. 1995. The great storm of 1995. Luis hit Antigua and tarnished the reputation of St Martin as a safe hurricane hole four years before Lenny came through and did even worse. Over 100 yachts were sunk in the Lagoon by Luis.

Marilyn. 1995. Followed Luis to give the Virgins and St Thomas in particular a good thrashing.

Debby. 1993. Not a hurricane but classed as a tropical storm, Debby caused loss of life in Dominica and washed away 80% of the island's vital banana crop.

Hugo. 1989. Causing massive destruction and loss of life. A catastrophe in the Virgins. The islands were lucky, though. Gabrielle, two weeks earlier than Hugo, was bigger and more powerful but missed the islands and history.

Gilbert. 1988. One of the worst ever recorded.

Klaus. 1984. Hit St Thomas as a tropical storm but put over 100 boats ashore.

David. 1979. An extreme Category 4 hurricane that did huge damage on Dominica. The island was ill-prepared, not expecting David to make a direct hit. However, it struck southern Dominica with 150mph winds. Huge rains caused landslides; hurricane winds eroded the coast; the capital Roseau was hammered: 80% of houses were destroyed and three quarters of the people left homeless.

Testing the predictions

One of the most eminent forecasting teams has for a long time been run by Professor William Gray at the Department of Atmospheric Science, Colorado State University, and is now headed by Philip Klotzbach. Their predictions are widely borrowed. Even the National Oceanic and Atmospheric Administration (NOAA) uses research from the Colorado team, although NOAA calculates its forecasts independently. Colorado University and NOAA websites are good sources of hurricane information.

The Colorado team has been building a data base of climatological indicators since the 1980s. They modestly say that after 20 years of hard work their predictions are still improving. The team not only forecast each whole season but try their hand at the much more difficult task of forecasting single months during the main period of the season. These are issued at the beginning of the month itself.

Their problem as forecasters is that hurricane seasons in the Atlantic basin (which covers much more than the Caribbean chain) vary more than those of other tropical cyclone basins. Major factors underlying future hurricane activity can vary unpredictably at critical times before and during the season, forcing forecasters to keep revising their projections even during the season.

The team puts out its initial forecast in December of the preceding year and then periodically during the forecast year. The table below gives us a picture of both the accuracy of the forecasts and the historic intensity of hurricanes in the last five to six years. The table shows mid-year forecasts and actual outcomes and compares these with the 50-year average of 1950 to 2000. Most of the last few years have been above average activity. The most active year (2005) and the least active (2009) have been the hardest to predict. The 2010 season was well above average but closely predicted by the team. The range predicted over this period is less than actually happens. The team is more conservative than nature.

Hurricanes compared with mid-year forecast and 50 year historical average

	1950-2000 average	2010 Actual (May/June forecast)	2009 Actual (May/June forecast)	2008 Actual (May/June forecast)	2007 Actual (May/June forecast)	2006 Actual (May/June forecast)	2005 Actual (May/June forecast)
Named Storms	10	19 (18)	9 (11)	16 (15)	14 (17)	9 (17)	23 (15)
Named Storm Days	49	88 (90)	27 (50)	85 (80)	35 (85)	50 (85)	103 (75)
Hurricanes	6	12 (10)	3 (5)	8 (8)	6 (9)	5 (9)	13 (8)
Hurricane days	25	38 (40)	11 (20)	30 (40)	11 (40)	20 (45)	45 (45)
Major Hurricanes	2	5 (5)	2 (2)	5 (4)	2 (5)	2 (5)	7 (4)
Major Hurricane Days	5	11 (13)	3 (4)	9 (9)	6 (11)	3 (13)	17 (11)

Figures rounded to nearest whole number

One clear message from the table is that prediction is a difficult business. One of the main elements in a hurricane forecast is whether this will be an El Niño or La Niña year and often this doesn't become clear until well into the season. As happened in 2010 when the strength of La Niña became apparent in about June of that year, forecasters will often find themselves running new predictions as late as August. This means their forecasts are only beginning to settle when the season is well under way. Nor is it the case that the forecasters always err on the same side, of too few or too many hurricanes. Half way into the season they can be correcting upwards or downwards from their initial predictions.

It doesn't help to have key elements in the forecasts so remote from the action in the Atlantic basin. El Niño and La Niña are events of the eastern Pacific. Over on the eastern side of the Atlantic, rain from the Sahel region of Africa can have major effects on convection in tropical storms and hence their ability to develop hurricane force winds. Above average rainfall in the Sahel is usually associated with above average hurricane activity. Hurricane predictions are raised or lowered as data comes in showing the level of rain in the Sahel but these rains are affected by the El Niño. Forecasting from inter-related variables is not ideal, since the model may enhance the direction of the predictions.

If we are now moving into a period when seasons vary even more from the average, as we might if we move into the more extreme weather of global warming, hurricane forecasting will become an even more difficult art.

The last decade has been the most active hurricane period on record and forecasters are not reckoning on this changing. They believe that higher levels of hurricane activity will persist through the early decades of the 21st century. The lower activity in some recent years does not change their overall argument since the major climatic changes towards global warming which underlie the changing frequency, timing, location and intensity of Caribbean hurricanes will persist.

A breath of a boy, and his shy little sister

El Niño, called the "Christ Child" or "Boy Child" because it occurs around Christmas, is a reversal of prevailing ocean currents in the eastern Pacific so that the cold currents off Peru and Ecuador are replaced with a weak warm current. At the same time there is a reversal of the normal winds so that the prevailing westerlies are replaced by weak easterlies.

El Niño is one extreme of a cyclical event known as the El Niño/Southern Oscillation cycle (ENSO). The other half of ENSO is La Niña (the girl child) when unusually cold sea surface temperatures occur in the eastern tropical Pacific and the easterly trade winds strengthen. The system oscillates from El Niño to La Niña on average every three to four years.

El Niño is associated with reduced Atlantic basin hurricane activity. La Niña is thought to bring more hurricanes. La Niña may, but does not always, follow El Niño. Since 1950 El Niños have occurred about 30% of the time compared to about 23% for La Niñas.

El Niño and La Niña bring such large-scale changes in sea-surface temperature that they affect atmospheric and climate patterns around the globe, with greater effect on month by month variations in climate than any other terrestrial event.

Global warming and/or extreme weather

The debate on global warming has often been side-tracked, with good science being squeezed out, but of late the debate seems to be making progress as non-scientists drop their opposition to the idea and scientists can get on with questioning data and conclusions and laying down new programs for better data and analysis. International cooperation is the key to this and much of the drive comes from humanitarian instincts to reduce the impact of extreme weather disasters around the world. In early September 2010 leading climate scientists from around the world gathered in Britain to finalize plans for an international databank that would revolutionize their ability to predict disasters. This initiative was in response to the 2008 drought in Australia, crop failure across central Asia, and floods in southeast Asia but it also come out of concern for the more recent events of record temperatures in New York and South Florida, heatwaves in Russia that sparked massive wildfires in the main grain growing areas, flash flooding in France and Eastern Europe, and floods in China. But nowhere was hit harder in 2010 than Pakistan where 2,000 people died and 4 million were affected by the torrential rains and immense flooding.

In early 2011 there was massive flooding and loss of life in Brazil, Sri Lanka and northern Australia from the unusual monsoon season. The rains in Brazil have brought lethal mud slides with probably more than 1,000 killed. The scale of the floods in eastern Australia is unprecedented, with huge areas underwater. The February cyclone that followed the January floods was the most savage in a century with its 180 mph winds. Thankfully there has not been large scale loss of life. The news of this cyclone in Australia may not have been getting through to some of you. It coincided with the worst snowstorm in the U.S. since the 1950s, as snow covered Maine to Texas and sometimes as thick as 20 inches. Sri Lanka has suffered three major flash floods since May 2010, affecting over two million people, but the events of January 2011 are the worst, bringing damage second only to the 2004 Asian tsunami. The UN Global Disaster Alert and Coordination System rates these floods as a 100-year event. But even as this was happening local meteorologists warned of yet more extreme weather in Sri Lanka as La Niña pulled down temperatures at the equator by 5°C. The earthquake and tsunami in Japan in March have only added to the human toll, as well as a nuclear crisis.

These events are real and horrific. The causes are less clear cut. These extreme southern hemisphere rains are thought to be linked to the extreme cold water in the Pacific from one of the strongest La Niñas in the last 50 years. This La Niña began in June 2010 and the Pakistan floods were just the first signs of trouble. The disastrous floods of Queensland, Australia were being forecast by late November. La Niña is likely to continue well into 2011.

Of course the Earth has always been subject to major temperature fluctuations, with fairly rapid swings between ice ages in the last three million years. The last ice age ended about twelve thousand years ago; we know that a "little ice age" occurred from the sixteenth century through till the nineteenth century; and the Milankovitch cycles based on James Croll's calculation of the Earth's elliptical orbit of the Sun forecast another major ice age in about 40,000 years. The jury is out on the exact timing of this next ice age but there is little doubt that astronomical influences on long term climate do not rule out man's ability to mess things up in the short term. Since 1945 one peak of higher temperatures has been exceeded by another. Spring now starts a week earlier in the northern hemisphere than it did in the 1960s.

Take to the hills

Forecasters say that the strongest hurricanes of the last few decades may be nothing compared to the more intense hurricanes of the 21st century if global warming continues. The unpleasant trick of global warming would be to help hurricanes reach their maximum potential. At present hurricanes run into land or the cooler waters of the northern Atlantic before they reach their maximum. With higher sea temperatures more storms will reach their potential, bringing stronger winds and much more rain. NOAA calculated that the winds of the strongest hurricanes could increase by 5% to 12% for a sea surface temperature increase of only 2° centigrade.

Measurements show that sea surface temperature rose as fast in the last decade as in the two decades before that, even taking account of the El Niño effects, and the 2010 sea surface temperatures hit a record twelve-month moving average.

As well as raising the ferocity of Atlantic basin hurricanes such global changes may play havoc with where hurricanes strike. The southern end of the Caribbean chain may become more vulnerable. A hurricane in Trinidad is reckoned to be a once-in-a-century event. Well, that and chaotic weather has suddenly become commonplace. Tropical storms have been recorded in the southern Caribbean in the past and global warming may mean they are more able to reach the higher strength of a hurricane.

The odds against a hurricane may be greater in the south but often that just means that the potential for damage is greater if yachts sit ashore for the hurricane season with masts and rigging up and jibs still on. Yards that know they are in the path of hurricanes have responded to the danger. Yachts stored ashore for hurricane season in Bobby's Marina, St Maarten, for example, have taken their masts down since Hurricane Bertha came through in 1996. Since then no boats have been blown over.

Yards in Grenada and Trinidad are close to the shore and just a few feet above sea level. I have sat in both places wondering what damage the tidal wave from a storm surge or the dome of water in the vortex would do, sweeping through these yards. It would certainly carry away the shores and chocks holding up some of the yachts. It would inevitably push a huge amount of equipment, such as dinghies and work benches and smaller hulls and oil drums and even some buildings, ahead of it like a bulldozer's ram. Perhaps we should be building boatyards on the tops of hills.

Picture this—a reading list for weather forecasting

Even professional forecasts are just the background to a sailor's weather knowledge. In the end, those of us wishing to go to sea in small boats must keep our eyes on the sky, the sea and the winds and make our own assessments of how observed conditions relate to the predictions.

There is certainly more to Caribbean weather than meets the eye of those used to North America or Europe. Spotting the unusual in the tropics is more difficult for those of us from the higher latitudes, but vital. There is useful information in the region's pilot books but you may feel the need to read a specialist weather book or two.

I like weather books with lots of photographs, such as Alan Watts' *Instant Weather Forecasting*. Mr Watts' book may already be familiar from your sailing back home. A useful little book which is very focused on what makes tropical weather and events over the island chain is *The Concise Guide to Caribbean Weather* by David Jones. It is just that.

5

The land that glows

Everything about the Caribbean is dynamic, including its geology. The land so far beneath your keel is in a state of flux, shaped (as science has relatively recently discovered) by the enormous forces of plate tectonics. These forces created the island chain itself, through a series of volcanic eruptions along an arc known as a subduction zone. Volcanic activity in this subduction zone cannot help but periodically break out on the surface of both the islands and the sea. This can add a certain spice to cruising the area, even if it just means you have occasionally to strike an island off your itinerary or take a wider detour around Kick-'em-Jenny off northern Grenada. Of more everyday interest to the sailor is the effect that the underwater shapes can have on the currents and wave heights on the windward coasts and in the passages between islands.

You are sailing over the eastern edge of the Caribbean plate. This segment of the Earth's crust is being squeezed by the North American and South American plates. These two much larger plates are older, and therefore cooler and denser, than the Caribbean plate and so are forced to slide under their younger neighbor. This sliding action, called subduction, occurs at an average rate of between one and two centimeters a year, not smoothly but in spasms and sudden thrusts. These thrusts produce huge forces at the boundary, the energy being released in volcanic activity and earthquakes.

The Caribbean chain of islands lies in an arc parallel to the mid Atlantic Ridge and about 1,000 miles away from it. This mid Atlantic ridge is where an upwelling from the Earth's upper mantle emerges along the line of a trench. The ridge is, in effect, an underwater mountain range rising about 13,000 feet from the ocean plain, only breaking surface in Iceland and as isolated peaks in the Azores, Ascension Island and Tristan da Cunha. The forces here are pushing the American and European continents apart at a rate of about five centimeters a year. Let us hope that the telephone cables running across the Atlantic ocean have a little slack built in to cope with this. It wasn't always so. These ocean ridges were first discovered in the 19th century by the engineers of the Atlantic Telegraph Company. When laying lines from Europe to America they had assumed the ocean bed to be flat. The first telegraph connection broke within weeks because the engineers had strung their cables across peaks higher than the Alps.

The activity along the arc of the Caribbean subduction zone is relatively mild compared to other subduction zones, but even a little of this sort of activity can go a frighteningly long way. Seventeen volcanoes have been active in the region in the last 10,000 years and there have been about 40 major eruptions in the recorded history of the last 400 years. This may not seem many but one was among the most deadly known to the world. In 1902 Mont Pelée erupted on Martinique killing about 30,000 people in what was then probably the finest city of the Caribbean, and giving its name to this type of blast. This was probably the first time in recorded history that such a blast had been seen, which is probably why vulcanologists still use the French term *nuée ardente* to describe the glowing-hot, ground-hugging, totally-destructive cloud of molten lava fragments and burning gas created when the highly viscous magmas erupt with unimaginable explosiveness. As well as these more explosive events, the current volcanic activity in the region creates boiling, bubbling lakes, hot springs and sulphur-ravaged landscapes.

The islands of Grenada, St Vincent, St Lucia, Martinique, Dominica, Guadeloupe, Montserrat, Nevis, St Kitts, St Eustatius and Saba have "live" volcanic centers. The rest, while not live or volcanic, are close enough to those that are to catch occasional severe ash fall and tsunamis.

The islands in the chain were created in two major periods of volcanic activity and their modern form reflects this. The first period, about 60 million years ago, created the eastern-most islands of the chain at about the same time as it created the Greater Antilles. These earliest islands gradually sunk below the sea, and when they later re-emerged had been covered by the limestone and sedimentary rocks laid down by marine life. These older islands are Anguilla, Antigua, the eastern half of Guadeloupe, Barbados and parts of St Martin. These were already flattened and dead volcanoes by the time the second series of eruptions occurred about 30 million years ago. The islands created then are still active or semi-active volcanoes.

From the gates of hell—the day St Pierre died

Mont Pelée gave its name to the Pelean eruption, the lethal and devastating combination of a hot sideways blast and incandescent cloud, as hot gas and red-hot rock fragments rip across the land at high speed. This is reckoned the most dangerous form of volcanic eruption. There is no way of diverting the lethal *nuée ardente* or pyroclastic flow. The erupting mass can be as hot as 700°C. A blast of only a few minutes can devastate areas of 20 square miles or so. Anchor in the bay and visit the museum up the hill in modern St Pierre to get a sense of what happened here over one hundred years ago.

The deadly eruption of Mont Pelée on May 8, 1902 came with little precedent. Two small eruptions had been recorded in 1792 and 1851. Early in 1902 hydrogen sulphide leached out of the volcano and in April that year a minor blast of steam warned that the volcano was becoming active again. Earth tremors and mud slides had already claimed human lives by now, but in the days before the first eruptions of May there were more warnings of potential danger as waves of yellow ants and black centipedes came down into the lower fields and even into houses, followed later by an exodus of snakes from the hillside, including the deadly pit-vipers.

The volcano gave off huge explosions in the first days of May 1902. The ash falling on the city of St Pierre in just one day was nearly two inches thick. Walkers climbing to the summit saw that the crater was no longer dry; a new cylinder cone was producing boiling water. Then two days before the final great explosion the crater rim gave way and the newly formed boiling lake sent a 30 foot mudflow down a river valley, carried a rum factory into the sea and raised a small tidal wave in the bay; 23 people died.

Problems worsened in the last days of St Pierre as electricity generators clogged with ash and food supplies ran short. This was the time of a major election on Martinique and the ruling conservative party feared losing power to the socialists. The mayor and governor were keen to calm their main electoral base of St Pierre and wanted to keep pro-government voters in the island's capital. The governor's Scientific Commission issued statements that St Pierre was in no danger of mudslides or earthquakes. No one realized that the red glow from the crater on the evening of May 6 showed that molten rock had finally reached the surface. Early on the morning of May 8 the whole mountainside blew out. The huge blast sent the gas, steam, scalding mud, scorching ash, drops of molten rock and red hot stones straight down on St Pierre at speeds of over 300 mph. Little survived. The rum casks in the distilleries ignited. The city became an inferno. In the bay, only one of the large sailing ships survived. The other ten or so, and all the smaller vessels, were overturned or smashed.

"Where have you come from?" asked officials in St Lucia. "From the gates of hell," replied the captain of the *Rodham*, his ship scorched and most of the crew dead or dying.

Nearly 30,000 people died in St Pierre; only about 70 survived, including the famous Auguste Ciparis, often described as the sole survivor of the eruption, who had spent four days in the city dungeon before being rescued.

Coastal villages were also hit. Four hundred people at Le Prêcheur were killed by a mudflow earlier on the morning of May 8. Four hundred others from Le Prêcheur climbed a hill to escape further mudflows but were killed by the *nuée ardente* which, ironically for them, missed the village. The eruptions continued during the rest of May.

Still too hot to handle

Six islands are currently active or have a recent history of volcanic activity: Dominica, Guadeloupe, Martinique, Montserrat, St Lucia, and St Vincent, but the greatest of these is little Montserrat.

The current volcanic activity on Montserrat, following the re-activation of the volcano on Soufrière Hills in the southern end of the island in July 1995, is the most disruptive in the island chain. About twenty people died. The island suffered near total economic collapse. The capital, Plymouth, has been completely destroyed.

Activity levels change from year to year but the volcano has continued to be active with rockfalls, mud and lava flows, earthquakes and the continued building and partial collapsing of the magma dome. In late summer 2000 a small explosion released pressure that had been building during the summer. Lava flowed and an ash cloud rose about 10,000 feet. Early in 2010 the volcano shot ash about nine miles high in what was probably the most dramatic event since the 1995 eruption. The volcano has been relatively inactive at the surface since then but sulphur dioxide emissions and evidence of continued activity deep beneath the volcano indicate another phase of lava flow and growth of the dome is possible.

I nearly called in at Montserrat in 1998 as we sailed south from St Kitts. We had the right wind and one of the crew was anxious to visit a disaster area and explain to the local population that not everyone in Britain was opposed to continued occupation of the island. The island remains a dependent territory of Britain and questions over the level of support to the remaining population and whether more should move to Britain while the dangers were assessed, were hot news that year. In the end I was against adding the burden of sightseeing tourists to the disaster that nature was inflicting on the island so that night, as my crew slept, I assumed the moral high ground and steered us several miles to the south of Montserrat. In the morning our throats were still raw with fine particles of smoke-borne dust and everything inside and outside of the boat had a coating of finest grit. Montserrat was creating its own nature tourism right there before us, but I wasn't ready.

Soufrière, from the French *soufre* for sulphur, is a recurring name for volcanoes in the islands. I can think of five Soufrières and would not be surprised to learn of others. The Soufrières on Guadeloupe and St Vincent are, like Soufrière Hill on Montserrat, stratovolcanoes. They have large, steep-sided cones made of stratified layers of lava flows.

La Soufrière on Guadeloupe is the first eruption to be recorded in modern times. It blew in 1660 and has erupted eight times since then. Its most recent eruption was in 1976–77.

La Soufrière on St Vincent, 4,000 feet high, is more dangerous. It erupted violently at the turn of the 18th, 19th and 20th centuries. The 1902 eruption, the same year as Mont Pelée, killed 2,000 people. Lesser eruptions occurred in the 1970s. The 1979 eruption started with only 24 hours' warning. The first event, lasting about two weeks, raised a steam and ash column 12 miles high. The second was a relatively quiet extrusion of a lava dome; 20,000 people (perhaps 20% of the population) were evacuated. No casualties but a lot of crop damage.

The summit of La Soufrière, Guadeloupe. *Photo: Courtesy of Ph Giraud, Tourist Office of Guadeloupe.*

Don't Kick-'em-Jenny

Volcanic activity is not confined to the land. Kick-'em-Jenny is the lovely name of a strange patch of sea a few miles north of Grenada and close by the small islets of Diamond Rock, Ronde Island and Caille Island. The name is possibly a corruption of the French *cay qui gêne*, "the troublesome cay," because the currents caused difficulties for the old sailing ships. They still cause trouble for today's yachts.

> Gordon was probably sailing too close to Kick-'em-Jenny when his near shipwrecking occurred. It was bright daylight and calm but he was busy with music and rum and realized too late that he was being sucked onto the rocky headland of Ronde Island. The slatting sails were not going to save him and the engine took longer to fire than his nerves needed. He was in the surf line before his yacht responded and began to turn offshore. I met up with him two days later in the sheltered harbor of Tyrell Bay on the nearby island of Carriacou. His behaviour was erratic, which at the time I put down to a problematic love life but which I later realized was due to the major fright he had experienced at Ronde Island. I've never felt comfortable with the place ever since. Coming south from Bequia a few years ago with a strong easterly wind G and I hit a patch of mean waves on the western, leeside of the three little islets. A huge current was flowing through the channels between the islets and we were pleased not to have tried to slip past on their windward side even though that would have allowed us a fast sail down the windward coast of Grenada.

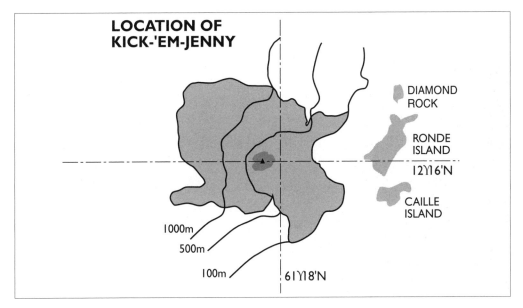

LOCATION OF KICK-'EM-JENNY

DIAMOND ROCK

RONDE ISLAND

12Y16'N

CAILLE ISLAND

1000m

500m

100m

61Y18'N

Fig.4 The location of Kick'-em'Jenny

Most charts show Kick-'em-Jenny as the second name for Diamond Rock but vulcanologists place it at approximately 12°18'N, 61°38'W, offshore and just west of The Sisters and Ronde Island. Nearby Caille Island is made up of two youthful craters and lava flows.

Kick-'em-Jenny is the southern-most active volcano in the Lesser Antilles and the only one below the sea. Its base is about three miles in diameter and rises 4,300 feet from the ocean floor. This major submarine mountain is itself sufficient to cause currents and wave disturbance at the surface, apart from the volcanic activity, but Kick-'em-Jenny has erupted 12 times in the last 60 years, making it the most active volcano in the region. The 1939 eruption (when the volcano was first discovered) sent a black cloud nearly 1,000 feet above the sea. The eruption lasted for at least 24 hours and generated a series of two-meter sea waves or tsunamis in northern Grenada and the southern Grenadines. These were not recognized as tsunamis at the time.

Eruptions since 1939 have not been as dramatic. However, the volcano has been in a state of continuous low-level eruption, with some nasty kicks in between. The 1965 eruption produced strong earthquakes on Ronde Island. The 1974 eruption threw material into the air, boiled the surface of the sea and produced spouts of steam. The 1990 eruption was thought to have blown its underwater top off and a similar event was recorded in 2001. No eruptions have been recorded since 2001 but a 2003 underwater survey discovered a second vent three kilometers from the volcano. This new crater is where the old dome used to be, meaning that the active vent is deeper than it used to be and Kick 'em Jenny has not grown closer to the surface since the early 1960s.

This restless period has been enough to make the Government of Grenada along with the Seismic Research Unit of the University of the West Indies establish a four-tier system of alerts during 2001 and a permanent exclusion zone for pleasure craft of 1.5 km. When the volcano becomes more active pleasure craft must keep at least 5 km clear.

Alert level	Exclusion zone	Symptoms
Green	1.5 km	All quiet. Below historic activity
Yellow	1.5 km	Restless. Activity observed or expected
Orange	5 km	Busy. Eruption may begin with less than 24 hours' warning
Red	5 km	Hot. Eruption in progress or expected any minute

During that first year of 2001 the alerts were at orange (severe) and yellow (less severe). In October 2001 there was an increase in seismic activity and in December 2001 an eruption, albeit completely submarine, and the area was put on orange alert for four days. Activity then quieted down and the area went back to yellow alert. By mid 2003 the periods between activity were lengthening.

The area seems to have been on yellow alert most of the time since 2003 but you can check the current alert on the Seismic Research Unit website, www.uwiseismic.com.

If Kick-'em-Jenny continues to grow at past rates, and doesn't blow its top again, it could emerge above sea level sometime this century. Best not to be tacking over it at the time.

More to the point for most yachts (as well as people living close to the shore in Grenada) is that with the summit so close to the surface any new explosions can have violent effects above the surface. Scientists are also taking the possibility of a major tsunami seriously.

The best monitoring technique for a volcano—visible inspection—doesn't apply with Kick-'em-Jenny. If she blows there could be a dangerous and rapid ejection of hot rocks and ash into the water column and air above the volcano. A sinister danger for passing yachts is that a concentration of volcanic gas bubbles may cause a drop in water density such that the yacht could lose its buoyancy and even sink. Recent studies have shown that the volcano is degassing continuously. If a big quantity of gas is blown off, it will happen without warning.

Care should be taken when sailing this area. The Seismic Research Unit has been pressing for a permanent exclusion zone, largely to save pleasure craft from themselves. Too many yachts continue to sail right over this danger. If you're reading this, don't go there.

Kick 'em Jack

Kick 'em Jenny has a brother. Geologists using a remote-controlled submarine found a 1.2 km high underwater volcano three kilometers from Jenny in 2003. It must have been there a long time. It seems inactive and looks like a completely separate volcano from Jenny.

Drive-in volcano

Volcanoes can be sights to visit too. Solfataras and fumaroles are the last stages of volcanic activity in some places. A great example of Solfataras is the famous "drive-in" volcano of St Lucia.

Visit the wonderful hot springs at St Lucia and the world famous boiling lake on Dominica. The so-called mud volcanoes of The Devil's Woodyard in Trinidad, well worth seeing with a name like that, are on a major thrust fault.

Get the book out

During 2003 the Caribbean Development Bank financed a Volcanic Hazard Atlas of the Lesser Antilles to give information on the nature and dangers of each active and potentially active volcano in the islands. The atlas is edited by Lindsay, Robertson, Shepherd and Ali of the Seismic Research Unit and was published by the University of the West Indies in 2005. It is a reference work for the region. See uwiseismic@uwiseismic.

6

A people to know

Caribbean cruising is a rich cultural experience and sailing a small boat guarantees greater exposure to local culture than any other way of visiting the islands. In the islands you will find two traits—the very local particularities of an island nation state, which when politicized can look and sound remarkably like nationalism, and the shared experience across the region of a broadly similar socio-economic and essentially agricultural reason for being. This shared Caribbeanness reaches back to the period when slave societies were created here on a scale never seen before or since, but it also comes right up to date in that all islands here are affected by the same worldwide economic trends.

Caribbeanness may seem deceptively familiar to you. After all, Caribbean people work in every English-, French-, Spanish- and Dutch-speaking country, just to name a few. I can only really speak of the English language countries. Caribbean artists, writers and musicians above all others give us access to their culture and language. Language means a lot here. Derek Walcot, poet and playwright born in St Lucia, won the Nobel Prize for Literature in 1992 largely for his inventiveness with language. V S Naipaul, one of the Trinidadian Naipaul brothers, was awarded the Nobel Prize for Literature in 2001. The French poet and writer St John Perse from Guadeloupe was awarded his Nobel in 1960. Jean Rhys, author of many fine books but none better than my favorite *Wide Sargasso Sea* was born in Dominica. Trinidadian Earl Lovelace has given one of the best introductions to the meaning of Carnival in his novel *The Dragon Can't Dance*. This is not an exhaustive list of writers. Just a curtain raiser to show the quality of writers in this region. I shouldn't really mention poet Fred D'Aguiar because he is from Guyana and so not from the island chain, but his razor-sharp poetic novel *The Longest Memory* happens to be the most moving story of slave plantations I have read. So there you go. I haven't even mentioned the music makers. The influence of the great Jamaican Bob Marley is everywhere in the Caribbean and the world. Few socio-political songwriters anywhere in the world can compare with Trinidad calypsonian David Rudder.

You might think that the Caribbean will be culturally familiar to you and their language readily comprehensible just because this West Indian diaspora is so large. It won't be. You will find much here that you recognize but the surface familiarity will catch you out.

Separated by a common language

The English-speaking visitor will struggle to understand the local dialects. It isn't just a different vocabulary, although you will find words from hip-hop modern American and 18th century rural Britain. It isn't just a different grammar, although you will notice more missing verbs and different uses of the first and third person. What strikes me most is how the different speech rhythms confuse my ear and cut me off from full comprehension. These are African rhythms to be heard in the French of Martinique and Guadeloupe and in the English of Nigerians and Ghanaians. In the Caribbean these rhythms remind me of calypso music rather than the pentameters of English.

Arguments about speech communities, language and dialect, concepts which I find elusive enough when I think about the way we speak on my ancient little island of Britain, never mind when I pontificate about British English compared with American English, seem simple compared to the task of classifying the English spoken in the Caribbean. I know from my journeys round the region that the English language has developed distinct dialects and different *patois* or *patwas* across the islands, so that even I can tell a Trini from a Bajan or a Vincentian, but there seems some essential Caribbeanness about it. Certainly, there is enough in this to generate support for the, as yet, tentative idea of a "Nation Language" for the region.

Trying to pin down or legislate for language is seldom a sensible use of anyone's time, despite the best efforts of some wonderful dictionary makers. From the standpoint of their own Englishes, natural speakers of English from Britain and North America will find the English of the Caribbean original, unpredictable and marvelously complex.

It is claimed that the West African slaves brought to the Caribbean for the hugely profitable labor intensive sugar trade were chosen from tribes with separate languages, as a way of preventing a co-ordinated revolt against the slave masters. These languages, separated by vocabulary, still had much in common in their grammar. As a result, the retained grammar is similar across the Caribbean islands while the vocabulary borrows heavily from English. The degree of this differs across islands. In Jamaica, for example, where plantations always had to import slaves to maintain their labor supply, the English language was continuously Africanized. In Barbados, an early British colony and long established sugar plantation, the work force was maintained by natural growth and Barbados English was less reinforced by African influences. Topographically too, on this flat island there was simply less scope for slaves to escape or avoid contact with the natural English spoken by the British.

English is not the only language of the English-speaking islands. Many have a French-based Creole language reflecting the time they spent under French control. St Lucia, for example, switched from British to French control 13 times before finally remaining British. A large proportion of the population there are bi-lingual in English and a patois understood across French-speaking islands as well as other English-speaking islands. Local Creole or patois, once stigmatized by the ruling classes as "bad English," is recognized by linguistic anthropologists as a language in its own right. The rich inventiveness, the vivid qualities that reflect the Caribbean itself, leads many local writers to use it. Half a millennium ago the English language made a quantum leap in richness as Shakespeare and his contemporaries made it their plaything. Something like that seems to be happening to the English language in the Caribbean.

As with language, so with culture. The region expresses its cultural traditions from the old countries of Africa, Europe, Asia and the Mediterranean in many ways but is also re-working those into new forms of its own. Perhaps the Caribbean felt like this 50 or 100 years ago—a region in transition, re-inventing itself. Perhaps it is always on the cusp of major change. I cannot know about this from my limited time here but I do know from the last half decade that there is a huge cultural energy that seems hell-bent on expressing its own identity.

Sugar and spice—no basis for an economy

Economic hardship has shaped the level and nature of the Caribbean diaspora. The islands began their modern life as prime agricultural colonies but not in what you would call a utopia of social harmony. The large-scale, slave-based plantations were ruled by the whip and worse. When abolition meant that slavery could no longer provide the kind of mass labor force that sugar planters demanded, indentured labor was tried. The largest source of these new workers was India. But the old cruel habits of being a sugar planter were to die hard. An official British observer reported to his government that jail for the indentured East Indian workers had replaced the whip used on the enslaved Africans.

The plantations grew sugar, cocoa, cotton and coffee but for the longest while sugar was king and made huge fortunes for the planters –"as rich as a sugar planter" they used to say in London. King Sugar struggled from the 1840s but the market for sugar cane was finally decimated by sugar beet and better technology in the 1880s. Other crops replaced sugar but this and the end of slavery meant that plantations declined to be largely replaced by small-scale, share-cropping, subsistence agriculture. In some smaller islands people turned away from the hardship of working the land to the sea; to boat building, whaling, fishing and inter-island trading.

Small island agriculture, even now, although spices are grown, is heavily dependent on banana crops. Bananas not only face uncertain futures in markets protected by Europe or the U.S. but are periodically ravaged by hurricanes and occasionally by volcanic activity. Even today, in the big French islands and Trinidad with their more noticeable commerce, industry and other natural resources, most islands rely relatively heavily on agriculture. The smaller ones have no manufacturing industry at all. Only the larger islands or those in the Virgins have a service sector capable of earning foreign currency. The lucky islands are developing tourism as an alternative economic base.

Tourism is a good source of external earnings in hard currency and one the islands are well suited to, whether luxury hotels or the rapidly growing eco-tourism. But it does make for something of a dual economy. The hotels and restaurants here, which range from pretty good to luxurious world-class, exist alongside deep poverty. The value of yachting tourism, from visiting yachts and charter yachts, is one that governments are

Not all is spick-and-span. This old plantation house in Guadeloupe, now fallen into disrepair, is still a fine building in a beautiful plot of land. *Photo: Courtesy of the author.*

beginning to recognize, especially with encouragement from international agencies. The United Nations Economic Commission for Latin America and the Caribbean recently commissioned a two-year study into the growth and development of the yachting industry in the island chain with the idea of devising a sub-regional strategy. Apparently you and I make up an industry and, would you believe it, yachting is "one of the least understood sub-sectors of the tourism industry." No matter, with a little more research and implementation you and I will soon be enjoying a "unified Eastern Caribbean yachting product" as the islands increasingly come to share St Lucia's view that "our product is actually enhanced by its location among other islands." Well, I think I know what that means.

Despite my natural cynicism I'm sure this is a good idea, especially if it means that visiting yachts will increasingly feel more welcome by officialdom. There has already been an Eastern Caribbean Yachting Summit to discuss a joint approach to using the UN findings. But if you fear that every island will soon feel like every other one, don't worry. There is a lot that could be improved by greater cooperation and none of it need ever turn yachting into a "product." And if you think that governments already appreciate the role of yachting in their local economy, just put these two facts together:

- The contribution of yachting to the St Maarten economy was one of the main reasons the UN study was set up and part funded by the Dutch government.
- Some months after the Eastern Caribbean Yachting Summit a member of the Dutch St Maarten Island Council felt under attack when hearing criticism from

cruisers. What did he say to these drivers of the important yachting sector? "Leave now. Do it today."

Whatever the contribution of yachting to the island economies, for most people living here the really hard days when agricultural workers were housed in sub-standard estate barracks and women as well as men would work in construction and road building—a halfpenny for a half day's work—and large numbers of men went abroad to support their families, are probably over. During the 1950s about 10% of Jamaicans emigrated to Britain. As one of the large islands of the Caribbean this group dominated the Caribbean population of Britain. The much lower emigration of Trinidadians to Britain reflects the greater wealth of that country in those years, when it was oil-rich. More English-speaking Caribbean immigrants are now attracted to North America rather than Britain.

The governments of many Caribbean islands describe their countries as Third World economies. I don't think they are as poor as that. Sure, pockets of severe poverty are not hard to find but that's true also in Europe and North America. While gross domestic product per head varies considerably from Caribbean state to Caribbean state, being highest in the larger more industrial islands, it is in general two to three times greater than that of the poorer African states or India. In turn, of course, it is anything from one tenth to one half the GDP per head of the most developed western economies, such as the U.S. and countries of Western Europe. One positive factor is that the growth rates for GDP are often high, even if coming from a low starting base.

The economic reality of being in a poor region is obvious on all but a few atypical islands like Mustique or St Barts, the tiny hotel island of Petit St Vincent or the affluent sub-region of the Virgins. Economically the Virgins stand out from the rest of the Caribbean. They are more like a tropical offshore state of the U.S., with well dressed people, smart cars, solidly built roads and houses, international shops, and world class restaurants and hotels. When I think of other Caribbean islands where there is comparable affluence it is limited to the pockets where the mega-rich locate. English Harbour and Falmouth Harbour in Antigua, for example, have mega-rich yachts beyond the dreams of the rest of the islands, but step outside and you are on dusty roads bordered by ramshackle houses on the way to the squalor that some mistake for quaintness in the capital city of St John's. Wealth is not just greater in the Virgins. It is more evenly distributed.

In practical terms, being in an economically poor region means massive income inequality and the resulting political and social tensions. It means more roadside slums and shanty towns and more blatant security shutters and armed guards in bars, shops and filling stations. It means pot-holed roads and beaten-up route taxis—a sort of bus-van working a defined route and carrying as many passengers as they can. It means administrative and communications systems that don't work as well as you, from the First World, would like. The equipment repair promised to you in seven days or the parts promised for tomorrow sometimes simply won't happen. Whether this is Third World or just life in the Caribbean I don't know.

A fisherman checking the waters of the quiet little anchorage at Anse la Raye, St Lucia. The exposed reef keeps out the swell from the north. *Photo: G. Jardine.*

Some features of socio-economic development reflect the past support and traditions of the old colonial powers. Literacy levels, for example, are high in most islands, indeed higher than that of the 97% level reported for the U.S. This puts Caribbean literacy at two to three times that of developing African countries.

Do not assume that because poverty so often seems to breed crime in the developed countries of the First World where you may live, that it does so here. The Caribbean seems to me to have an old fashioned, highly moral culture. This is not an unreservedly good thing, since not all old fashions in morality are better than new ones. There is crime here, that is undeniable, and on the rise. But to me it seems a strangely different incidence of crime to the type I have grown familiar with in Europe. It can be massively petty—the theft of two coconuts, widely reported in the press in Trinidad—and senselessly violent. But relatively little is directed at yachts even though I read and hear of more thefts from yachts. The huge surprise to me sailing in the Caribbean is that the unintentionally but nonetheless flaunted wealth of visiting yachties does not attract more theft.

Giving back—community relations

Long-stay foreign yachts often like to involve themselves in the local community. In many of the small and independent countries of the Caribbean the scope is often limited. The restrictions on work permits and periods of stay, especially in the ex-British islands, are interpreted in ways which only allow foreign sailors to make a contribution through some charitable project. I think this is a shame for both the local communities and the yachties. Many live-aboard yachties have advanced and valuable skills and hard-won experience from the various professions: administration and management, business enterprise, media, computing and communications technologies, research, education and academia, all of which would be of immense value here in leap-frogging the problems of under-development. They bring different ideas and values as well as practical contacts back to their worlds. These offerings are all likely to be welcome to individuals in the Caribbean islands as opening broader horizons but seem less welcome to government. To yachties, getting involved in practical ways that draw on their past enables them to reach more deeply into the ways and values of the Caribbean, and so give something back to the countries they are visiting.

Foreign yachties are probably best organized to contribute to the island communities on those islands where there are large numbers of long-stay yachts. In St Martin this may be deflected into working in the marine industry, since the island has developed this massively in the last decade or so. In Trinidad, the contribution comes by virtue of the large number of longstay live-aboards based there and the very positive reaction and affection of most of them to the people and culture of Trinidad and Tobago. Crews are involved in considerable educational projects as well as organizing fund raising for groups in special need.

The Boaters Charitable Giving Project set up in early 2003 helps cruisers channel their donations and skills to greatest effect on each of the islands. Look for them on www.caribcruisers.com and find similar projects in the pages of *Caribbean Compass*.

The good, the bad and the boat boys

If you have only sailed in the U.S. or Europe you will not have direct experience of, or even heard of, boat boys. You will, probably on the first day you sail out of the Virgins into the rest of the Caribbean chain.

Boat boys are vendors who make their living performing a range of services to visiting yachts, not all of them welcome when offered. The term, by the way, does not imply any age or disrespect. Boy is a common adjective among people in the Caribbean, as common and harmless in its use as it is in many parts of Britain. It carries none of the insulting associations which a Black American male might feel. A boat boy may well turn out to be a boat-person of mature years and fine social standing.

Many expressions in common use in the Caribbean may feel a little archaic or insensitive. You don't have to use these expressions if they carry resonances that make you feel uncomfortable but bear in mind that those are not the resonances that locals know. These words simply reflect the different roots of English here, just as American English has words which British English finds archaic or loaded with different nuances and vice versa. But sometimes the newer, supposedly neutral expressions miss the target by a country mile. Please stop me and complain if you ever hear me using the recent official term for boat boy—Beach-Front Service-Provider.

And as for the boat in question, this may be anything from a leaking skiff with a broken oar to a powerful pirogue with a 30-horse engine on the back of it. The services you are offered may range from taking a line ashore, diving for conch or lobster, being offered fine French wine or guided to local tourist sites. Boat boys are a source of good information about their island—good walks, tour guides, bus timetables and so on.

Take a little care with boat boys themselves but more especially take a lot of care with the stories you hear of them. Many visiting yachts regard boat boys as a canker in paradise but they are not. At worst, they are a manifestation of the economic poverty of the islands. Their pestering of boats is part of their survival. At best, you cannot do without them. Start out with an open mind and a generous appraisal of boat boys, and try to stay that way. I know they often arrive when you are stressed or busy with anchoring or mooring and you would rather they just went away, but that is no reason to be rude to them as some cruisers are, to the detriment of us all. Be courteous to them, as you would be to anyone whose island you are visiting, and they will be courteous and kind to you.

Not all islands have boat boys. I haven't seen them in Trinidad or Tobago or Grenada, nor in Antigua or the islands north of there. I am not sure that I would call the man who delivers fresh bread and croissants on a water bicycle in The Saintes, ringing his bell to attract attention and picking the delicacies out of his basket with tongs, a boat boy. More of a *bateau garçon*. You can decide that when you meet him. Almost all the islands of the Grenadines have boat boys offering supplies. On some islands the boat boys have very specific interests. At the Pitons, St Lucia, for example, they will be ready to take your line ashore. In Prince Rupert Bay, Dominica, the boat boys really want to take you for a trip up Indian River but they will also bring you provisions or taxi you ashore. One may meet you more than a mile offshore and then come to visit when you have anchored.

Strict rules and procedures apply with boat boys, as is so often the case in the Caribbean when to the visitor the system seems anarchistic and haphazard. Unless you already know a boat boy and want to continue to use his services, the etiquette is to deal with the one who first contacted you and the code for the others is to respect this. So if Spaghetti or Respect or Jesus Lover is the first to speak to you even though far offshore or in another bay, wait for him to turn up.

> "Welcome to Paradise", the boat boy said as we lay at anchor in Prince Rupert Bay. He was preparing to leave, now that he knew Spaghetti had met us offshore. "I've been to Dominica many times," I said. "Then welcome return to Paradise," he replied. No one has more natural charm than the people of this island.

In some islands or bays the procedures may be less solidly established and some furious arguments will take place as the boat boys argue over precedence. Don't get involved. There will be some code which will be honored. You may mistake a fierce argument for what is no more than the local style. St Vincent, for example, is currently going through a period of bad reputation with charter fleets because of the aggressive behavior of its boat boys but then people from St Vincent have a reputation throughout the islands of being noisy and a lot of noise can often sound aggressive. Perhaps there is some truth in it. Charter companies know these things. It pays them to keep their finger on the pulse. They also recently warned their clients against visiting St Lucia because the boat boys there were becoming too pushy.

> It was our first time in the Cumberland Bay anchorage of St Vincent and the old man made it clear to the others that we were his client. However, after he had instructed us in tying bowlines round trees and gone, grumbling because we were not going to eat ashore at his cookhouse, a younger man on a surfboard began to chat. G asked about some fruit and the man said he could get it for us but not till the morning. I said we were leaving early and named some ridiculous time in case G needed an excuse to say no, but instead she did what I took to be a very foolish thing. She gave the man money and told him to deliver before our sailing time. Come the morning, I had given up on the man and our fruit and berated G for her naivety. I mean, I am the naïve, trusting one on this boat, not her. G is always berating me for the risks I take with local people and reminds me that she is a Trini and knows the Caribbean better than an Englishman. Just after I had cast off our tree line a board came paddling out from the shore. The fruit and small change was delivered with apologies for being late. I was so pleased to be proved wrong that I let G lecture me on her superior ability in assessing human character.

You might think that paying someone to take a line ashore is not worth very much, but it is if it also involves advice on where best to drop your anchor and where best to land your dinghy. More to the point, it is certainly worth the money if it means that the security of your yacht at anchor or your dinghy ashore is guaranteed. A short while ago a spate of dinghy thefts on Dominica came to an end when the boat boys started their own security watch. After all, it is in their interest to have yachts visit rather than sail by to a more secure anchorage. In this case, the boat boys even met the prime minister and persuaded the government to improve policing in the area. In international St Martin, there are no boat boys but there are dinghy thefts on a scale that would be unacceptable if visiting yachties thought it was down to the locals.

Whatever you think, boat boys are just part of sailing in the Caribbean. The bottom line is that through them you make a direct and immediate contribution to the local economy and usually get something back in return. The boat boys are making a living and that is a positive gain in this economy. Beyond that, though, they are part of maritime life and as close to its pains and pleasures as any sailor.

> When in November 1999 Hurricane Lenny hit the usually secure bays along the lee side of St Vincent boat boys in Cumberland Bay rowed bareboat charterers ashore in hair raising conditions, carried their luggage over swollen rivers and waited with them for local buses to take them to safety.

7
Island passages

Sharp points of perspective

The Caribbean islands are the peaks of great mountain ranges thrown up by the action of plate tectonics on the Earth's crust. Imagine a relief map from the deep sea-plains to the high mountain peaks. You are floating around the tops of mountains to match the Alps or the Appalachians.

The sea driven by the North Equatorial Current has to suddenly change direction to flow round these massive obstacles. What it does on the surface depends on whether it is flowing over the relatively shallow plateau on which a number of islands stand or through the deep channels that divide these plateaux.

Once past the island chain the sea deepens to something like 6,000 to 8,000 feet until it meets another but lesser underwater mountain chain, the Aves Ridge, running north-south from Saba to the Isla de Margarita off Venezuela. The only point at which this ridge breaks surface is Aves Island, a tiny uninhabited place about half a mile by quarter of a mile and no higher than 12 feet above sea level.

The limestone half of Guadeloupe, the islands of Antigua and Barbuda, St Martin and St Barts, are part of the older volcanic period and on more of an outer arc than the more recently volcanic Nevis, St Kitts and Statia on the inner arc. Two volcanic crescents is a useful way of visualizing these islands of the northern Leewards. Although Antigua and Barbuda make up part of the same nation, Antigua is further from Barbuda than it is from Nevis. However, between Antigua and Nevis is a deep water channel, separating them from their distinct ridges.

These older islands, though less mountainous, rise just as sharply from the ocean floor and influence the Equatorial Current just as much. Knowing the relative depths of banks and deeps is important:

* The flow of currents and the sea state in the inter-island passages varies by the depth and obstruction of shoals and banks.
* The large area of a shallow bank acts as a heat sink. Its absorption and release of heat energy affects the sea state over and around it in ways curious and novel to sailors from higher latitudes.

It was calm enough to anchor and go ashore to visit this little lump of rock, normally off our beaten track. But we drifted by towards the Virgins, and in the night the wind that came would have made the Saba anchorage unpleasantly rolly. *Photo: G Jardine.*

Bouncing checks on the banks

Banks of shallow water act rather like the land in storing heat. They release this heat at night to give a lee-effect. Channels along these banks can be protected at night and passages there are in smoother conditions, but in the day when there is no protection the water can be rough with a jumble of waves. The wide and shallow Saba Bank is one to be avoided. It is a fine example of what an old West Indian schooner-man might call "a vexing piece of troublesome water."

Shallow banks also act rather like headlands in refracting waves. When the depth of the bank is less than half the wave length it produces a drag on the waves, causing them to slow down. Their wave length then reduces, but their height remains the same and they must steepen and finally become unstable and break. In rough conditions this can produce dangerous seas in the lee of the bank.

At the northern end of the chain the Virgin Islands sit on the most obvious of all the banks, and in a way not found elsewhere in the Caribbean chain. St Martin, Anguilla, and St Barts also sit on an extensive shallow bank but not one that offers the kind of scale and protection of the Virgins. They are separated from the shallower Antiguan and Barbudan bank to the south by a channel 1,000 meters deep. Further south, the channels between Antigua and Guadeloupe, Guadeloupe and Dominica, and then Martinique and St Lucia are between 500 and 600 meters deep but in the middle of these, the channel between Dominica and Martinique is over 1,000 meters deep. These are immense depths where the sea can push the Equatorial Current very hard.

Road map of the ups and downs

The main topographical features of the Leeward and Windward islands of the chain are:
- St Martin, St Barts, and Anguilla, islands of the older volcanic period, sit on the same shallow bank north of St Kitts and Statia. Depths are mainly less than 50 meters.

- Antigua and Barbuda sit on a shallow bank with depths mainly less than 80 meters. The ocean depths approaching this bank come up from about 4,000 meters to about 400 meters in 10 to 20 miles and then very sharply to the last 60 to 80 meters.
- Montserrat and Redonda are high points on a small bank with 800 to 1,000 meter depths between them and the larger bank on which Nevis, St Kitts and Statia sit. The shoal patch of 20 meters due south of Nevis rises sheer out of the 800 meter deep passage between Redonda and Nevis. The depths on the windward side of Nevis and St Kitts rise almost sheer from 600 meters.
- South of Guadeloupe is a four-mile wide channel 200 meter deep between Guadeloupe and The Saintes, until the 60 meter bank of The Saintes.
- The 10 mile wide Dominica Channel between Dominica and The Saintes has depths of 600 to 800 meters but drops to less than 200 meters a few miles west of a line from Terre d'en Bas and Cape Melville.
- St Lucia and Martinique sit on the outer curve of the arc of the island chain. This is the point at which the winds and currents can change for you. If you had adverse winds when going north or south you can expect them to become freer from here. Going south you usually command the wind. Going north, you command the current. In the 18 or so miles between these two islands the ocean bed rises from a depth of 1,200 meters to a bank of 600 to 800 meters and then drops off again to the west to depths from 1,300 to 2,000 meters. Contrast this with the 400 to 600 meter depths in the 25 mile wide channel between St Lucia and St Vincent, with its shoal patch of 100 meters mid way across before the great depths of 1,800 meters just five miles north of St Vincent.
- Over the extensive area of the Grenadines from Grenada to St Vincent the shallow bank ranges from 20 to 60 meter deep but the eight mile wide channel between Bequia and St Vincent has depths of 400 to 800 meters.
- Between Grenada and Trinidad the depths vary considerably. The shallow plateau off the southern end of Grenada extends for some 10 or 15 miles and then the ocean deepens to 1,000 meters or so until the 200 meter contour line that circles round the north of Tobago and extends due west of that island, roughly one third of the way from Grenada to Trinidad. As you come up on to the mainland shelf and Trinidad the depths drop to 50 meters and less.
- Between Tobago and Trinidad, in the Galleons Passage, the current is obstructed by shoals and banks but still runs hard.

Easy days among the Virgins

The topography of the Virgins is very different from the Windwards and Leewards. The main problems for the passagemaker are all in the approach and entry into the protected waters of the Virgin Bank. The charts show such a density of land, rocks and reefs that even a clear thinking brain may glaze over. At first sight from the sea these islands appear like a single piece of land with no clear channels. The pilot books, with their infinite listing of different harbors for breakfast, lunch and dinner, only serve to compound the mental confusion. Take heart: once up on the bank the pilotage around the islands is wonderfully straightforward.

When approaching the Virgins bear in mind that all vessels must clear in. Even U.S. vessels entering the USVI must clear in. Later, when you travel between the USVI and the BVI you must again clear in and out, but that does not involve any great passagemaking.

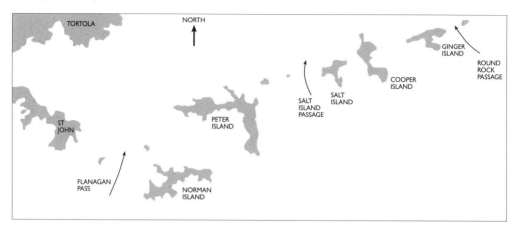

Fig 5 Useful passages and anchorages in the Virgin Islands between St John and Virgin Gorda.

You should plan your approach to arrive at one of the six ports of entry but do not be a slave to this. With the possible exception of Great Harbour on the BVI island of Jost Van Dyke none of the ports of entry are places I would choose as pleasing anchorages. Rather than be caught in one of these overnight, for lack of daylight to find an alternative, and rather than pushing hard to make the port of entry before daylight fades, I would rather find my good anchorage while I still had a lot of day ahead of me and go through the official clearance early the next day. The Virgins are famous for fine overnight anchorages in which you can relax and swim and generally sort the boat and yourselves out after your passage, and I am sure my friends in Customs and Immigration would not deny this to an honest skipper who is only seeking to put the safety of the ship and crew first. And anyway, this is not an area where you should be sailing at night until you are very familiar with it, and not even then.

The Virgin Bank is open to the prevailing Equatorial Current with its westerly set but is subject to some notable exceptions. In summer the current is predominantly northwest or north but can run strongly to the south in a reversal known locally as the "Saint John's tide."

Tides will affect your sailing here more than in the Leewards and Windwards. Though the rise is not great the flows can be strong in the narrow channels. The time and rate of flows, however, as well as the height of tide, is more likely to be influenced by winds and other meteorological influences. Bear in mind that where the tide is the greater influence you will be subject to periodic reversal in the flow of the water. The tide, unlike the Equatorial Current, turns.

Personally I love the challenge of tacking to windward against a tide and the satisfaction of a tricky bit of pilotage made under sail, but more than that I love the steady beat of my diesel engine pushing me through one of these little Virgin passes in half an hour instead of the half a day it would take me to sail. Most modern cruising yachts come with a reliable marine diesel which is more than a match for a couple of miles of one-knot or even three-knot current.

Go with ease

Some of the passages between islands in the Leewards and Windwards need a full day even when starting before dawn. Precious sailing time on the day itself should not be spent in preparations that could have been done yesterday. This doesn't just mean taking sail covers off the evening before, checking the engine, jotting down navigation notes and preparing food. It also means getting as close to your departure point as you can commensurate with a good night's sleep.

You may have spent some time exploring the island of departure and have chosen a quiet little bay from which you can safely leave in the dim light before dawn, rather than leaving from one of my prime harbors. This is good, so long as the bay is quiet and the exit is safe in poor light. Make transits or bearings or enter GPS waypoints before you go, just to make sure.

It is always vital to arrive in daylight whenever possible, hence the value of leaving early when you can more comfortably cope with poor light. Also, when calculating your passage time in the prevailing conditions, and with the hindsight of how long the last similar passage took, remember to calculate your journey from anchor up to anchor down, rather than from headland to headland. The channel separating St Lucia and Martinique, for example, is about 20 miles across but the sail from an anchorage in Rodney Bay, St Lucia, to the anchorage off the city of Fort-de-France, Martinique is the best part of 40 miles.

Sailing between islands at night is nothing to be afraid of here and is often to be preferred to, say, a planned eight hour beat which turns out to be longer and leaves you five miles offshore on a new island, with an anchorage you don't want to risk in pitch black. The absolute rule of small boat pilotage also applies here: if in doubt, stay out.

A night at sea can mean a dawn landfall, when visibility is usually good and the full day is ahead of you to arrive or enjoy ashore. Battling in late in the afternoon just means you don't do anything till tomorrow anyway.

If coming to an island or anchorage where there are lights ashore, these will be visible a comfortably long distance away and usually further than you can see details and judge distance in bright daylight. Night time can mean calmer conditions for sailing and calmer conditions for arriving. Night also saves you from the worst of the sun.

There is relatively little night traffic at sea here although local schooners may not bother to show lights until they are close to you or until you flash yours to encourage them. Make sure you are keeping a watch and running with lights, *pour encourager les autres*. More of a problem is closing the land where fishing nets and pots have been laid across the track of the unwary.

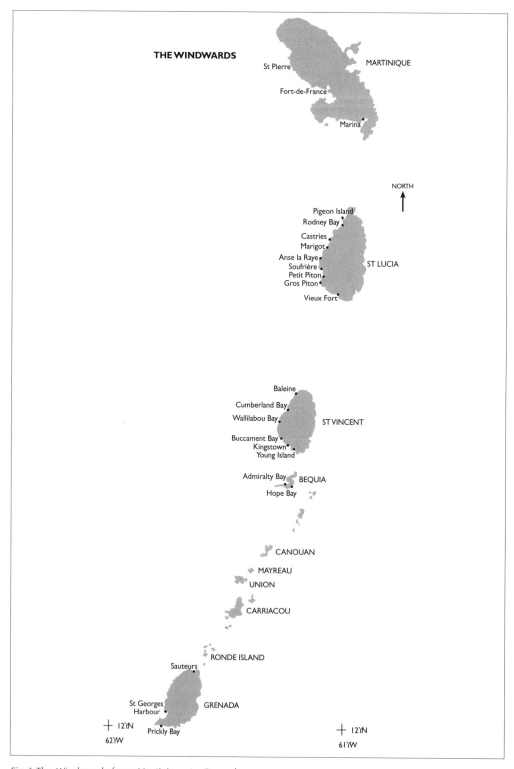

Fig 6 The Windwards from Martinique to Grenada.

Arriving is also as important as leaving and you should plan time to recover before you set off on the next leg.

Making passages that are longer than from one island to the next is a simple matter here in the island chain, and wonderfully enjoyable. If the wind is unusually north or south one year then the best strategy may be to make long hops along the chain in one direction and come back visiting each island the other way.

The tips that follow in this chapter offer guidance on passagemaking between islands as you sail from one prime harbor or anchorage to another. Of course, if you choose to skip an island or two, as can be done with ease, the tips can be adapted to help on these longer passages.

The long goodbye

Given the scale of the geology it may seem an anti-climax that much of your sailing will be timed to catch the opening hours of Customs and Immigration. You are, however, sailing from one nation state to another and while the logic of such frequent official clearance may often escape you, it is the logic of nation states the world over. Not all the states charge to let you in or out of the country but some, the ex-British islands in particular as well as those which are still British Dependent Territories, will charge port fees, clearing out fees, cruising permit fees, extra for charter yachts and fees for other things they may just have thought of yesterday.

One of the great burdens we sailors must bear is the inconsistency in Customs and Immigration policies. Despite the recognition at a political level of our contribution to local economies the systems we suffer seem designed to maximize hassle and chase us from the region. Ah well, perhaps we shouldn't grumble. Is it really such a heavy burden for so much pleasure?

Take, for example, fees. Fees are changing particularly fast just now, as island governments realize that, on the one hand, yachting is a growing source of tourism to be encouraged further and, on the other hand, that they can raise more revenue from it. Some new fees seem either confused or misguided, as well as painful. The pilot books may already be out of date so check in *Caribbean Compass* or with another cruiser.

British Dependent Territories apply the rule back home in Britain that until the skipper has officially cleared the vessel and crew, no one else should go ashore. I find this is a rule more on paper than practice, but it is best not to flaunt it openly. A similar procedure applies in the U.S. territories, but is somewhat more restrictive. In the USVI the skipper must go ashore to obtain preliminary clearance, after which all crew can then go ashore taking their completed papers to Customs and Immigration. One crew is allowed to remain on board on anchor watch but they too, if not a U.S. national, will also have to personally clear in.

In some islands you will be told you must report to clear in the minute you arrive. Trinidad and Tobago, since they have written their regulations particularly clearly, is a good example of what you may also find elsewhere. Once a vessel enters their territorial waters it must come alongside the Immigration/Customs jetty and may not proceed to

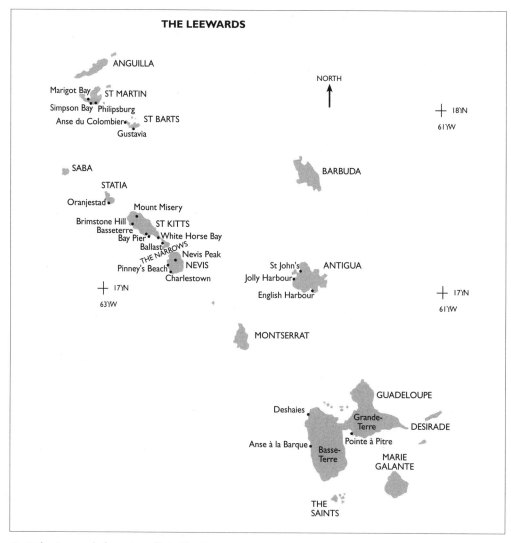

Fig 7 The Leewards from Anguilla to The Saintes.

a marina or anchorage without permission. You can be fined for anchoring or landing crew before checking in. Skipper and all crew must proceed immediately to Immigration and then to Customs. In case you were wondering what "immediately" means it means "No Delays," on any day, at any hour of the day or night. Actually the UN Convention on the Law of the Sea allows 24 hours on arrival and 24 hours on departure and 24 hours refuge. And as long as no immigration or quarantine laws are broken it allows a vessel to leave without any need to check in during that 24-hour period. You may one day find yourself reminding officials of these laws.

Those who sail the Caribbean year after year become particularly concerned to avoid the overtime charges for Customs and Immigration. It may not seem a lot to a new visitor, even a worthwhile contribution to the local economic development fund, but the experienced passagemaker doesn't much care for the standard charges and can become incensed when a minute's delay means it is doubled to overtime. The U.S. and French islands do not charge for Customs and Immigration.

Unfortunately, along with entry and exit charges you may find enough subtle rules of deportment to baffle a professional diplomat. Never be any less respectful and courteous than you would be to your own Customs and Immigration officials. Always present yourself in smart clothes as an explicit signal of this respect. If not, you may be accused of insulting the uniform. You will certainly not be helping yourself to a friendly, trouble free clearance.

Make your first task ashore the visit to officialdom with your briefcase of papers. It isn't really so difficult. You will need a document to show you are a foreign registered vessel, such as your certificate of registration, and identity papers for each person on board.

North Americans can offer a birth certificate or voter's card as valid identity papers when re-entering their own country or coming into a British territory, but the Caribbean is a chain of many different nation states and the one document that identifies you in all of them is your passport. North Americans do not need visas to enter any of these countries.

Non-U.S. nationals entering the USVI by boat will need to have obtained a visa in advance. Don't assume you will automatically be issued with a visa on arrival as may have happened if you ever flew into the States. Sailing in is different. There is considerable confusion about where you can get these entry visas. Some yachties claim to have obtained visas from countries in the Caribbean but the official word is that the U.S. embassies in the Caribbean will only issue such visas to Caribbean nationals. For the rest of us, be safe and get one before coming into the region. You will also need to be able to show the clearance papers from your last port. This is vital. So don't go visiting these different countries without officially clearing in and out. You may carry lots of other papers relevant to your boats, from radio certificate to weapon certificates, but these are extras, special to your circumstances. Don't show papers you innocently think might interest the official. Why raise a hostage to fortune?

When you enter a port of entry it is best to fly your yellow Q flag from the starboard spreaders unless you know for sure that the Q flag isn't needed. If an official concludes your clearance with "And now you may lower your Q flag," don't tell him you haven't raised it. You might offend his sense of irony. Now you may replace your Q flag with the courtesy flag for that country.

You will soon have written the passport details of your crew often enough to know them by heart and may be thinking that a prepared crew list would be a good idea. Indeed, you will sometimes be asked for a crew list as though you should have prepared one in advance. Don't bother. This is seldom a good use of your time, since whatever format you have used will usually be unacceptable and you will have to fill in the local one. Read this local form and the other papers carefully for two reasons. First, they may look the same as the previous island's but they aren't, and you win no brownie points for spoiling a form and having to ask for another. Second, some of the English is a tad archaic and I for one think some of the key words mean the opposite of what they intend. In the more visitor-friendly offices you will find examples of completed forms pinned to the wall to help you. Follow the way they are completed. Sometimes you have to put NIL against everything you don't have; sometimes you can put a single NIL across them all. Believe me, you won't guess this right. The model on the wall is how the officials want the form done, and it is after all their form not yours. Don't choose this moment to helpfully point out that it is always better to re-design forms that users can't understand.

In some islands, not always the poorest, you will be charged for the official forms. In some, you will be asked to go across to the nearby shop to make, at your own expense, a photocopy of the last remaining form in the office. Do it and do it with good grace. This is not the time for you to tread on someone's local sensibilities.

Usually one form is not enough to satisfy official appetite, and nor is one copy of any of the many forms. Trinidad and Tobago Immigration entry forms win the prize for progeny. There are more forms and more copies of forms than anywhere else despite an announcement back in 1999 by the Immigration Department that they were "on the verge" of introducing a new single form for yachts clearing in through Customs and Immigration. While the Department gets closer to the verge you can always ask a fellow-sailor in the long queue if you have the right forms. They don't have much else to do but chat with you. Also, watch for helpful visual hints. The forms are usually in pigeon hole shelves. Take all of those under the relevant heading for you ie "clearing in" or "departing yachts." Look for sheets of carbon paper. This is always the best sign that multiple copies are needed. If five copies happen to be beyond the power of carbon paper, don't point this out to the officers. Just make sure you are seen to be pressing hard.

At no time assume that you can bluff your way out of not having the correct papers. If, say, you are trying to enter Antigua from St Lucia but haven't got papers, don't say you weren't given any just because you weren't or you lost them; and certainly don't offer old papers from somewhere else as an alternative. Every officer knows the routines of the other islands. If you spent three days lounging around Grenada instead of heading straight to Trinidad, don't think you can explain the lapsed dates by engine failure unless you have the broken bits in your oily hands, and possibly not even then. These officials have heard all the stories before and they don't want to think you are treating them like fools. Think of the sensibilities of the other yachties in the queue. None of us like to see a fellow sailor caught out telling an untruth and being made to squirm on the hook of officialdom, like an object lesson for the rest of us.

These are my hard-earned lessons of the past. But what can be said of the future?

All hail to e-clearance

Actually, e-clearance isn't strictly the future. It is here already or at least coming up fast on the rails. A system called eSeaClear—the Caribbean Pre-Arrival Notification system—has been developed to help small vessels clear in and out more quickly and more pleasantly. You must register to access the system and keep your vessel's information up to date, and then you can electronically submit your details to the Customs officers of participating countries.

This is a giant step forward for the region but it is also a massive task, as any shift from paper forms to computerization usually is, but especially when it involves the co-ordination of separate nation states and their already very creaky systems. I'm sure you have already spotted some of the potential flaws in eSeaClear.

Not all countries participate. At the time of writing the ones covered by this book are: British Virgin Islands, Dominica, Saint Kitts and Nevis, Saint Lucia, Saint Vincent and the Grenadines.

Not all who do participate have got the system to work. It isn't always just a matter of the computers being down, although that is always an excellent excuse for most bureaucratic failures. There are reports of desk officers not having yet been told about eSeaClear or who prefer their old "easier" system. Some countries that haven't joined say they lack the money for a computerized system. And this must also be the case for some of those who have joined.

But there are reports of eSeaClear working in places, although not consistently so. However, it is a step forward, makes enormous sense for a relatively small region, and would be an enormous benefit for yachts.

Check on www.eseaclear.com for an update of the participating countries and try using it yourself. I have tried it in theory but not in practice. I probably would have completed the registration if a glitch in the system hadn't thrown me out, right at the end. You can usually find sailors writing of their eSeaClear experiences in *Caribbean Compass*.

Times of change

In the time I have been sailing here, some places have changed out of all recognition and many of those that haven't are on the verge of change even as I write. Sailing is becoming a major activity throughout this region as the success in places like the Virgins and northern Leewards knocks on to the islands further south. Do not expect things to be exactly as I describe them by the time you lower your sail in a prime anchorage, or sound your way into some hide-away to explore a bit of paradise. Don't even expect your pilot book, even if it is the latest edition, to be up to date either. Pilot authors are good, but they don't have a crystal ball.

Where I can see signs of change in my prime harbors and favorite places I have mentioned this in the text below. The good thing is, most of these changes will bring more convenience to the cruising yacht. The bad thing is they bring more yachts and push up prices. But that's the nature of development, I suppose.

It's already too late to experience the Caribbean of years ago. Even the tiny islands of the Grenadines are catching up with modern standards. If you want to experience the Caribbean as it is today, get down here now. Tomorrow is already on its way.

8

Tips to easier passages

I have arranged this chapter in two separate parts: passages from north to south and then passages from south to north. Passages in the island chain are not symmetrical. Wind and current, journey lengths and the location of prime harbors make this so. Your south to north passage is not the converse of the one you made when coming from north to south. I personally hate it when I struggle through highly detailed, 20-step instructions on how to take a piece of kit apart and then read a one-liner telling me that re-assembly is simply that procedure in reverse. No, it never is, not even if it were natural for us all to read instructions backwards. This approach smacks of laziness by someone somewhere. I don't want you, as you come northwards from the southern end of the chain, turning to the end of the chapter and reading from right to left, page 100 before page 99 and so on, and then not getting the warning about a particular harbor until it is too late. So be grateful for having two sets of instructions.

Going south through the chain

Into the Virgins

Boats coming from North America to the Virgins, once they have reached Florida, have really two choices to deal with the straight line of 900 miles against wind and current. They can either make this into a delivery trip, going outside all the Bahamas, or they can have a holiday and come down through the islands of the Bahamas in easy stages. The problems are of time and depth, respectively.

If you make this a delivery trip you have to protect yourself when at sea from the first of the local winter gales coming out of the Gulf of Mexico, known as Northers, and from the last of the summer hurricanes coming in from the Caribbean. You have a window which is really just November. If you cruise through the Bahamas you are less exposed to bad winter weather and your window expands accordingly. But you then need to plan a route carefully, since boats drawing more than two meters are limited to where they can cruise in this shallow region. You will need to practice eyeball navigation and pilotage. The tides and currents are often unpredictable and you should seek out as much local knowledge as you can.

Modern cruising boats are usually capable of hard sailing to make ground against wind and current but that doesn't mean the crew are. You will be sailing much further than the 900 mile rhumb line to the Virgins, possibly double that. One of the greatest of British sailing writers, Eric Hiscock, said of his own strategy on this passage: "I would stand out to sea from Nassau on the starboard tack until I thought I could make the Virgins on the other tack, and then go about. Bermuda might even be a convenient stop."

South and east to USVI and BVI

St Thomas port of entry	Charlotte Amalie
Jost Van Dyke port of entry	Great Harbour
Tortola port of entry	West End/Sopers Hole

To St Thomas

Boats coming from the west to enter the USVI at St Thomas will approach the harbor of Charlotte Amalie from Virgin Passage or Savannah Passage off the northwest end of the island.

Virgin Passage is clear of danger except for Sail Rock. Savannah Passage has a strong tidal flow near the northeast corner of Savannah Island. Beware the reef. The harbor is about halfway along the island. The entrance is well marked. Leave Water Island and Hassel Island to port.

To St John

Coming from the west to St John you need to enter Pillsbury Sound through the Cays at the northern entrance. The tide can run fast here, sometimes up to 4 knots. It is strongest in the Windward and Middle Passages.

Of the three passages through the Cays the easiest is Middle Passage between Thatch Cay and Grass Cay. Once through the Sound is clear of danger since you should be well clear of the Two Brothers, a marked rock, and Stephen Cay just south of the harbor entrance is also marked.

Boats coming from the west to enter the BVI have a choice of Jost Van Dyke or West End, Tortola. I think these are more attractive than either Charlotte Amalie or Cruz Bay and certainly offer an easier landfall than coming through the Cays of Pillsbury Sound.

To Jost Van Dyke

The approach through the passage between Little Hans Lollik Island and Little Tobago or between Tobago and the western end of Jost Van Dyke is straightforward. Great Harbour is easy to recognize. It is the only bay with any substantial buildings.

To West End/Sopers Hole

Come through The Narrows or Thatch Island Cut. Tidal streams are strong in The Narrows and Thatch Island Cut, and you may encounter eddies.

When tides are flooding (running north) the stream runs through Thatch Island Cut, across The Narrows and along the north coast of St John, sometimes at three knots. It runs less strongly along the coast of Tortola. Local advice is to keep to the St John side when heading east and the Tortola side when going west.

Out of the Virgins—USVI and BVI to Nevis; St Martin/St Barts to Antigua

Tortola port of entry	Road Harbour
St John port of entry	Cruz Bay
Nevis prime harbor	Pinney's Beach
St Martin prime harbors	Simpson Bay & Marigot Bay
St Barts prime harbors	Gustavia & Anse du Colombier
Antigua prime harbors	St John's & English Harbour

Boats leaving the USVI from either St Thomas or St John have clear access to open water.

Boats leaving Tortola will cross the Sir Francis Drake Channel to leave the Bank through Flanagan Passage or one of either Round Rock or Salt Island Passages.

On any passage out of the Virgins south or east into the Leewards the main problem will be to make some comfortable easting. The best tactic during the winter season is to watch the cycle of cold fronts coming down from the north. Pick a weak front, where the winds and gusts are not strong. Wait for the front to stall and the winds to veer to the north and northeast, and go, making the best east you can. You have about a day before the regular Trade Winds return but by then you may have made all the easting you need.

Above all, be patient. Remember that these winds are cycling, sometimes as rapidly as every three to four days. Waiting is easier than going with the wrong wind.

At this northern end of the Leewards you have two routes south which later recombine in the vicinity of Antigua or Guadeloupe. Briefly, these are:

- South to Statia, St Kitts/Nevis.
- South to Antigua.

If you choose to go towards Statia *et al* you will be unlikely to sail from there to Antigua, unless you retrace your steps to St Martin.

South from St Martin/St Barts to Antigua

St Martin prime harbors	Simpson Bay & Marigot Bay
St Barts prime harbors	Gustavia & Anse du Colombier
Antigua prime harbors	St John's & English Harbour

The trip from St Martin to Antigua usually has the wind free but the Equatorial Current forces you to stay close hauled. You might make life a little easier by splitting the journey with a short up-wind hop to St Barts since this puts you at a better sailing angle for Antigua and adds a few more hours of light on the day. Also, the current doesn't feel quite as strong on this short leg, perhaps because the island of St Barts and the various fangs of rock on the way help block the current. Between St Barts and Antigua the current runs strong and despite the better angle you should still stay tight on the wind.

Even starting from St Barts you are looking at an overnight passage to Antigua to ensure a daylight landfall. Antigua, though the major center for yacht racing in the Caribbean and a popular cruising ground, is one of the most dangerous islands to approach. The low-lying northwest offers poor landmarks from the north and off-lying reefs run almost uninterrupted from Diamond Reef on the northwest corner to halfway round the east coast. Take great care on the east and north coasts. Eyeball navigation is essential, so make sure you have good light and use polaroids to reduce the glare.

On this route the obvious harbor to aim for on Antigua is the capital of St John's, up a very well protected bay. However, there are dangers in the entrance from Warrington Bank and then Sandy Island as you line up for the buoyed channel. When you get there you may, like me, find St John's an unattractive and commercial harbor. I would rather park the boat in one of the many wonderfully pretty anchorages on this island and go to St John's by bus.

South from St Martin/St Barts to St Kitts/Nevis and Statia

St Martin prime harbors	Simpson Bay & Marigot Bay
St Barts prime harbors	Gustavia & Anse du Colombier
Statia prime harbor	None—see notes in Chapter 9
St Kitts prime harbor	None—use Nevis—see notes in Chapter 9
Nevis prime harbor	Pinney's Beach

If the wind direction is not favorable to sail from St Martin or St Barts to Antigua consider reaching down to Statia and St Kitts instead. If you do this, you will then prefer to go on to Guadeloupe rather than make the 50 mile beat dead upwind to see Antigua.

Going south from St Martin or St Barts to St Kitts *et al* the thing most in your favor is the distance. It is only a day sail. The current will be against you from St Martin and across you from St Barts but the wind should be free. My plan would be to sail down the windward side of St Kitts if the wind allowed and through The Narrows, and then decide on anchoring in tiny Ballast Bay on St Kitts or crossing to Nevis. If unable to sail a course down the windward side you will need to come round the leeside of Statia or through the channel between Statia and St Kitts and then down the leeside of St Kitts. Neither is difficult but if forced to do this I would probably take the opportunity to visit Oranjestad on Statia, even if it meant a rolly night on a buoy in the harbor there.

If the lack of wind initially forces you to motor south down the leeside of St Kitts you may later, somewhere in the vicinity of Brimstone Hill, run into a head wind, adverse current and choppy sea that makes progress slow. Allow time for this, so that you are not approaching an anchorage in Basse-Terre, the capital, in the dark.

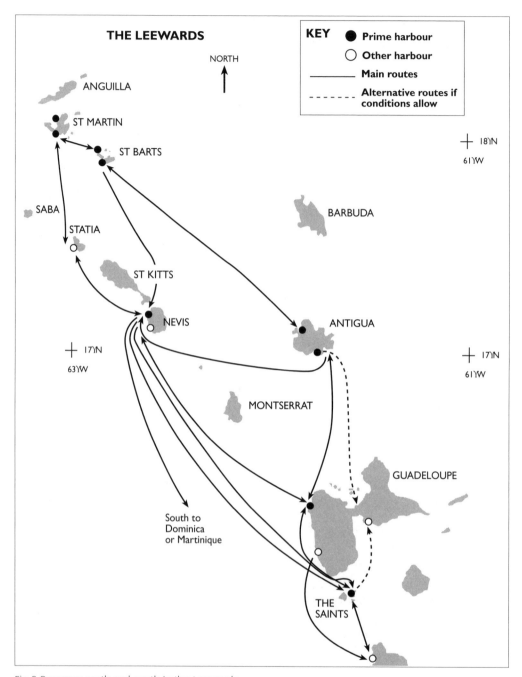

Fig 8 Passages north and south in the Leewards.

South from Antigua to Guadeloupe

Antigua prime harbor	English Harbour
Guadeloupe prime harbor	Deshaies

The 40 or so mile passage from Antigua to Guadeloupe is usually a single tack. The bend in the arc of the island chain helps and you may now have the prevailing wind fairly broad when coming south. At this point, if you have a northerly wind, you have the choice to make a lot of ground to the south and miss out Guadeloupe and even Dominica and then come round to the leeward side of Martinique to visit that island.

Sailing south from Antigua to Guadeloupe, my preference is to go down the west side of Basse-Terre rather than into La Rivière Salée. We draw two meters and this is rather close to the minimum usually available in this channel. I would hate to arrive and discover our extra cases of beer meant we couldn't get through and had to sail back round. Deshaies is usually a fine harbor to stop in.

South from St Kitts/Nevis to Guadeloupe

St Kitts prime harbor	None—use Nevis—see notes in Chapter 9
Nevis prime harbor	Pinney's Beach
Guadeloupe prime harbor	Deshaies

From St Kitts south to Guadeloupe the fly in your 70-mile passagemaking ointment is Montserrat, since it lies on your direct line. Ideally you want to pass this to windward, both for the better course this gives you and because you may still be required by the exclusion zone to pass at least two miles to leeward. The passage is an easy one in a northeast wind but a struggle in a southeasterly. In my various efforts here I have never yet managed to get to windward of Montserrat. The current has always pushed me too much to the west and forced me to sail down the leeside of Montserrat and then beat across to Guadeloupe in what I hope is the weaker current from the lee of that big island. In the seasons when I have been doing this I have never managed to make the northern end of Guadeloupe or, therefore, the straits of La Rivière Salée. Get into the lee of Guadeloupe and motor into the coast. My plan on this route, if I can't make Deshaies in comfort, is always to make The Saintes, or failing that, Dominica. By extension, if conditions make this a hard sail, then the trip to Antigua from Nevis or Montserrat would be a very wet upwind beat directly into the current.

South from Guadeloupe to The Saintes and Dominica

Guadeloupe prime harbors	Deshaies & The Saintes
The Saintes prime harbor	Bourg des Saintes
Dominica prime harbor	None—try Prince Rupert Bay—see notes in Chapter 9

The Saintes, the *Iles des Saintes*, is a small group of eight islands a few miles off the south coast of Guadeloupe. The Canal de Saintes, the 10-mile passage between Guadeloupe and The Saintes, is mainly 250 to 400 meters deep but in places shoals to 12 meters. The sea is usually choppy in the Channel although I find it calms nearer The Saintes, perhaps because of Marie-Galante or the shoaling between Marie-Galante and Guadeloupe.

To make The Saintes from the Basse-Terre coast of Guadeloupe in one tack stay close to the leeside of Guadeloupe. There is a calm patch about 200 meters offshore from Basse-Terre to Southern Point lighthouse which makes motoring easy. Trying to sail from Basse-Terre to Point Vieux Fort will leave you a long way to leeward when you clear the land, with a lot of hard work to do in the Saintes Channel when you meet the strong west-going current and a wind which always seems to be accelerated by the land.

Come between La Pate Island and Ilet à Cabret. Avoid the marked shoal between Cabret and Terre d'en Haut as you come across to anchor off Bourg des Saintes. The Saintes make a good jumping off point for a passage to Dominica by shortening the distance and giving you a better angle across the Equatorial Current.

Coming south from Guadeloupe to Dominica your main problem will be the strong current through the Dominica channel. In most conditions you will have the wind broad enough to allow you to command the west-flowing current in a direct passage to Prince Rupert Bay.

As you close Dominica, the headland of Prince Rupert Bluff on the north side of Prince Rupert Bay is an unusual and therefore distinctive landmark.

South from Dominica to Martinique

Dominica prime harbor	None—try Prince Rupert Bay—see notes in Chapter 9
Martinique prime harbor	Fort-de-France. Try St Pierre as your arrival point

Starting from Prince Rupert Bay means you are at the northern end of Dominica, so allow for this in planning your passage time and leave early if you want to make harbor on Martinique in good daylight. This is not usually difficult since once clear of the land this 26 miles of open water should be a fast, steady reach albeit with periods of rough seas. The wind, accelerated by the high lands, can be 10 knots stronger at each end of the passage. Be brave here when leaving the land and expect the true ocean winds to be more manageable. The shoal off the north to northeast of Martinique gives protection from the current when you come within five miles of Martinique.

Steer a course which takes account of the strong west-running current but also point-up to take account of the wind shadow you will get from Mont Pelée. The lee from this high volcano stretches about ten miles out to sea. To minimize time under engine you might try to come right in to the tiny Islet de Perle and motor from there.

St Pierre, a wide bay with easy access, is usually a good overnight anchorage though subject to rolling. Stopping here on passage ensures a daylight arrival on Martinique and lets you more calmly view the coastline the next day as you motor round

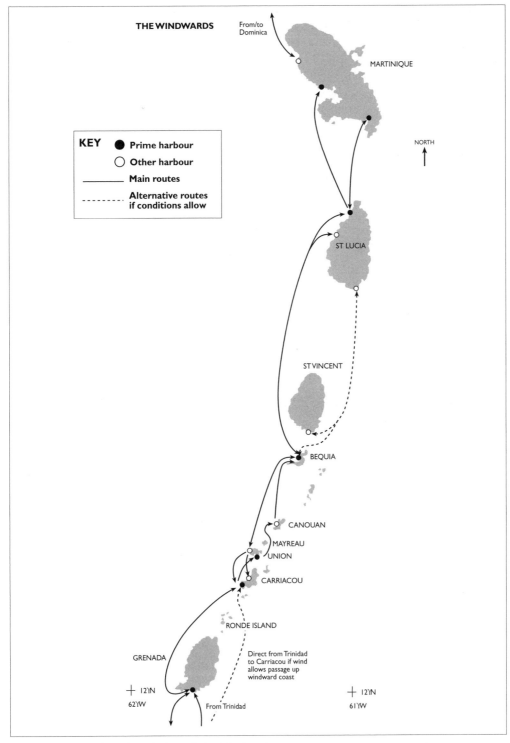

THE WINDWARDS

From/to Dominica

MARTINIQUE

NORTH

KEY
- ● Prime harbour
- ○ Other harbour
- —— Main routes
- - - - Alternative routes if conditions allow

ST LUCIA

ST VINCENT

BEQUIA

CANOUAN

MAYREAU
UNION

CARRIACOU

RONDE ISLAND

GRENADA

Direct from Trinidad to Carriacou if wind allows passage up windward coast

+ 12°N
62°W

From Trinidad

+ 12°N
61°W

Fig 9 Passages north and south through the Windwards.

to Fort-de-France. Also, take this opportunity to visit the museum and see what little remains of old St Pierre.

South from Martinique to St Lucia

Martinique prime harbors	Fort-de-France & St. Anne/Le Marin
St Lucia prime harbor	Rodney Bay

This is an easy day hop. You will be leaving Martinique from one of three locations: the main bay at Fort-de-France; the small harbors on the southwest corner of the island; the main yacht center at Le Marin or its outer anchorage at St Anne. The open water channel between the islands is about 18 miles across, but from St Anne to Rodney Bay on St Lucia is about a 22 mile passage and from the southern headland of Fort-de-France bay about 26 miles.

Whichever point of departure, point high initially to allow for the current and also because the wind flows round the southern coast of Martinique and only becomes freer when you clear the land.

The passage should end with an easy entrance into Rodney Bay. Pigeon Island on the northern end of Rodney Bay is a good landmark but beware: this has not been an island for a long time. From the sea you can look right over the causeway connecting the island to the mainland without seeing it and may mistakenly believe that the blue roofed hotel on the northern side of the causeway is on the southern side, ie inside Rodney Bay. It is not and Gros Ilet is not Pigeon Island. The blue roof of this hotel is equally conspicuous as you come south from Martinique or north up the coast. Pigeon Island is a distinctive landmark. It looks to me rather like a Sphinx.

Rodney Bay is a fine wide and deep bay, good holding off the beach and a steady refreshing wind coming offshore. Easy to enter in daylight and possible at night. At night, take care to avoid the tiny islet off the southern headland. Do not attempt to enter the lagoon and marina at night. The entrance to the lagoon is a wide, straight canal dug across the beach. Easy in daylight but not for a first or even second timer at night. Once inside, the lagoon opens up into a wide and protected harbor. Yachts may anchor between the pontoons and the boatyard as well as further into the lagoon.

South from St Lucia to St Vincent

St Lucia prime harbor	Rodney Bay
St Vincent prime harbor	Bequia—Admiralty Bay

You may have worked your way down the coast of St Lucia to Anse la Raye, or, if you feel like a spot of palm tree anchoring, as far as the Pitons. Any of these will substantially shorten your passage to St Vincent. Departing from Vieux Fort does not achieve enough to be worth the journey there in the first place.

If this is your first visit to St Vincent then on this inter-island passage I advise sailing by and going straight on to Bequia. Then you can make a much shorter trip back from Bequia to begin to explore St Vincent and still have time to return to Bequia or another St Vincent anchorage if the first one you choose is uncomfortable.

From the Pitons to St Vincent it is sometimes possible to sail down the windward coast of St Vincent on a reach and then have an easy dead run to Bequia. This avoids the calms and adverse current along the leeside of the high mass of St Vincent.

If you end up on the leeside of St Vincent then you will have the chance to look into a number of the palm tree anchorages on this stunningly beautiful coast, and try one if you feel up to it. I mean, we have done it so it can't be *that* hard. If you don't want to be adventurous just yet, then sail on to Bequia rather than into Kingstown. It probably doesn't take much longer to sail across the Bequia channel than it does to beat your way against wind and current around the headland to Kingstown.

South from St Vincent to Bequia

St Vincent prime harbor	None—use Bequia—see notes in Chapter 9
Bequia prime harbor	Admiralty Bay

This is a pleasant and short passage of eight to 10 miles, taking less than two hours on the usual fast reach south. In the deep water channel between St Vincent and Bequia the current runs much stronger than most other parts of the Grenadines so expect to be set west. Sometimes big seas are raised. The view of white horses from the north end of Bequia can chill the heart of even a fearless sailor like me. If the tide is running counter to the current the seas can be especially rough off Bequia Head. Close in, coming south, catch the adrenaline high as you surf into the lee of the Head.

Avoid the Devil's Table shoal and Wash Rock off North West Point, the northern side of the entrance. The rock should have a buoy but sometimes it doesn't.

There are no reliable lights for a night entry into Bequia but it is usually easy to make out the high land of the long peninsula running out to West Cay on the southern side of the entrance and follow it in. There are no dangers off this side of the entrance and the land leads you into the anchorage.

Bequia is a jewel in the crown of Caribbean anchorages. If coming in late, anchor off the back of the moored yachts and find a longer stay position in the better light of the next morning. Some of the best anchoring spots close into town are now taken with visitor (and permanent) mooring buoys. Help to pick one is usually not slow to arrive. If you prefer to anchor, try Princess Margaret Beach.

South through the Grenadines

The Grenadines is a sailing experience not to be missed. This chain of small islands, islets and rocky reefs provides well sheltered anchorages, wonderful diving and excellent walks. The islands are economically poor and not good places to provision a boat. Once you have arrived in the area, the Grenadines is an easy place to explore in short hops, when daylight is good enough to navigate the reefs (not always well charted) and to see how the strong local currents are running.

Coming south into the Grenadines your command over the wind means you are more likely to manage all your passages in fast day sails. But if the wind has south in it, don't rule out making your longer trips overnight. On a windward beat that begins to look like ending in darkness, the skipper's day becomes more fraught by the hour.

From the north you are likely to stop first at Bequia or go on to make Union your base. Remember that at some point you will be crossing from the state of St Vincent to the state of Grenada and must therefore check in and out of Customs and Immigration. You can check in and out of St Vincent at Bequia or Union Island, and in and out of Grenada at Carriacou.

Bequia to Union via the islands

Bequia prime harbor	Admiralty Bay
Union prime harbor	Clifton
Carriacou prime harbor	Tyrell Bay

Union Island is the southern-most inhabited territory of St Vincent to have a Customs and Immigration office. Any yacht heading south that did not check out in Bequia will need to check out here. From Admiralty Bay to Union Island is usually a beam reach or near run. The long reef of islands well to the east of you, of which Mustique is the largest, usually help flatten the seas to give fast and dry sailing and a passage easily done in daylight.

A course to Clifton Harbor brings you to the eastern side of Union and you pass so close to Canouan and Mayreau that you might choose to call at either or both, whether for the spirit of exploration or because your journey is slow and in danger of running into the night.

If you visit Canouan then sort out your pilotage on leaving so that you know for sure which island is which. It is easy to mistake Union and Mayreau for a single island. The small, flat island of Mayreau can be lost against the dramatic humps of the more distant Union, and the height of Union can make it seem nearer than it is. If you can't distinguish Mayreau there is a danger that you will mistakenly think Tobago Cays are Mayreau. The consequences don't bear thinking about.

Mayreau has three bays on its leeward side where boats on passage might stop. The most enclosed of these is the pretty but usually crowded Salt Whistle Bay. Most yachts anchor in Saline Bay. Good holding in four meters of sand but tends to have swell. If coming in here, or even if sailing close along the coast, beware of the inadequately buoyed Grand Col Reef between Trios Anse and Saline bays. The tiny buoy is further offshore than you will guess.

Coming round the eastern side of Union take care to identify and follow the markers for Union's outer reef.

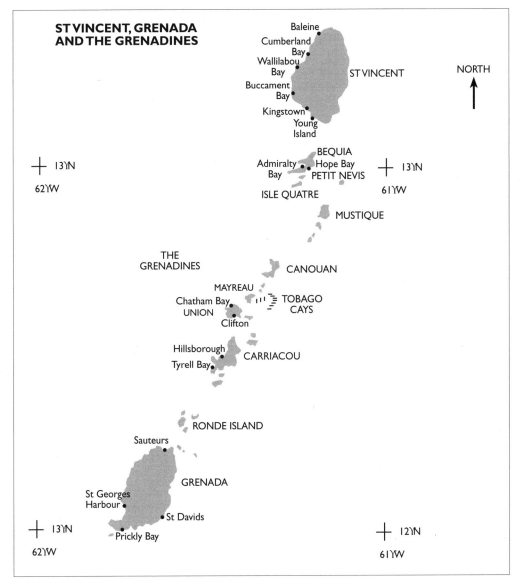

ST VINCENT, GRENADA AND THE GRENADINES

Baleine
Cumberland Bay
Wallilabou Bay
Buccament Bay
Kingstown
Young Island
ST VINCENT

NORTH

13˚N
62˚W

13˚N
61˚W

BEQUIA
Admiralty Bay
Hope Bay
PETIT NEVIS
ISLE QUATRE

MUSTIQUE

THE GRENADINES

CANOUAN

MAYREAU
Chatham Bay
UNION
Clifton
TOBAGO CAYS

Hillsborough
Tyrell Bay
CARRIACOU

RONDE ISLAND

Sauteurs

GRENADA

St Georges Harbour
St Davids
13˚N
62˚W
Prickly Bay

12˚N
61˚W

Fig 10 From St Vincent to Grenada via the Grenadines.

Yachts heading for the west side of Union Island, whether to clear all the reefs and sail direct to Grenada or perhaps to anchor in Chatham Bay, need not pass close to either Canouan or Mayreau. This will be a broader reach or run and fast. On this course I would pass west of Catholic Isle and Catholic Rocks, those dramatic if small lumps of hard, weathered rock catching the perennial current and the waves.

Chatham Bay is easy to enter from north or south, but if coming from the south take care not to mistake it for the first bay you see. This is probably a good anchorage itself, but is not as protected. Chatham Bay is deserted apart from a small fishing camp used by nearby villagers, has a fine beach and good holding in the north corner, where you get most protection from the down-blasts off the hills. A track leads you into town. We bought a large and fine fish, freshly caught to order.

Between Union and Carriacou

Union prime harbor	Clifton
Carriacou prime harbor	Tyrell Bay

This is a short and very pleasant sail in either direction. I could happily spend a month doing nothing more than this. The wind, tamed by the little islands of Petit St Vincent (PSV) and Petite Martinique as well as by the northern end of Carriacou, is usually a gentle sailing breeze and the sea is flattened by the reefs. Even my own dear *Petronella* flashes along in these conditions. Your timing on so short a journey is largely dictated by the opening hours of Customs and Immigration. Beware the overtime charges if you are outside office hours.

Tyrell Bay on Carriacou is one of the best anchorages in the island chain and much to be preferred to the main town of Hillsborough. Walk or get a bus to Customs and Immigration in Hillsborough, or just anchor off the Hillsborough jetty long enough to make your clearance.

While in this area you may want to visit the tiny Palm Island, Petit St Vincent and Petite Martinique. Remember that these are not all in the same country. You may be committing the illegal technicality of not having cleared in or out of either St Vincent or Grenada.

South from Carriacou to Grenada

Carriacou prime harbor	Tyrell Bay
Grenada prime harbor	Prickly Bay

An easy sail and usually possible to choose either the leeside or windward side of Grenada.

Coming from Carriacou down the windward side of Grenada means more pilotage initially to get through the rocky archipelago of Ronde Island, Diamond Rock, the Sisters and Les Tantes, and then a wonderful reach down the east coast of Grenada and a rolling dead run along the south coast. Keep track of your position along the south coast because the many headlands can be confusing, there are reefs some way off a few of them, and you must make sure you are passing north and clear of the Porpoises as you come up on Prickly Bay.

Sailing to pass down the leeside of Grenada is usually a good broad reach, with a wind that allows you to sail wide of the archipelago and Kick-'em-Jenny, before you run out of wind and have to motor. With luck you may find a sailing breeze later on, and almost certainly once you are off the bay of St George's. Like St Vincent, the leeside of Grenada is high, green and beautiful but with even fewer comfortable or pleasant anchorages.

The little group of islands around Diamond Rock and the underwater volcano of Kick-'em- Jenny are more of a problem to boats beating north and east of north from Grenada to Carriacou, so I have described them in more detail in the north-bound passages below.

South from Grenada to Tobago

Grenada prime harbor	Prickly Bay
Tobago prime harbor	Charlotteville

No, really, you are unlikely to make this journey. This trip is usually a lot of hard down-wind tacks straight into current. Sailors from Grenada who need to get to Tobago for its famous Race Week don't enjoy the trip so why should a cruiser like you. If you want to visit Tobago, and I have to say it is one of the most wonderful islands of the eastern Caribbean, then wait till you have a wind in your favor or start from further north. Perhaps from Bequia. Perhaps from Mustique, after calling in there for the Wednesday barbecue and jump up at Basil's Bar, as part of a side trip of exploration.

If you do attempt this trip and don't make it, stay within territorial waters so that the Customs and Immigration officers won't charge you an unnecessary departure fee when you eventually reach back to Grenada.

Charlotteville on Tobago is right at the northwest corner of the island, just where you might hope to arrive, and is the most comfortable of all the harbors on the island. Charlotteville is a port of entry of sorts, which is to say they have Customs and Immigration there but sometimes they seem to think you should have gone to the capital of Scarborough on the southeast side.

South from Grenada to Trinidad

Grenada prime harbor	Prickly Bay
Trinidad prime harbor	Chaguaramas

This is one of the longer sails between islands and for most boats must involve a night sail if you are to make landfall in daylight. We always sail overnight. The usual approach for this 90-mile passage is to leave in late afternoon, between 1500 and 1600 hours. The Grenadian plateau extends its long, shoaling, underwater tail southwest for nearly 15 miles. The seas over this tail are nearly always lumpy. We prefer to cross them in daylight and settle down for the night after that. Daylight also means we can locate and avoid the breaking rocks called the Porpoises, a little way off Prickly Bay Harbor. Avoiding the Porpoises is especially important if the wind at this stage allows you to head up to the southeast. It is always worth making ground to the southeast in case you are set down to the west later in this passage.

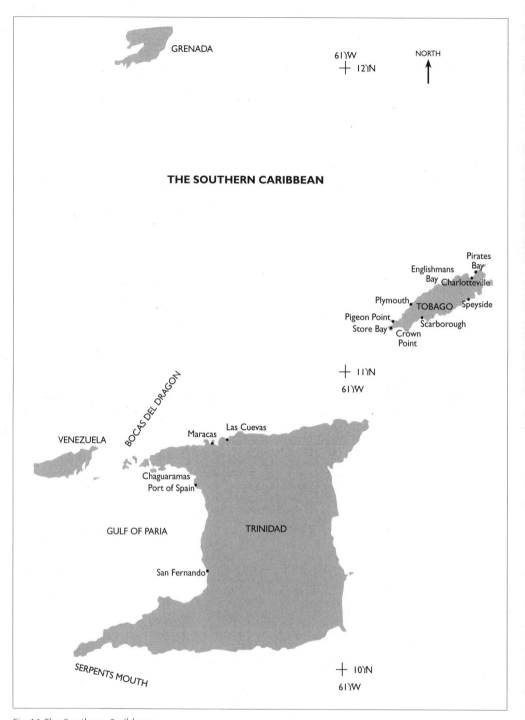

Fig 11 The Southern Caribbean.

A foreign yacht passing luxuriant trees as it heads for an anchorage in Trinidad and Tobago. *Courtesy of Trinidad & Tobago Tourist Authority*

White necked Jacobin Florisuga mellivora, a tiny hummingbird pausing briefly before feeding. *Courtesy of Trinidad & Tobago Tourist Authority*

Grande Anse, Martinique, is a good anchorage and destination for one of our favorite walks. *Courtesy of Hanna-Marja Niemi of s/y* Canace

Salt Island Channel beyond the quiet anchorage of Deadman's Bay, Peter Island.
Courtesy of BVI Tourist Authority

English Harbour, Antigua. *Courtesy of Antigua and Barbuda Tourist Board*

Silver Spotted Flambeau, Agraulis vanillae vanillae. It is one of the 123 species of butterflies on Tobago. *Courtesy of Trinidad & Tobago Tourist Authority*

Tranquillity on the tiny island of St Barths. *Courtesy of the author*

Sandy spit off Little Jost. *Courtesy of BVI Tourist Authority*

A spectacular view of The Pitons from Soufrière, St Lucia. *Courtesy of St Lucia Tourist Board*

You can step back to Nelson's time in the wonderfully renovated English Harbour, Antigua. *Courtesy of Antigua and Barbuda Tourist Board*

The Baths, Virgin Gorda. Huge volcanic boulders make this the most visited site in the BVI, but don't be put off. Stunning and thought provoking scenery. *Courtesy of BVI Tourist Authority*

Sunset on North Sounds, Virgin Gorda. *Courtesy of BVI Tourist Authority*

Looking down from Fort Napoleon onto the sheltered anchorage of Le Bourg on Terre-de-Haut. *Courtesy of Guadeloupe Tourist Office*

Foxy's watering hole, Jost Van Dyke. *Courtesy of BVI Tourist Authority*

How the island chain was made—Soufrière Hills in Montserrat are still erupting. *Courtesy of Montserrat Tourist Board*

Gustavia, St Barts at night. Truly the St Tropez of the Caribbean. *Courtesy of Guadeloupe Tourist Office*

Virgin Gorda—plenty of room to go sailing. *Courtesy of BVI Tourist Authority*

Sopers Hole, Tortola—the famous Pusser's Landing. *Courtesy of BVI Tourist Authority*

A friendly welcome from Skipper on the front line welcoming committee at Union Island in the Grenadines, Place your orders now! *Courtesy of Hanna-Marja of s/y* Canace

This is a night passage to enjoy. Once off the southern shoal, seas ease as the water deepens to 1,000 meters or so until you are due west of Tobago, roughly half way to Trinidad. You will have good conditions most of the way. Beware the occasional wave that wants to join you in the cockpit. On many of my trips the later part of the night brings black squalls. These often carry more rain than wind, and often miss the boat anyway. Some time after the half way mark you may benefit from what G calls the "Tobagonian effect." I've no idea about this, but perhaps the long island of Tobago, some 40 miles east of you, gives a lee to the wind and current. Certainly, you can usually expect flattish seas and easy winds here.

About 30 miles off Trinidad you will pick up the high, powerful light of Chacachacare. This wonderful light is on the peak of the western-most of three islands off the west coast of Trinidad. These three islands, Monos, Huevos and Chacachacare, create the Dragon's Mouth channels called Bocas that lead into the Gulf of Paria. I find sailing almost down the line of Chacachacare light more relaxing navigation than GPS or compass, and more reliable than following a star when there are a million on display. It gives a visible line to your destination which allows for all the variations in water flows. Despite the strong prevailing current the tide, especially around springs, may for a while set you to the east. Don't, of course, sail straight for the light. It marks the western end of the Bocas and you will get pulled that way by the current.

About 10 miles north of Trinidad you may find more confused seas. Even in light winds there will be low breaking waves and rips and eddies, although the chart shows no shoal patches. Not serious but strange. This is now the time to take care with your navigation. You don't want to end up downwind and down-current of the Bocas.

About five miles off the coast the swell will become more obvious as it gradually turns to follow your course into the Boca. As the wind strengthens along the coast you will get an exhilarating ride to the Boca until finally you get the lee of the coast, just before you enter the channel. You will need to motor through the first Boca, the Boca de Monos, but if you take the second and strike lucky you will have a beautiful broad reach on a light steady wind that carries all the way through—the icing on the cake for your sail into Trinidad.

Petronella is a slow boat and we find that traveling slowly reduces the slamming and adds enormously to the comfort of the crew trying to sleep, but even sailing slowly we expect to arrive off Trinidad by 8 or 9 am. A fast boat in ideal conditions and making a dawn start might make this trip in daylight but, if it didn't, I wouldn't recommend trying to make harbor in the dark. On the one hand, I might consider entering Trinidad's second Boca, the Boca de Huevos, at night in strong moonlight; but on the other hand I have never had to and might bottle out of it at the last minute. There are no other landfalls on Trinidad that I would consider at night. I would certainly heave-to rather than attempt any of the little bays on the north coast.

On my very first trip to Trinidad I hove-to rather than attempt the first Boca before dawn and have never regretted this seaman-like decision. The first Boca, the usual entrance for most boats making this trip to Trinidad, is bad enough in daylight. The seas offshore are always lumpy; a heavy swell usually runs into the entrance; there are rocky ledges off the headlands on either side; and a 40-foot high rock just off the northwestern end. The current almost always runs out of the Boca. The tidal effect is to stop the current for a period on the flood but add to it on the ebb, so that you can meet a north-running current of two to three knots. There are no lights in the Boca. Even in daylight, because of the dog-leg shape of the channel, you cannot see right through until you are northwest of the entrance. Finally, the floating debris, which ranges from plastic sacks to rafts of sea hyacinth, could shut your engine down. I've gone into the first Boca and stood still on a standing wave. I hadn't even heard of standing waves till then. I slithered across the wave with full sail and full throttle until I found a weak point in the current and managed to break free. I wouldn't like to be surfing up there in the dark.

I don't really understand why the first Boca is the preferred entrance to the Gulf of Paria for most yachts. Yes, it's the first and most direct channel for boats coming from Tobago or Grenada and comes out closest to the Chaguaramas anchorages, but the current can run out at a couple of knots, there are always some rips over the uneven sea bed and the wind usually changes from northerly to southerly about halfway through. The second Boca is straighter and wider and its shores are cleaner. The scenery is dramatic, the current less aggressive and I have always managed to carry a sailing wind right the way through.

I was single-handing back from Dominica otherwise I might have got the photograph to make me famous. Slipping through the second Boca under working sail I saw what at first I took to be a submerged log and second a rock awash. I was still trying to recall whether this was a clean 300-meter deep channel or whether a rock might have gone unnoticed all these years when I realized I was looking at a large sea creature unlike any I had ever seen. A manatee, sea cow, fabled mermaid of times past. This isn't where they usually swim but when I got in G and her friends from a Trinidad wildlife group confirmed that my description fitted this rare sea mammal. Next day G and I quartered the second Boca in *Petronella* but it was gone by then. I had been too busy looking, steering and panicking to find my camera and so missed earning a footnote in the natural history books of Trinidad and the Orinoco basin.

Once in the Gulf of Paria turn east for the anchorage of Chaguaramas. If coming through the first Boca, beware a reef extending from the headland just as you turn east. This is marked by a very insignificant red buoy. Pass between the island of Gaspar Grande and the mainland shore, passing either side of Gasparillo, a tall heavily wooded islet usually smothered by corbeaux (pronounced *kobos*), the local black hooded vultures, and so enter the bay of Chaguaramas. You will see the forest of masts over in the eastern corner, where yachts are anchored or moored in the marinas or hauled out ashore. The boundaries of the preferred yacht anchorage are shown on a chartlet you will be given when you clear in.

The Gulf of Paria is a very protected patch of water and the bay of Chaguaramas is almost land-locked. It is certainly better than the anchorage around the headland at

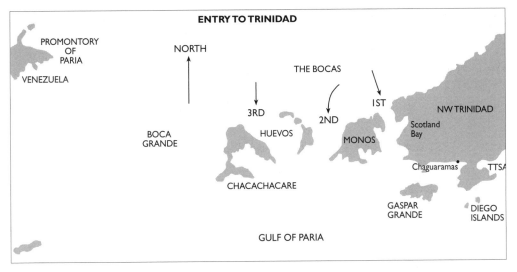

Fig 12 Entering Trinidad through the Bocas into the Gulf of Paria.

Carenage Bay where TTSA (the Trinidad and Tobago Sailing Association) have laid moorings. This pretty bay is subject to a stiff onshore breeze most afternoons kicking up a nasty chop, and loud heavy music from the popular nightclub at weekends or fetes (pronounced *fett* by the Trinis).

Despite its protection Chaguaramas is far from being a wonderful anchorage. The bottom now is well stirred by yacht anchors and the holding is poor. Anchors can drag. The wonderful pond-like calm of the mornings is usually replaced by gusty winds and slapping waves in the afternoon and the chaos of the Chaguaramas tango. Changing afternoon currents break up the previously consistent lines of moored yachts, swinging them in different and unpredictable directions. Yachts that were far apart can suddenly be nuzzling up. If you are deep in the crowd, anchored close in to shore, then stay with your boat for at least a full day until you have some idea of how she swings in relation to your neighbors. And even then don't assume that she won't find a new angle tomorrow, or that some new arrival won't take up your swinging room.

In usual conditions the tango only happens in the afternoon. On top of this, there can be tidal surges of up to five knots during July and August through the channel between Gaspar Grande and the mainland. I have been here during July but haven't seen such a surge myself.

An alternative to anchoring is to take one of the buoys laid by YSATT (the Yacht Services Association of Trinidad and Tobago). Twelve moorings can take boats up to 15 metric tons and three can take boats up to 25 metric tons (late 2010) at U.S. $5 per night or less for longer periods. The ground tackle is checked every three months. Moorings are such a good idea here that I'm sure more will be laid.

If you have serious work to do or want to leave the boat for a few days or longer you may wish to moor at a pontoon in one of the yards (about the same price as hard standing).

Arrival procedures in Trinidad are slightly different from most other islands. The authorities in Chaguaramas require you to come alongside their pontoon and remain there until you have cleared in. The pontoon is in the inner bay, close by the tower of the Lighthouse restaurant at Crews Inn. It is easy to come alongside here and to turn to go back out to the anchorage. Underneath the restaurant is a well stocked Hi-Lo supermarket. The food store in Powerboats is also well stocked and open seven days a week, serving as it does the local boats which go down to the islands of Monos and Huevos at the weekend.

Arrival procedures are also slightly different in that this is a large island and the officials are usually very professional in their manner.

Going north through the chain
North from Trinidad to Grenada

Trinidad prime harbor	Chaguaramas
Grenada prime harbor	Prickly Bay

Aim to come through the Boca with a couple of hours of daylight left so that you can see what you are doing when clearing the bumpy seas during the first few miles. Sometimes these seas are no great problem and you are through the worst in half an hour; sometimes it can take an hour or more to ease your way through the big swells, motoring until you have left the blanketing effect of the north coast headlands. After that you will usually have a fair sail to Grenada, although it is normal to stay hard on the wind to avoid being pushed west by the Equatorial Current. On one trip I managed to make landfall to the southeast of Grenada and had the pleasure of a broad reach for the last 10 miles. On another occasion I was pushed 10 miles west of the island and motor-sailed to get into the lee of the land. I have also been lucky enough to sail straight into Prickly Bay Harbor without a single tack. It all depends on what shift there is in the Trade Winds that year.

If you get a wind with enough east or south in it to let you sail the windward side of Grenada, take it. You can reach Carriacou or Union more easily than the usual wet beat from the northwest tip of Grenada, and it is quicker to sail the windward coast than motor the leeward side. But beware the effect of the south-running current.

We had a fine sail hard in the ESE5 and surprised ourselves to be east of Grenada at nightfall instead of the usual west so we grabbed the chance to sail up the windward side for the first time ever. In the pitch black, pitching seas with waves crashing into jagged black rocks I disconnected our self steering to hand steer. It is a rocky lee shore and we were getting a tad anxious about a low lying unlit island that seemed to be on collision course but remained stubbornly invisible. The big bright moon was lighting where we had been, not where we were going. I swear the wind had risen to a Force Six. We had such odd seas out here. Sometime we seemed to be in vicious tidal rips and back eddies, probably caused by the depth changes from 1,000 fathoms to about 100 fathoms. We slammed massively or hobby horsed at three knots with tons of white water on the foredeck. At other times we slipped over flat seas at an easy seven knots. In the morning G conned us through the confusion of islets into Tyrell Bay. We had saved at least a whole day of sailing.

There is an excellent light on the southwest corner of Grenada, but beware, this is some distance north of Point Saline. The loom of St George's town will come up if you are approaching the island in darkness, and there are now usually plenty of domestic lights along the south coast (including the growing university campus between the runway and Prickly Bay) to warn you of its proximity. But don't come right up onto the south coast of Grenada in the dark. You need to locate tiny unlit Glover Island, the old whaling station just a little southeast of Point Saline, and special care is needed to identify and avoid the Porpoise rocks about three quarters of a mile south east of Prickly Bay. These are a group of mean-looking rocks, not all of which are showing their backs above the sea. There is usually plenty of spray flying but this is often lost in the white caps of the waves in daylight. At night there is nothing to warn you of them. In daylight, once you have located the Porpoises, you can easily pass inside them as you go either east or west along the south coast.

Prickly Bay is my harbor of choice for a first and last landfall on Grenada. It is easy to enter, usually wonderfully sheltered, has enough ashore to keep you entertained, and has a Customs and Immigration office to clear in and out.

If you have come east of Prickly Bay you can have a sleigh ride along the south coast, inside the Porpoises, but take care to avoid the reef, with swell and breaking waves, just inside the eastern edge of Prickly Bay. If you have been pushed west of Grenada you will need to tack along the coast against wind and current. Expect both to always be running east to west along the southern coast. You can beat up inside Glover Island but beware the reef off the island. Usually visible with breaking water.

Yachts anchor in the northern end of Prickly Bay, avoiding the no-anchoring area 200 yards off the hotel beach. There is usually plenty of room to anchor in the bay. Holding is good and yachts tend to all lie steadily to the breeze off the cliff. It is common for incoming yachts to come close on the stern of an anchored yacht before letting their anchor drop. You have Customs and Immigration, a supermarket, laundry, showers, travelift, chandlery, sail-loft, restaurant, and Internet lounge. Other very good places to eat are just a short walk away.

North through the Grenadines

Heading north you are more likely to be sailing against the wind while being close-hauled to counter the current. Consequently, you are now in some classic examples of passages short enough to be a day sail but long enough to end in darkness. The nervous skipper will try for a day sail, and become more nervous as the day progresses. Don't rule out making these overnight. Your first passage northwards out of Grenada is also the first of those best suited to overnighting.

Grenada to Carriacou

Grenada prime harbor	Prickly Bay
Carriacou prime harbor	Tyrell Bay

Coming to Carriacou from Grenada you will probably aim for Tyrell Bay. The little island of Carriacou is worth more attention from passing yachts than it usually gets. I find Tyrell Bay one of the best anchorages in the Grenadines and easy to enter. I rely on this for passagemaking because it is snug under most conditions. Although only about 15 or so miles across from Grenada, regard this as a full day sail because there are no prime anchorages on the lee coast of Grenada, and the passage must usually therefore start from St George's or Prickly Bay with the whole lee coast of Grenada ahead. There are lunch-anchorages on the way to Carriacou and the chance to do some exploring around the little archipelago of Ronde Island and Diamond Rock, the Sisters and the Tantes, but take care that as soon as these islets come into view you immediately establish which is which, and whether or not you can already see Carriacou or even Union.

Take care when tacking on and off these islets, as you inevitably must on this windward trip. This little archipelago is part of a shallow 40-meter shelf running to Laurent Point on the northern tip of Grenada. The shelf falls away rapidly to the west, with depths dropping to 400 meters in less than half a mile. The bank can provide protection from the Atlantic but sometimes the seas here can be disturbed and lumpy. The strong currents, tide rips and eddies must always be treated with respect.

Kick-'em-Jenny is not Diamond Rock as some charts would have it but a submerged and increasingly active volcano nearby. Before you leave Grenada check with the marina or Customs and Immigration to see what level of alert has been set by the government, and the range of the exclusion zone.

In a normal winter with a lot of north in the wind and a lot of west in the strong current the sail from the north end of Grenada to Carriacou can be tiring and wet, with the boat hard on the wind all the way. Local advice to avoid being set far to the west is to tack east as soon as clearing David Point at the northwest end of Grenada, where the current is less. In these conditions, or if short handed, I would probably leave Grenada at night to motor up the leeside in the dark, have the full day for the passage to Carriacou and the guarantee of daylight when coming into Tyrell Bay. It is rarely possible to sail on the leeside of Grenada so if you have to spend five hours or so motoring you might as well do this at night. The land is high, clear and visible. There are no offshore dangers.

Entering Tyrell Bay at night must be possible because I have done it more than once, but I can't recommend it. The long headland to the south of Tyrell Bay is uninhabited and there are no good lights even from the village to guide you in. Just half a mile offshore on the headland between Tyrell Bay and the larger more open Hillsborough Bay are The Sisters, two jagged rocks that are hard to see against the unlit headland and must be avoided. There is a light on one of these but I would not rely on it working. When coming from the south the town lights of Hillsborough make this light hard to identify until you are almost under it.

> Nine o'clock and as dark a night as I have sailed in. No moon. Heavy cloud hides the stars. Rm kept telling me we were being set north by the current but I couldn't believe that I should steer the southeasterly course he was giving me. I wasn't happy. We were less than two miles off Carriacou and I couldn't see any lights from the village in Tyrell Bay nor the headlands either side of it. We seemed to have a good transit on some lights, one of which was flashing, and I went below to see if I could match them to the chart. I plotted our GPS position and yelled at Rm to turn hard southeast. My plot put us on top of The Sisters. I had unwisely been steering towards Hillsborough. To hell with Hillsborough. I came up to the cockpit and only now could I see what my "good transit" had been. The nearer transit light was the flashing white on top of one of The Sisters, not mentioned on our chart or pilot. The pinnacle of rock under the light had been lost against the blackness of the land and I had thought the light was a couple of miles away on shore. We could see The Sisters clearly now that we had slid past them and they were silhouetted against the sea. The light was so high above us on this 22-meter rock because we were so damned close. I conned us into Tyrell Bay, aiming for the gap in the middle of the bay between the northern reef and the southern reef. I steered on the blinding lights of a fishing boat that I remember had been parked in the middle of the bay last time I came in here. I was opening a calming beer even before the anchor went down.

Once in Tyrell Bay anchor in sand as close to the shore as feels comfortable. Most yachts anchor in the southern part of the bay. Holding is good, and there is seldom any rolling. The wind can gust hard at times through Hillsborough Bay but usually all you get in Tyrell Bay is a gentle breeze off the land. From Tyrell Bay you are in easy range to begin exploring the Grenadines.

You must go to Hillsborough for Customs and Immigration. This is a rolly anchorage with little to recommend it other than its access to Sandy Isle, so you might prefer to walk into Hillsborough from Tyrell Bay or take the local bus.

Carriacou to Union

Carriacou prime harbor	Tyrell Bay
Union prime harbor	Clifton

Sailing between Carriacou and Union is usually a quick and pleasant affair thanks to all the protection to the east. Clifton is a well protected harbor almost fully enclosed by its outer reef. Entry is easiest through the western-most entrance, marked by beacons, but take care not to find yourself tacking too close to the reef which runs from Frigate Rock to this western entrance.

Clifton Harbor is increasingly taken up with mooring buoys although anchoring is still possible in the main channel and the secondary bay over by the eastern reef.

A good alternative to Clifton is Chatham Bay. Easy to enter in daylight, quiet and pretty but subject to strong wind blasts from the hills. Anchor in the northern corner.

Union to Bequia

Union prime harbor	Clifton
Bequia prime harbor	Admiralty Bay

Bequia's Admiralty Bay is usually a fine, well protected harbor and although often crowded there is always room for another boat. The harbor is occasionally subject to swell, with most protection being found on the northern side. Unfortunately this is where local and long-stay boats moor and where many of the old anchoring spots are now taken up with mooring buoys. If you don't wish to take a buoy and the places near town are taken, anchor off Princess Margaret Beach.

There are no reliable lights for a night entry into Bequia but from the south, once around West Cay at the western tip of the island, it is easy to make out the high land of the long peninsula and follow it in. There are no dangers off this shore and the land leads you into the yachts at anchor. By following this shore you avoid the Devil's Table shoal and Wash Rock off the northern side of the entrance. At night, anchor at the back of the fleet and find a longer-term spot in daylight.

If arriving from Union you will already have cleared into the nation state of St Vincent and the Grenadines so you don't need to clear in at Bequia.

North from Bequia to St Vincent

Bequia prime harbor	Admiralty Bay
St Vincent prime harbor	None—use Bequia—see notes in Chapter 9

North from Bequia to St Vincent the current usually makes this a beat to windward, but Kingstown or anywhere further west up the lee coast is usually easy to make. Young Island usually requires you to tack to windward because of the strong current. If going to Young Island and finding the seas rough, sail to wherever you can on the St Vincent side and try working your way along the south coast to Young Island.

I do not think that any of the harbors on St Vincent deserve to be rated as prime. Young Island, which I like, is hard to reach from the south in prevailing conditions. Kingstown, which I don't care for, is too deep and insecure. The little bays on the west coast all need palm tree moorings. None of this should stop you from visiting St Vincent when the conditions are right and you have daylight to spare when coming into an anchorage, but my usual tactic on passage is to sail past this beautiful green island.

North from Bequia/St Vincent to St Lucia

St Vincent prime harbor	Bequia
St Lucia prime harbor	Rodney Bay

The 30-mile passage from the north end of St Vincent to the Pitons can be a hard, wet sail, and a long day even if you leave from Cumberland Bay or Wallilabou part way up the leeward coast of St Vincent. These are not prime harbors but you might try them as departure points if you have been exploring the island.

The Pitons, those striking sugar-loaf volcanic plugs, are a wonderful landmark when sailing north from St Vincent but they can play havoc with the wind coming off the southern end of St Lucia. They confuse the seas but rob you of any wind to drive the boat. Try very hard to lay the Pitons otherwise you will get pushed a long way west by the one knot current. If you choose to sail past Dark Head on St Vincent it is unlikely that you will be able to lay the Pitons in one tack. Motor-sailing very close under the cliff till you bring De Volet Point abeam gives you a better sailing angle for the Pitons but you may also catch some fierce downdrafts if the Trades are strong. You may be catching hard gusts from the land anyway until you get a few miles off St Vincent. Think about reefing in advance and shaking the reef out when you have the true ocean winds.

It is a long trip up the west coast to the prime harbor of Rodney Bay. You could use the small bay of Anse la Raye to overnight.

North from St Lucia to Martinique

St Lucia prime harbor	Rodney Bay
Martinique prime harbors	Fort-de-France & St Anne/Le Marin

From Rodney Bay, Martinique should never be more than a day sail. From the north end of St Lucia point high to begin with to allow for the current. Sail the 22 miles to St Anne and Le Marin hard on the wind all the way to counter the current. The 26 miles or so to the headland of Fort-de-France bay is usually a fast, almost broad reach.

To Le Marin/St Anne

The current runs strong in the channel between St Lucia and Martinique and the land mass of Martinique bends the wind so that as you sail for Le Marin the wind comes more on the nose and less constant as you close the coast. Unless you have some north in the wind you must sail close-hauled to avoid being pushed down onto Diamond Rock, as we usually are. When beating along the coast from Diamond Rock beware the reefs that come out a long way from the shore. The anchorage at St Anne, at the mouth of the estuary, is easy to enter and we usually spend the night here before going up to Le Marin. Holding is good and the bay is well protected by the land although the wind can gust here. Many yachts anchor here but there is always room for more.

To Fort-de-France

The passage to the headland of Fort-de-France Bay is straightforward since the wind and current are in your favor most of the way. As you approach the land you may get the wind coming ahead of you, out of Fort-de-France Bay, but the current will help you up the southwest coast and the hard beat should only start after you open the bay.

> We had lazed our way towards Martinique since lunch and now I realized that this gentle wind from astern meant it would be dark before we reached the anchorage under the Fort. I took the helm just a few minutes before the breath of a giant hit our sails right on the nose. We went over on our ear and took off at seven knots. I didn't know *Petronella* could heel so far. I would have dropped sail and motored but we had engine problems and we wanted to keep it for the final approach. I played the sails and tiller. At times we were sailing upright; at other times we had the side decks under. We beat into the south west corner of the bay and tacked for the Fort-de-France anchorage about five miles to windward just as day turned to blackest night. A flotilla of four yachts motored along behind us all the way across like ducks on a string, tacking as we did, even though I sailed the boat so slowly to force them to overtake. I desperately wanted one of them to lead us in, this being our first time on Martinique. But they must have thought we were experienced gung-ho locals. I mean, who else would have full sail up in that wind and that much darkness.

If too much wind is coming out of the bay you might use one of the small harbors on the southwest coast or save some work in the bay by making for the shelter of Anse Mitan rather than Fort-de-France itself.

On your passage from St Lucia the small harbors on the southwest corner of Martinique are really only there as your fallback for when the current and wind don't allow you to make Le Marin and you are not yet ready to visit Fort-de-France. In normal conditions you will find these easy to reach since you have the current with you and good wind until you get into the lee of the island. You should have no problem with Diamond Rock or the shoals to the south of it, since these should always be upwind of your course.

North from Martinique to Dominica

Martinique prime harbor	Fort-de-France
	Try St Pierre as your departure point
Dominica prime harbor	None—try Prince Rupert Bay—see notes in Chapter 9

Although St Pierre is not one of my prime harbors we often use it as our departure point when heading north from Martinique and it is a little town you should visit, just for the history there. It is too unprotected to always be comfortable, but it saves several hours and makes the passage to Dominica an easy day sail. The combination of motoring or sailing along the land and sailing the wide channel can make for a perfect day.

I cannot bring myself to declare any prime harbors on Dominica, but the least worst in usual conditions is Prince Rupert Bay, and we have never had so bad a time of it there that we would condemn it out-right. Somewhere there may be sailors who find Roseau comfortable but I am not one of them. And nor is the great Cap'n Slocum.

> The great Joshua Slocum had some sore trials in the Caribbean, not least in Dominica. He dropped anchor in the quarantine section off Roseau, not liking the heavy roll in the commercial roads. He so disliked the look of the rolly anchorage that when he was ordered to move to it he upped anchor and went direct to Antigua. His brief account of Dominica is well worth reading. I wonder if the attitude of Customs officials to visiting yachts has changed much since then.

The sail from Martinique to Dominica itself is usually an easy one even though you are going north, because the angle is just that much easier for you to cope with the current if you have the usual Trade Winds. We have always had to motor up the leeside of Dominica for lack of wind but the current runs with us. The island is one of those magnificent massively green and high islands with clouds whirling round the peaks. After the distinctive and high Rollo Head, the opening into the large expanse of a deeply indented bay with a greater concentration of shoreline buildings than anywhere since Roseau, and the headland of Prince Rupert Bluff away to the north, tells you that you have arrived at Prince Rupert Bay. If in doubt, ask the boat boy now motoring alongside you.

North from Dominica to The Saintes

Dominica prime harbor	None—try Prince Rupert Bay—see notes in Chapter 9
The Saintes prime harbor	Bourg des Saintes

Prince Rupert Bay is a very convenient departure point, being at the north end of Dominica. The sail to The Saintes is short and usually a beam reach, though the seas can be bouncy in the channel.

From Dominica the easiest route into The Saintes is to come through the southwest passage (Passe du Sud Ouest). As you close The Saintes the different rocks and islands open up and the pilotage becomes clear. You may be able to sail right through to Bourg des Saintes, short tacking.

North from The Saintes to Guadeloupe

The Saintes prime harbor	Bourg des Saintes
Guadeloupe prime harbor	Deshaies

We usually sail up the leecoast to Deshaies and base ourselves there but The Saintes put you in a good position to explore the south coast of Grande-Terre and the bustling city of

Pointe à Pitre, where the main marina and yacht services are based on Guadeloupe. The approaches to Pointe à Pitre are dangerous and this is not a destination I would recommend to you when passagemaking unless you have most of the day to find your way in.

If planning to go through the Rivière Salée check the opening times of the bridges. They used to open automatically on Saturdays and Mondays but only by prior request on other days. The usual opening times are around 5 am, so you need to be ready to go straight through a little before this. Whatever, you will be going through the bridges in the dark and may want to find a spot to anchor till daylight. Also check the draft and buoyage in the channel. It should always be enough for a boat drawing seven feet but the conditions may allow a nine-foot boat to get through. The bridge gives you a better angle to reach Antigua.

North from Guadeloupe to Antigua

Guadeloupe prime harbor	Deshaies
Antigua prime harbor	English Harbour

From Guadeloupe the current gives you a slightly favorable lift and the wind should make for a comfortable sail. Your prime harbors are perfectly placed—Deshaies at the north end of Guadeloupe and English Harbour on the south coast of Antigua. The wind is often gusting heavily at Deshaies and you wonder whether you dare leave harbor, but this is a local effect and once clear of the northwest corner of Guadeloupe you are back in the honest ocean Trade Winds.

West from Antigua to St Kitts/Nevis and Statia

Antigua prime harbor	English Harbour
Nevis prime harbor	Pinney's Beach
St Kitts prime harbor	None—use Nevis—see notes in Chapter 9
Statia prime harbor	None—see notes in Chapter 9

Antigua really commands the islands to the west and north of it. Sailing to Nevis or St Kitts or Statia should be a broad reach or a run downwind and down-current. I suspect the landmass of Antigua, low though it is, can block a light breeze on this trip. I have been so dead on the wind while making this passage that we broad-reached southwards to lonely Redonda and then broad-reached northwards to Nevis in the hope of stopping the sails slatting in the light winds and rolly seas.

Leaving from English Harbour does not make this passage any less of a day sail, but if you have been exploring Antigua you might be leaving from Jolly Harbour or one of the anchorages on the west coast.

Your natural destination of the three islands is Nevis, the nearest one. As you come up the west coast of Nevis beware the reef extending offshore just after the recently built commercial dock on this coast and before the headland of Charlestown Bay. The reef only extends a few hundred yards but by that time you might have become too blasé about hugging the coast. Charlestown is a very distinctive landmark. Just look for the only big settlement along the coast, and that is it. Your anchorage off Pinney's Beach is immediately after Charlestown bay.

North from Antigua to St Barts/St Martin

Antigua prime harbor	English Harbour
St Barts prime harbors	Gustavia & Anse du Colombier
St Martin prime harbor	Simpson Bay

I have sailed from English Harbour to St Barts but I made it an overnighter. It is likely that if you have spent time on Antigua you will have explored other anchorages, in which case you might be leaving from Jolly Harbour or St John's.

The passage is straightforward. Sailing to St Barts and St Martin the wind will usually become increasingly free and the current has a helpful vector in it. For part of this journey you may benefit from being in the lee of the Barbuda bank. Take care on approaching since the current can run strongly through these islands and reefs, pushing you to the northwest. Take special care with your navigation if coming in here in the dark. There are some rocky bits above water between St Barts and St Martin that you would not want the current to drive you on.

Coming in to St Barts you should aim to arrive at Gustavia, the capital and port of entry, but if this is busy or rolly you might then move on to Anse du Colombier to recoup. I find the sea over the southern tail of St Barts is often lumpy. Coming in to St Martin there are no dangers and the obvious harbor is Simpson Bay.

North from Guadeloupe to St Kitts/Nevis and Statia

Guadeloupe prime harbor	Deshaies
Nevis prime harbor	Pinney's Beach
St Kitts prime harbor	None—use Nevis—see notes in Chapter 9
Statia prime harbor	None—try Oranjestad—see notes in Chapter 9

On a broad reach and the current pushing you with it this is an easy sail. You command the sea so it should be simple enough for you to stay outside the exclusion zone round Montserrat and avoid the rocky peak of Redonda. Your prime harbor is on Nevis.

North from St Kitts/Nevis and Statia to St Martin or St Barts

Nevis prime harbor	Pinney's Beach
St Kitts prime harbor	None—use Nevis—see notes in Chapter 9
Statia prime harbor	None—see notes in Chapter 9
St Martin prime harbors	Simpson Bay & Marigot Bay
St Barts prime harbors	Gustavia & Anse du Colombier

You have probably been exploring here, so you may well choose to leave from one of the little anchorages at the southwest end of St Kitts or from Oranjestad on Statia. If Oranjestad becomes rolly while you are visiting you will certainly be pleased to be leaving it. The passage to St Martin is likely to be close hauled on the wind but with a helpful current to compensate. Once clear of Statia your only problem may be to avoid visiting Saba, either because the current is sending you there or your navigation is. Make sure you know which island is which while you are still sure you know which one is Statia.

The passage to St Barts is just that much closer on the wind. If the wind has a lot of north in it this will not be a sail to make for pleasure, but only if duty calls. You are bouncing into the Trades and the current will make it hard for you to get that little bit further east than you needed for St Martin. Wait for a winter front or a summer wave and the winds to shift into the south or west. Then seize your moment.

North or west into the Virgins from St Kitts/Nevis or St Martin

The wind and current will be in your favor. The most uncomfortable aspect of the passage will be if you have light following winds and a rolly swell. In which case the Virgins will really feel like paradise.

Coming up from St Kitts beware the Saba Bank. This can be a rough piece of water and you have no reason to be cutting across it. As you approach the Virgin Bank take care to avoid Baracouter Shoal.

Most boats will find it easiest to enter the BVI first. You have a choice of Road Harbour on Tortola or Spanish Town on Virgin Gorda. In most cases Tortola will be the more convenient landfall in the prevailing winds. Enter the Sir Francis Drake Channel through Flanagan Passage or one of either Round Rock or Salt Island Passages.

If my timing was wrong to reach Customs in Road Harbour I would take one of the Peter Island anchorages and finish the trip the next day. If a northerly makes this unwise, go direct to Road Harbour and tuck up into the anchorage off Burt Point. There are charter company buoys here but usually plenty of room to anchor inside the reef.

Northwards out of the Virgins

Boats bound for North America have a choice of routes depending on their destination, but all of them will have fair winds and currents. The route through the Bahamas is easier from east-to-west because you have the prevailing wind and current with you. You still need to take care with eyeball navigation and need to master the unpredictable currents and tides.

Going outside the Bahamas bound for Miami or Fort Lauderdale, you will need to take account of the unpredictable wind-influenced currents as you turn through North West Providence Channel, and then make full allowance for the Gulf Stream running at three to four knots in the Florida Strait.

If bound further north to Charleston or Morehead City or Newport you will pass further outside the Bahamas and must aim to cross the Gulf Stream at right angles, coming out at the right point for your destination without having to beat into the

Stream. The window for this passage is April to May, avoiding the last of the winter storms from the U.S. and the first of the Caribbean hurricanes.

Boats bound for Europe may consider leaving from the Virgins rather than St Martin or Antigua. The sail northwards from Tortola to pass inside Anegada should be a comfortable reach in the prevailing Trades and you can expect to enjoy a further few days with good beam winds until you leave the Trade Wind belt.

9

Island guides

This chapter gives more detail on my prime anchorages and the islands themselves, geographically arranged from north to south. It covers topics of particular interest to sailors.

Every island has its own tourist information services and these provide plenty of glossy guides on what to do and how to do it. Usually information can be picked up where you clear in, or nearby. In addition to tourist information, many of the islands provide free guides to local yachting services and these are vital to the visiting yacht. These can be picked up from tourist offices when you arrive, and from chandlers or boat yards.

There are international airports throughout the region with frequent connections to European and North American cities and an excellent (if rather expensive) network of inter-island flights.

The region is being discovered by more and more cruisers and the economic value of yacht tourism is increasingly realized. This means major changes to the region are underway and being planned even as I write. Goodness me, even the United Nations Economic Commission for Latin America and the Caribbean has got in on the act, with a project snappily entitled "Development of a Sub-Regional Marine-Based Tourism Strategy." You and I are part of this. We are the candle flames that the businesses and investors in tourism will use to ignite the sluggish resolve of the island governments. So don't expect things to be quite like I describe. Fortunately, as we lazy navigators say when we justify our use of out-of-date pilot books and charts, the rocks don't change. Nor, I hope, do the hearts of the wonderful people of these islands.

Not all the island names are pronounced the way they are spelled. I have put a clue to the most unlikely ones at the head of each section. Not all the towns mentioned are pronounced the way they are spelled either.

St Thomas

St Thomas Harbor is one of the finest natural harbors in the Caribbean and has an easy-to follow buoyed channel to get you to Charlotte Amalie. It has been popular with sailors since the pirate era. Unfortunately, not all the pirates left.

The harbor is relatively large. It is protected from all wind directions but can suffer from swell, especially when the wind is in the south. This makes tying up to the town quay dangerous. There are several anchorages but the area is heavily buoyed. If you are lucky you may find one of these many moorings free. If not, beware of them when you drop anchor. All the protected locations have marinas. The larger ones offer a full range of marine services. Recent marina developments have made much greater provision for mega yachts.

The area is covered by the U.S. Harbor Pollution Act which prohibits the discharge of sewage, refuse or oil in the navigable waters of the USVI, and the Act is strictly enforced by the U.S. Coast Guard. You should have a holding tank or a device that prevents you discharging any visible floating solids of sewage. I think the Act can also be read to say that you should also have an engine drip tray to prevent oil polluting your bilge water. Also, you must not bring rubbish, fresh vegetables or fresh meat into the USVI.

St Thomas is the largest of the USVI islands, the most densely populated and commercially developed. It is a major location for U.S. tourists, with the cruise ship facilities, airlift, shops and even ski-lift style trams to prove it. In season this is a major seaport and there will be many cruise ships on the move. The busy traffic makes it uncomfortable. The capital, Charlotte Amalie, has some fine old Danish step-streets and buildings which make for an interesting walk around the town.

The waterfront is heavily developed and overflown by planes using the nearby international airport.

There are many reasons for cruising yachts to visit St Thomas. Big chandleries and supermarkets are located there, with the main focus being around Charlotte Amalie, and prices are duty free. You can find all the services and things your boat needs, but much of the shopping is clothes and jewelry and high luxury goods directed at passengers from cruise ships. Apart from the big bulk-buy supermarkets prices are not much different from supermarkets in Road Town, Tortola, now that these have expanded in the last few years. People who have been around the USVI for many years tell me that the decline in yacht services make this a less attractive cruising destination than it was, and less than the BVI currently are.

Much of the island is still heavily wooded and there are good walks in the national parks and many good anchorages in the bays and off-lying islands. It is an island with so many small and rarely used anchorages that it repays exploration. I would avoid Red Hook and the southeast end of the island, since this is very busy with charter yachts and the very frequent ferries that run across Pillsbury Sound. In the winter beware of the west and north coasts when swell can make the anchorages untenable.

Although the main population center is Charlotte Amalie on the south side of the island, the impression when looking at the north coast from the sea, especially at night, is of almost continuous heavy development.

St Thomas is a place where American sailors might come to find work to fill their cruising purse without having to obtain expensive work permits. But it isn't a place that attracts me. Like St Croix, St Thomas has high crime levels in general and violent crime in particular compared to other Caribbean islands and especially when compared to the very low crime levels across the water in the BVI. Hotel-based tourists are often very protected from the local low-life. Not so sailors or their boats. A pilot book written in the early 1980s was advising sailors even then not to go into town at night. Take all the precautions you would when out in any big city back home. This is definitely a place where you must lock your dinghy when you go ashore and even when anchored overnight. The word is that even some charter yachts based there prefer to sail straight across to the open spaces of St John or the BVI.

On the whole, this is the sort of place that most visitors to the Virgins and expats now living in the rest of the Virgins have come to get away from.

St John

St John is a beautiful, largely unspoilt island. Laurence Rockefeller put it on the path to being a nature island when in the mid 1950s he bought and gave much of the island to the National Park Service. Since then large portions of both the USVI and BVI have been designated national parks but nowhere to the extent of St John. Nearly 70% of the island is a national park and virtually all the population live in or near Cruz Bay. One effect of protecting so much of the island from development is that the pace of life is slower and people have more time to be friendly.

St John depends on tourism. As with St Thomas this is upmarket North American tourism, with international standard restaurants and hotels.

The main town and port of entry, Cruz Bay, is a small protected harbor really only open to the northwest, and then fairly protected by the cays at the north end of Pillsbury Sound. Cruz Bay harbor entrance is marked by two sets of green and red buoys. The harbor is very busy with passenger and car ferries and their channel to the dock must be kept clear. Once inside the harbor there are mooring buoys either side of the channel. Many are occupied by local boats. Many look to be of dubious holding. The harbor is usually crowded, anchor where you can. The wash from the ferries is an added reason not to stay in Cruz Bay longer than necessary.

Just to the north is Caneel Bay, a fine wide anchorage off the beach and only a mile walk from Cruz Bay. I think I would prefer to anchor there and walk back to clear Customs.

Coming into Cruz Bay from the south, or leaving to the south, go outside Steven Cay. There is an inside route but you need to be a ferry pilot to know it. Take care at the western end of Steven Cay. The fine big beacon is almost but not quite on the end of the cay. Watch for breaking water about 50 yards further out.

Environmental protection on the land has allowed some excellent walking trails through the hills. Protection has also reached the bays and reefs through the declaration of the Virgin Islands Coral Reef National Park. This is a way of protecting the reefs from the rising number of charter boats as well as the more careless of us cruisers. When chartering began to take off in the 1970s the bays of the Virgins were empty and boats could anchor where they chose. One drawback to this freedom was that reefs were damaged when boats dragged their ground tackle or even deliberately chose to drop anchor on the reef to give more secure holding during a midnight blow. Now mooring buoys are laid in most of the popular anchorages, color coded for their different uses, and yachts are expected to use them.

The U.S. Park Service, managers of the Virgin Islands National Park, provide buoys free for daytime use but charge U.S. $20 to U.S. $25 for an overnight stop. Pay stations are onshore in Caneel Bay Watersports shop, Hawksnest Beach, Cinnamon Bay Beach, Haho Beach, Leinster Bay, Saltpond Bay and Great Lameshure Bay.

Buoys are a great convenience even if they are not cheap for most of us on a long-term cruising budget as distinct from a week's chartering budget. A night on a park buoy will often be the same as anchoring and much less than a privately laid buoy. Sometimes I appreciate tying to a buoy for the peace of mind it brings compared to a potentially dragging anchor. As well as this private benefit to us anxious skippers the buoys have brought a greater public good. The park wardens say that thanks to the buoys the reefs are now in much better shape than 30 years ago, despite the worldwide problems of the death of coral reefs.

St John's wonderfully indented coastline gives anchorages for every season. Also, the headlands and rocks add a little *frisson* to getting into them. Not many are marked on the charter charts as off limits to charterers, and I for one take comfort and encouragement from this in my own pilotage. Thanks to the wonders of GPS I have only had one of those blindingly terrifying moments of "where are we and what rocks are those????" G thought I'd just taken a short cut. I can't imagine better sailing conditions for close quarters pilotage.

The north coast of St John, in particular, is beautiful and deserted and the bays provide wonderful anchorages under most conditions. There is little sign of habitation now but some ruined chimneys and mills from the great days of sugar. Outside the relatively crowded national park with its mooring buoys you can find rarely used anchorages, such as Mary's Creek in Leinster Bay. Check your pilot books and charts for some of the one-boat anchorages and get there before someone else does.

Remember the U.S. Harbor Pollution Act: no discharge of sewage, refuse or oil.

Tortola

Rumors of over-development seem exaggerated. True, this isn't Carriacou or Mayreau in the Grenadines. It is the biggest of the BVIs, an offshore financial center in its own right and rivaling the affluence of the Caymans, as well as being the major charter yacht base of the Virgins. Huge numbers of offshore companies are registered here and the island claims to be one of the largest such centers in the world, which means there has to be lots of offices for the many lawyers and financial advisors and big homes for these high earners. Yet the impression you get of the land as you look from the sea, even of the environs of Road Harbour, the capital of Tortola and largest town of the BVI, is not of dense development. It is of well spaced and proportional buildings set apart from one another in the hills. These buildings are architecturally attractive, built to a high standard and, unlike many places in the rest of the island chain, are made more attractive by being completely finished rather than left with the top floor still to be added.

We heard much about the relative levels of crime between the BVI and the USVI. The proof is in the pudding. The BVI lacks the razor wire fences and burglar proofing that spoil many of the other islands. The BVI do not seem to have a crime problem.

We have spent most of our time ashore in the Virgins on Tortola. It just seems the nicest of the big islands. We began by thinking it very un-Caribbean but after a while we saw through the thin veneer to the essential Caribbeanness beneath. It isn't just the chickens on the main roads or the little timber shacks between grand houses, or even the overpowering smell of drains. It's the brilliant colors of the flowers, the songs of the birds, the scuttle of lizards in the dried leaves and the openness of the local people.

There is also a high proportion of incomers to these islands. The older expat British and Americans are often semi-retired or running a small business. The youth are from all over Europe and North America and the old British colonies, working for a spell on yachts or diving. And then you will hear Spanish from Puerto Rico, the long vowels of Jamaica and the lilt of Guyanese from the deep south of the Caribbean in the voices of economic migrants escaping the poverty and misery of their own countries for the two-job, twelve hour days of just managing to make a living here where life, though immeasurably better, is expensive.

Road Harbour is not just a major yachting center, it is also a cruise ship destination. Many of the shops in town are geared to these visitors. Yacht services, repair and maintenance workshops exist around the island and I am sure you will find everything you need eventually. The main concentration in Road Harbour is at the back of The Moorings. Although of good quality, it is limited in scope and does not compare in scale with St Martin and the bigger islands to the south.

Making up for this, we found the people here helpful and friendly. Not, of course, as friendly as islanders further south but still very helpful. I would say that Road Harbour is probably the best base for a prolonged stay in the Virgins, especially if you have maintenance to do.

Work here is not cheap. Labor rates vary from U.S. $30 to U.S. $70 an hour, depending on skills. Haul-out is U.S. $10 a foot for a monohull and storage starts at around U.S. $14 per foot per month with water and electricity metered and extra.

Road Harbour is not always a comfortable place to anchor. The Trade Winds blow straight in. Strong Trades bring a lumpy sea with them. The best shelter is inside the cruise ship terminal by the marinas of The Moorings and Village Cay, but there is little room to anchor here. The anchorage for the Customs is definitely subject to swell, but you might find relief inside the reef at Burt Point, where Conch Charters and some others have moorings. Yachts also anchor or take buoys in Fish Bay on the northern side but there is commercial traffic and not much room for yachts.

One of the joys of Road Harbour is that you don't need to stay there. The off-lying islands of Peter and Norman, in particular, provide excellent quiet and almost remote anchorages. When the weather is right I would choose Deadman's Bay on Peter Island as my anchorage. This is the only island where I have seen such generous treatment from a beach hotel to visiting yachts, all in the spirit of enlightened self-interest.

> The sign on the beach invited us to use the chairs and palm frond covered tables. They were put there for us, the visiting yachties. They were not for the hotel guests because they had their own facilities a mile away, yet they had been put there by the hotel and every morning a member of the hotel staff came to clean the beach and rake the sand. "Please respect the facilities" the sign said, and I certainly felt like doing just that. After all, they were there for me.

At the west end of Tortola, Sopers Hole is a wonderfully sheltered bay and port of entry. This is busy with small boats rather than big ferries and attractive, but so densely buoyed that you may have difficulty finding an anchorage. Customs is on the north shore of the bay, almost opposite the well-signed Frenchman's Cay shipyard on the south shore. Watch out for the red and green navigation buoys close to the northern shore, possibly marking a wreck site. There is a marina but Sopers Hole is also used by cruising yachts and some live-aboards.

Inland Tortola has good walking and wonderful countryside to visit. The National Parks Trust set up in 1961 led to the creation of 19 national parks, one of which is the offshore site of the wreck of the *Rhone*, a Royal Mail Steamer which foundered in a hurricane in 1867. This is now the most visited dive site in the region.

The BVI is also very concerned with protecting the underwater environment. The Association of Reef Keepers was set up here in 1996 to preserve and conserve the marine environment. They provide advice to sailors on how not to damage corals.

Sopers Hole, Tortola—the famous Pusser's Landing. *Photo: Courtesy of BVI Tourist Authority.*

Environmental protection laws in the BVI are similar to those of the U.S. Harbor Pollution Act: no discharge of sewage, refuse or oil.

Virgin Gorda

This is a long tongue of an island, with mountains in the north and low-lying land in the east. The southwest is a flat peninsula connected to the central part of the island by a low isthmus. From the sea it looks like two islands.

The main harbor in St Thomas Bay is easy to enter. Stay close to the headland of Collision Point to avoid the long reef projecting from Fort Point and blocking off much of the wide open bay. The rocks off to the west of Collision Point are marked by a green buoy. Follow the line of moorings up to the ferry quay, or take the leading line from the radio mast and the ferry quay. The channel is well marked by green and red buoys which will take you inside the reef and even right up to the entrance of the marina. This is a very protected yacht harbor in an old lagoon but usually full. A little local knowledge would give comfort when going in here. Fortunately, to clear Customs you only need to anchor off the ferry quay. This should be comfortable in all but northerlies. The yacht harbor has been under renovation for several years and probably will be for several years more.

This is a tourist island with only a small year-round population. All land over 1,000 feet is designated as national park and laid out with walking trails. The two wonderful things for sailors about Virgin Gorda are The Baths and Gorda Sound.

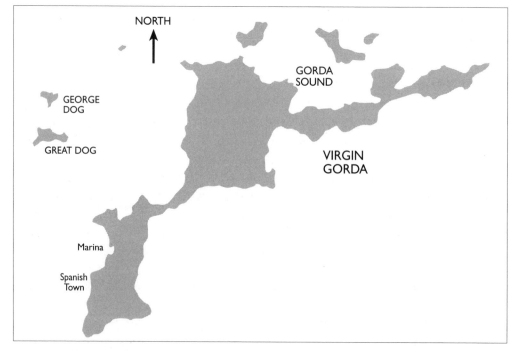

Fig 13 Virgin Gorda.

The Baths are huge blocks of granite scattered about the southwest coast following some immensely violent act of nature. The pilot books all rate these as the prime site to visit in the whole of the Virgins, and I must agree. Don't miss them. They make a stunning seascape as well as landscape. The colors of the water are wonderful, the warm salt water pools are relaxing, and the walk between the broken granite and the broad-leafed almond trees is magical. The water is so translucent that the anchored yachts seem to float in the sky.

You will almost certainly find The Baths crowded with other yachts, even out of season. Once this was a difficult place to anchor because of the broken and uneven nature of the bottom but mooring buoys have been laid for daytime use. In the high season you won't find room for a rowing dinghy to get in here after 9 am, but then why are you cruising here in the main charter season?

Gorda or North Sound is a wonderfully protected bay, almost land-locked. We came into it from the east, through Colquhoun Reef and Prickly Pear Island. The reef is largely uncovered and easy to see. The channel is close in to the island but the green and red channel buoys take you through between Colquhoun Reef and the dangerous hidden reefs off Prickly Pear Island. Pilotage to arrive at the channel is not difficult and once through into the Sound you have plenty of open water. There are plenty of anchorages, surprisingly empty in the low season. The hotel development is tightly grouped so that most of the surrounding land is undeveloped. I claim that if Gorda Sound is too busy with other boats I would take us through into Eustatia Sound, but this brave boast has not been put to the test.

In the winter months, when Tortola's north coast is exposed to northeasterlies and a swell is roaring passed Colquhoun Reef, North Sound should still be comfortable.

Jost Van Dyke

This small, sparsely populated island due north of Sopers Hole helps give a sense that the sound to the north of Tortola is protected by land on all sides. Certainly, from the anchorage at Sandy Cay off the northeast end of Jost Van Dyke all the land to the north, west and south merges to seem continuous.

The main habitation and location of Customs is Great Harbour, a beach settlement on the south side of Jost Van Dyke. This is protected from the northerlies but also, thanks to the mass of Tortola to the south, from the usual Trade Winds. The beach is cut off by a reef close inshore. Dinghy through the channel to the quay. It is a quiet place to clear Customs.

Jost Van Dyke has a more desolate feel to it than the west end of Tortola. The vegetation here is sparse and scrubby. The other anchorages on the island, such as Little Harbour, are less crowded than those on Tortola.

Green Cay, a beautiful rocky hillock of green vegetation and white-gold beaches just off the east of Little Jost Van Dyke, looks like the most beautiful remote anchorage in the area until you see Sandy Cay a mile south of it.

Jost Van Dyke—the jetty at Foxy's popular watering hole. *Photo: Courtesy of BVI Tourist Authority.*

It is places like this that make the Virgins the antidote to the rest of the Caribbean. For all its charm the Caribbean can be a rough old bit of sea that stubbornly refuses to live up to advertising executives' hype. The Virgins can restore a sailor's faith in glossy brochures.

We used the flat seas behind Tortola as a race track, beating east and then beating west, the fine breeze pushing our heavy old ketch to full speed and no nasty swell or waves to slow us down. After Sandy Cay we beat eastwards to the narrow channel between Guana Island and Tortola and motored through to find ourselves in yet another almost landlocked sea. Guana Island, Tortola, Beef Island and the Camanoes surrounded us, leaving the only major break in the land up to the north. Wonderful. We motored east, carefully plotting our position to take us through the dangerous off-limit waters (off limits to charter yachts) between Beef Island and Little Camanoe. The red and green buoys shown as marking the rock south of Little Camanoe and the reefs north of Beef Island were not there. Instead I could see a yellow and black buoy that was certainly not IALA. Which side to pass it? Leave it to port, I reckoned. I conned us from the foredeck, signaling to G until I had her steering closer and closer to the buoy and finally we slid by leaving it very close indeed to port. I had seen the submerged danger by that time, a flat rocky shape off Beef Island, and knew we should have left that buoy to starboard. The charter yacht coming up fast was obviously going to overtake us well to port of the buoy and probably smack right into that big rock. I waved wildly at the skipper. The yacht turned hard to starboard, shot across our stern at right angles and went well clear of us before coming back on course. I assumed the skipper was too stressed to wave thanks to me for saving the bottom of his boat. Perhaps he didn't know the etiquette. Ahead of us I could see another non-IALA yellow and black buoy. Let's leave this one to starboard, I muttered to G.

Minor islands of the BVI

A most useful group of minor islands runs along the southern edge of the Virgin Bank, as though part of the ridge between Virgin Gorda and St John. They lie a few miles off Tortola and mark the southern boundary of the Sir Francis Drake Channel. Ginger, Cooper, Salt, Peter and Norman Islands, and the greatest of these is Peter. In the right conditions these islands provide a change of anchorage.

St Martin/Sint Maarten

Unusual in being two countries on one small island. French and Dutch. The official name is Saint-Martin/Sint Maarten. This is an island that went out wholeheartedly to embrace tourism and succeeded, managing to retain beautiful natural features alongside intense commercial developments. The local economy is more heavily and explicitly dependent on tourism than any other island in the chain, and this tourism includes some major charter fleets and several hundred live-aboard cruisers during December to May. The large scale of tourism supports some fine supermarkets and specialist shops, such as auto-spares, that are of immediate interest to visiting yachts. Laundries and laundry services seem to be on every corner—certainly more available and at lower prices than most islands to the south I can think of other than Martinique and Trinidad. Water is available from marinas and boat yards as well as from a water tender contacted on VHF channel 72.

St Martin and nearby St Barts and Anguilla are probably the most popular location for bareboat charter in the whole of the Leewards because of the short passages, varied anchorages and pretty beaches. They are less populated than the nearby Virgins but much busier and probably less challenging than further south. These low-lying islands never had enough natural rainfall to support intensive agriculture and so were never developed like the taller islands. Their drier climate, like that of St Kitts and Nevis, makes them attractive to modern tourism.

The Dutch side has some very large and well stocked food supermarkets but we found the range and quality as well as price better for us on the French side. The Dutch side seems better for hardware and chandlery, but this may change as the French side develops its yachting industry. It may also depend on what chandlery you need. The Dutch side tends to stock American products while the French side stocks European. Because the island is duty free chandlery prices often beat those in the U.S.

I'm of two minds about St Martin, just as St Martin seems to be of two minds about itself. On the one hand I have always enjoyed the island and love sailing at that end of the Leewards. On the other hand I am never going to be a long-term resident Lagoonie or sail a mega yacht, so as a cruiser on a small yacht I don't feel at home there. Of course, I am not at home on any of the other islands either, but I feel welcome as a visitor there. In St Martin I feel like I should be a member of the main tribe, since we are all visitors there, but it isn't my tribe and when the tribe of sailors makes an overture to the tribe of non-sailors it sometimes gets a slap in the face. It's the price of being an outsider and occasionally thinking you aren't. If I'm going to be an outsider, let me be one in the real Caribbean.

St Martin is strangely un-Caribbean and strangely lacking in rootedness. The pre-tourism population of the 1950s was about 5,000 compared to about 60,000 now. About 40 different nationalities live here and only about 20% of the population is reckoned to have been born on the island. The Dutch half of the island is more international than the French, possibly even more American than Dutch, although both sides are very international. The line of advertising hoardings and shop fronts along the road from Simpson Bay and the Dutch airport reminds me more of the approach road to an American town than anything I have seen in the islands to the south. The wall of six-story timeshare apartments lining the Simpson Bay approach to the Lagoon are like some *Costa Inglesa* in Mediterranean Spain although they are wholly American in terms of who stays there and their facilities.

The island has two currencies and at least four languages but on both sides of the island the language of the street is English and the U.S. dollar is the dominant currency (and in 2011 became the legal tender of the Dutch side). Crossing between the French and Dutch sides by land is not complicated by any formalities of Customs or Immigration but yachts must clear in and out on both sides. Also, if you are taking your boat through the bridges into the Lagoon you will need to inform the harbor authorities. Procedures are simple. Local buses around the island are cheap and comfortable, good for sightseeing or shopping. Buses are like maxi taxis. Routes are displayed on their windscreen.

The island is small enough to get to know well in a short time. The coast is low lying and indented with some very beautiful bays and beaches and some fine walks along the headlands. French St Martin, like many other islands, has declared an underwater nature reserve to preserve its coral reefs from carelessly dropped anchors. These reserves protect various outlying islands. Mooring buoys are laid here. The island has many fine natural harbors to explore but the obvious ones for arriving passagemakers are Marigot and Simpson Bay, both of which are gateways to the Lagoon, arguably the largest concentration of yachting in the whole Caribbean chain.

The Lagoon
Approached through bridges opening at set times morning and evening on both the French and Dutch sides. A wide, shallow stretch of water with well buoyed channels. A mass of anchored yachts and the main center for chandleries, service firms and marinas.

Well sheltered, although the shallow water can kick up into a short chop in strong wind. The reputation as a safe hurricane hole was dented in 1996 and again in 1999. Neither of the hurricane hits were expected and much of the damage was due to badly anchored boats dragging on others. The wrecks of yachts driven ashore are still visible. The area under the runway of the Dutch airport is intensely noisy and I would want to wear earplugs if anchored there.

Demand for dockage in the Lagoon has led to the development of several new marinas, including some specializing in mega yachts. St Martin now claims to be one of the world's leading super yacht destinations. The Simpson Bay Lagoon Authority Corporation oversaw the widening of the bridge and channel from 38 feet to 55 feet to allow mega yachts into the Lagoon. The Corporation levied fees to repay the bridge loan, much to the anger of smaller-boat sailors, some of whom even claimed the Corporation was contravening the UN Law of the Sea. It took several years for the hottest disputes to settle down, though matters are still simmering as ordinary yachties object to the way that the small number of marina developers and managers use their financial clout and influence to obtain concessions from island governments (not just in St Martin) to restrict anchoring near their marinas.

The wider marine industry, including mega yacht owners, were also unhappy with the Lagoon Authority when it finally, in January 2008, set its bridge fees. It did so without consultation. Concerns had been voiced that the fees and the way they were being applied would drive yachts away from St Maarten to other islands. Many yachts had also, quite predictably, shifted from the Dutch to the French side. The Authority's actions were jeopardizing major investments on the Dutch side.

Feeling you should be consulted and have a voice in what is happening comes when you feel part of a community, when you engage in the politics of the place. There is every reason why sailors in Sint Maarten should wish to engage, though they may not anticipate or enjoy the cost of fighting your own corner that often comes with engagement. Many have been on the island for long years. They and visiting sailors are an important sub-division of the major economic sector of tourism. The widening of the bridge and channel and the levying of fees touched them directly and, through them, the employment and earnings and other economic variables of Sint Maarten. Sadly the debate between the government minister and the yachting community, as it was with other groups, was continuously acrimonious. There was no sign from the minister that the fees were inequitable, that yachties should have a voice or that by living and working and spending on the island they made a contribution to his community.

Low season rates apply in most marinas here between July and November, but so do stipulations for hurricane conditions. Boat owners rather than the marina must take all responsibility for any damage to the dock or other boats. Boats must be moved by the owner or someone they appoint whenever the marina management decides there is a hurricane threat. Boats left unattended during hurricane season must be moored as if a hurricane is expected. Curiously, one marina stipulates as a hurricane season condition that it will not accept ferro or steel yachts. So that's my last two boats heading offshore.

Simpson Bay

Gateway to the Lagoon from the Dutch side. The best protected bay on the Dutch side and easy to enter. Good holding in three to four meters off the conspicuous timeshare hotels. Push up into the bay to reduce rolling but beware the rapid shoaling close in. The bay, heavily developed on the shore, is busy with all forms of water tourism—dive boats, ferries, day tripper boats, jet skis and kayaks. Sometimes noisy but always interesting. Noisy also when big jets take off from the Dutch airport. There is a small commercial berth for ships loading with aggregates close to the entrance channel to the Lagoon.

Marigot Bay

Main bay on the French side and with the most interesting town on St Martin. Head inside the headland of Fort Marigot towards the market place and town center and anchor in two to three meters north of the lifting bridge into the Lagoon. The town bustles and the shoreside market can be noisy during the day. There is a very French atmosphere despite the accelerating growth of tourism. We found the anchorage here less rolly than Simpson Bay.

After entering the Lagoon from Marigot Bay you can follow the dredged channel to the very urban marina of Port la Royale.

Both Marigot and Simpson Bay anchorages can be crowded but yachts seem to come and go frequently so there is always room for a new one. Also, both anchorages are cooled by the Trade Winds.

Philipsburg

The main town on the Dutch side is a mecca of duty-free jewelry shops and casinos. Groot Bay, though deeper than Simpson Bay, is more open to swell and yachts roll heavily. The water here and the views across the bay are stunningly beautiful. Bobbie's Marina and Groot Bay Marina are here. Bobby's, the oldest of the marinas on the island, was built in 1968, and underwent a major facelift in 2005 aimed at accommodating mega yachts and encouraging them to stay longer.

On clearing in to St Martin pick up from the harbormaster's office the excellent guide to the island and list of yacht services and the local yachting free-sheet for stories and ads. St Martin is always undergoing change. Together these will help you organize your stay on the island.

St Barts, Saint-Barthélemy

Officially known as Saint-Barthélemy. Ruled by Sweden for a century, St Barts is now the smallest island in the French department of Guadeloupe. Volcanic with beautiful scenery and beaches. Approaching from the south the island looks like a messy archipelago of rocky islets, most of which are lying to the north, but all this falls into place as you get closer.

The local economy is now largely dependent on wealthy visitors. Average earnings and standard of living are more European than Caribbean. Unusual in that its 5,000 or so population is predominantly white.

St Barts is well worth a visit. It is usually a comfortable sail from Antigua or Nevis/ St Kitts and a short distance from St Martin. It is quite different from the Caribbean islands to the south, unmistakably French (despite reminders of its Swedish past) and fiercely independent. The island has a history of economic struggle and hard times but today it is a luxury holiday resort with villas and second homes for the seriously rich. Superyachts fill the middle harbor. The people in the streets of tiny Gustavia could be straight out of St Tropez or Biarritz.

On my visits there has always been some European-type cultural event rather than a Caribbean one. Art, cinema, classical music. One of the few times in my life I have watched ballet has been here, at the music festival in 1997. A warm dark tropical night, sounds of cicadas and tree frogs, a small stage growing more treacherous as the night dew fell more thickly, and dancers from Ballet France performing pas de deux and stunningly athletic solos. A male dancer performing a particularly vigorous set of leaps got double applause as he leapt and skidded on a floor without traction.

Despite its tourism, St Barts remains a real place with real people who connect to their history. It is not another Mustique, although it attracts the super-rich. Wealth from tourism has probably only arrived here in the last generation. The old families, some of whom have been in St Barts for 300 or 400 years, struggled to make a living from land and sea. They give the island a feeling of coastal Brittany or Normandy rather than the French Riviera.

Gustavia

The capital and main harbor. Coming from the south this will be the first anchorage. Busy and often crowded. The buoyed inner harbor is reserved for locals, which can mean long-stay foreign yachts. The best stern-to moorings along the quay in the middle of the harbor are usually taken by the superyachts. The outer part of the quay is subject to swell and waves. Most visitors and long-stay yachts anchor in the outer harbor off the headland, coming inside the rocks of The Saintes and Les Gros Islets. This too is crowded. The row ashore encourages sailors to get themselves a decent dinghy with a powerful outboard. Competition to be in the lee of the land is strong but even then the place feels exposed and the holding doubtful. We dragged almost immediately. Long-stay yachts usually put down a heavy sinker. The other town anchorages of Anse Corossol (about a mile from town) and Anse de Public (about half a mile from town) are closer inshore but off an industrial area and power generating plant. They look just as rolly and lack the pretty outlook.

Anse du Colombier

The first anchorage as you come from the north or St Martin. The anchorage at Colombier is remote from facilities but quiet and beautiful. Holding in sand is good. Boats on the southern side of the bay seem to swing a lot, even in steady winds. Boats anchored offshore roll more than those closer in. The anchorage is popular with cruising yachts and as a holiday for the long-stay yachts, as well as with tripper boats bringing sunbathers to the beach, but the bay seldom seems crowded. Since free moorings were

There is no road. Only the narrow, rough track links the quiet anchorage of Anse du Colombier to the little village of Flamand, St Barts. It's one of our favorite walks. *Photo: G Jardine.*

laid in Anse du Colombier there has been an improvement in the marine environment. Seagrass has recovered and turtles can be seen.

There is no road to Colombier. A rugged coastal footpath with stunning seascapes leads to the resort area of Flamand. The boulangerie in the village is one of the most general of general stores I have seen. A wide range of food and drink as well as hardware. The shop is less than a half hour walk from the anchorage along one of our favorite walks. This little shop makes yachts anchored in Colombier independent of the shops of Gustavia.

Statia, Sint Eustatius

Pronounced *Stay-shah*. Known generally as Statia but officially as Sint Eustatius. Changed its status in October 2010 to become an autonomous special municipality within the Kingdom of the Netherlands. English is spoken almost everywhere. The U.S. dollar is now the legal tender.

Easily approached from its very near neighbor St Kitts. From St Kitts the island looks like a single peak. From the north or northeast it looks like two islands, with the high peak to the south and a lesser peak to the north. The 2,000 foot high Quill is a wonderful example of a dormant volcano, with a rainforest inside and around its cone. A good walk.

From St Barts or St Martin, yachts usually pass round the northern end to make the main town and anchorage of Oranjestad. From this direction take care not to come inside the pipeline and the half-mile long jetty used by oil supertankers. Statia oil terminal is the biggest fuel store I have seen on any small Caribbean island. I have seen two large tankers at the jetty and four more at anchor.

The only anchorage on the island is at Oranjestad in a weakly indented bay behind a headland that offers little protection from the swell. The harbormaster has laid visitor moorings to give yachts more security than their own anchor. The best spots are in the southern end of the bay near a small harbor where the breakwater gives more protection, but all things are relative and yachts seem to roll as much here as anywhere else. Yachts that had given up an outer buoy for one closer in still left as early in the morning as we did, and presumably for the same reason. Severe discomfort. Best to avoid Statia if there is a ground swell from the north or the wind has south in it.

Oranjestad deserves to be visited. The main town, built on the clifftop plateau rather than the narrow strip of land along the shore, is barely visible from the anchorage or as you approach. Don't be fooled into expecting to see a town or you will sail straight past. The town center has some well preserved old buildings and one of the best local museums we have visited in the Caribbean. The clifftop fort and what looks like an ornamental waterfall suggest the significant role and wealth of the island in its heyday, as do the buildings along the shore, now almost all in ruins. Apart from these relics it is hard to imagine that this island was once one of the major trading centers in the region. The waterfront buildings sit with their foundations in the sea, like warehouses able to be loaded directly from the waterside. Perhaps they had some protection from the swell that went missing at the same time as most of their upper floors. Paintings from the period show the bay crowded with commercial and naval vessels.

The British may well be to blame for the ruins. The people of Statia upset the British at the time of the American War of Independence. Although The Netherlands was neutral, the island had an illicit arms trade to support the American rebels and was one of the first to salute the flag of the new republic. When Britain and The Netherlands later went to war with one another Admiral Rodney plundered Statia, fired the warehouses and breakwaters and dismantled the harbor. There was probably more protection from the sea just after Rodney than when we visited.

We landed at a half-ruined jetty belonging to a dive center. We timed our landings so that we each scrambled out at the top of the two-meter swell and none of us got our shore clothes wet. Thank goodness we have such a small dinghy. We hauled it out of the water and carried it up some handy steps. It would have been a burst balloon if we had left it tied on the jetty. People with outboards came ashore in the protection of the breakwater harbor.

Check in at the harbormaster office by the breakwater. There are no facilities ashore and few shops for provisions.

Statia and its near neighbors St Kitts and Nevis, which also lack secure natural harbors, were historically not easily accessible for shipping. This has allowed a degree of isolation which has given them a more individual character.

St Christopher (St Kitts) and Nevis

The Federation of St Christopher and Nevis, two islands separated by a two mile wide strait, the Narrows. The islands became independent in 1983.

St Christopher and Nevis are a bit off the track for most sailing passages up or down the island chain. A yacht visiting the islands from St Martin to Antigua would need to make a deliberate diversion to the west. This isn't too difficult although the wind at the time may decide whether you come north about from Antigua or south about from St Martin or St Barts.

It would be a shame not to visit this group of islands in the inner arc of the chain, and in which I include the Dutch island of Statia. (But not the island of Saba. While this belongs geographically to the group it lacks an easy secure anchorage and is a destination for the explorer rather than the passagemaker.) St Kitts and Nevis have a rich cultural heritage and are among the most charming and, outside the hotel complexes, some of the least spoilt islands in the chain. Their relative isolation as far as cruisers go is either cause or effect of their lack of a yachting center and their few facilities for yachts. Most of the visiting yachts we have seen here were private yachts flying American and British flags, rather than the charter boats seen so often in the outer arc of islands from Grenada to St Martin. Facilities for sailors may increase if Port Zante marina prospers and the planned marina off Ballast Bay is completed.

These islands are reputed to have a drier (i.e. healthier) climate than others in the Caribbean. Certainly in our March visit, during the dry season, the days were free of rain although some heavy rain came at night from clouds blowing off Nevis Peak.

St Kitts, St Christopher

Officially known as St Christopher, St Kitts, the larger of the two islands, has an important role in Caribbean history. British colonization of the Caribbean began with a settlement here in 1623. St Kitts has the feel of a very British Caribbean island despite having at times belonged to France. Brimstone Hill, one of the great buildings on the island and one of the great fortifications in the Caribbean, dates from the wars between Britain and France and was once known as the Gibraltar of the Caribbean. There is much to see here. Some of the "great houses" of the plantation days now provide tourist accommodations and the island has become an increasingly popular destination for tourism. There has been large scale hotel development on the coast north of Basseterre, the main town on St Kitts, massive investment in the Port Zante complex in Basseterre, and a huge scheme is underway on the southern peninsular of the island.

Basseterre lies towards the southern end of St Kitts. Even when coming to Basseterre from the north, you may find it more comfortable to come round the southern end of the island, through The Narrows, if weather allows. Otherwise you are likely to have ten miles of wind and current on the nose as you motor south down the leeside of the island.

We had a wonderful sail through The Narrows but this is a bit of pilotage that should be done with care as neither the shoals extending from Nevis nor the isolated rock patches close to St Kitts are marked. When sailing southwards down the windward side of St Kitts to arrive at The Narrows take care as you come close into shore, as you must, to sneak your way into The Narrows. The seas can become lumpier as you close the coast, due probably to a combination of shoaling and the backwash of waves reflecting off the land. Also the wind seems to reflect off the land and become fluky. Only sail through here in good light.

St Kitts and Nevis, with their high peaks (Mount Misery on St Kitts is 3,700 feet and Nevis Peak is 3,232 feet), can become confusingly overlaid on one another as you close the southern coast of St Kitts from the east. The low hills on the southern tip of St Kitts are connected to the rest of the island by a very low lying neck of sand. This is invisible from a few miles offshore and the low hills look closer to, and part of, Nevis rather than St Kitts.

Basseterre is a picturesque old town with colonial style buildings centered on a small square called the Circus, with its oddly Victorian clock fountain. The waterfront has spent many years undergoing massive new development for the Port Zante cruise ship complex and this may shift the economic center of the town.

Basseterre is a poor place to anchor. This is a wide but shallow indentation in the coast, apparently getting most of its protection from the south from its deep water port. The bay seems well sheltered from the prevailing winds but I find the swell too uncomfortable, even when tucked in to the eastern end by the unattractive commercial docks. By coming inside the long commercial jetty of the deep water port, you might avoid the worst of the swell and the fetch when the wind blows along from Nevis and The Narrows. A stern anchor holding you in the direction of the swell may make life more comfortable but you will have a hard time of dinghying ashore. The old rule of thumb here is that when the anchoring at Charlestown on Nevis is bad, it will be good at Basseterre, and vice versa.

Given the swell in the bay, a marina here would be a good idea. In principle. The ambitious 1995 Port Zante project to redevelop the waterfront with a new cruise ship dock and shopping center also included a 56-berth marina to take yachts up to 70 feet and 12 feet draft. Perhaps Port Zante will make life for the visiting yacht more comfortable in the future, and it is certainly handy for downtown Basseterre, but from my own experience of putting in there I would regard any marina here as a potential trap, to be left at short notice.

Rb proved unexpectedly heroic that spring of 1997. We had berthed in the newly opened marina at Port Zante and I for one thought we would lose my precious boat that second night. Massive surges came into the harbor without warning. One of our inch thick nylon stern lines snapped at 3 am leaving us with the uncomfortable question of what happens if the other stern line parts. At huge personal danger Rb dinghied out a cat's cradle of extra lines to the mooring posts and jetties. These added no sense of extra security as the surge worsened. We were in a box-type berth for a boat twice our length. We had long stern lines out to mooring posts and at our bow we had a pontoon between us and the dock wall. We were lucky to get out of the berth without tobogganing up the pontoon and embedding our bowsprit in that wall. Our inch thick lines were firing us forward like catapult elastic at full stretch. I had wondered, as we came into the marina, about the unusual dogleg entrance. As we came out I could make more sense of it. All those ad hoc bits of concrete and steel had been stuck on later to prevent swell entering the marina. Unfortunately, some condition on this swell-infested coast was able to trigger a *seiche*, the sort of resonating wave commonly called slosh when we see it in the bathtub. With hindsight I calculated the slosh wave had a period of less than a minute in the most enclosed part of the marina, where the box berths were laid roughly parallel with the coast of the island, and such a rapid surge doesn't have to be much to wreak havoc. I have been much re-assured since to learn that engineers routinely consider the phenomena of *seiche* in the design of harbors and marinas. Consideration is one thing; effective design is another altogether.

When we visited Port Zante in 2001 we could see that much of the building from the 1995 project had been blown away by Georges in 1998 and Lenny in 1999. Massive works were going on offshore. The character of Port Zante was becoming clearer. It is a fairly small marina of about 36 berths, although they can take yachts up to 70 feet in length. The marina is an integral element of the Port Zante shopping center rather than the other way round. I was pleased to hear that the breakwaters have been redesigned to make the marina more protected from surge and that the new Port Zante will be hurricane proof this time. Now there's a claim I wouldn't like to make in case that crazy old god Huracan is listening. Although some yachts were moored somewhere in the construction works, we chose to continue on our way.

The best anchorages on St Kitts are the little sandy inlets of Ballast Bay and Whitehouse Bay at the southwest end of the island. These bays are remote and in an arid, rugged and not overly attractive landscape but easy to enter and relatively free from swell. I prefer Ballast Bay, the larger of the two and with a comfortable breeze through the hills and flat land behind it. Good holding. A stony beach to land on. Beware the reef off the northern headland.

If you don't see Ballast Bay in your pilot books anymore look for Christophe Harbor. The whole southern end of St Kitts has been bought for a 2,500-acre development with marina village, hotels, oceanfront homes, luxury villas, a golf course, shops, streamlined Customs and Immigration services and, among other things, a full service marina with berths for 250 or so yachts and 50 to 60 mega yachts, to be ready sometime in 2011. Advance publicity said the marina would pamper yacht owners by providing a heliport. That's my sort of marina.

The little cut that provides access to the salt ponds from Ballast Bay will be dredged to allow the mega yachts into the basin currently known as Little Salt Pond. This will have the 20-foot depth needed for the mega yachts it plans to accommodate. The Greater Salt Pond will, I think, mainly provide the landscape for harbor front villas. Christophe Harbor will have a protected entrance and safe inner harbor.

Whitehouse Bay is blanketed by the high hills behind it. It is just as isolated as Ballast Bay but shows some signs of developing water sports. A line of kayaks on the beach suggest a base here.

> We had sailed to Statia from St Kitts. The American couple had sailed there from St Barts. "So which is the best anchorage in St Kitts?" they asked. Rb and I looked at each other instinctively. "Nevis," we replied in untutored unison.

Walking to Mount Misery is a fine day out. Take a guide. The 1,000 feet deep crater is still venting.

Nevis

Pronounced *Neevis*. A round island dominated by the 3,232 feet high volcanic mountain of Nevis Peak. Part of the Federation of St Christopher and Nevis and with its own separate parliament.

The leeside of Nevis is a rolly place for much of the year but we have never found it too bad and this is a fine unspoilt island to visit. The anchorage at the main town of Charlestown is busy and subject to too much swell, although the new landing stage is an easy place to come ashore, and handy for Customs and Immigration and shops.

We prefer Pinney's Beach anchorage just north of Charlestown, close in to the beach. It is convenient from north or south. It is within easy reach of St Kitts or The Narrows as you come from the north, and only a little further on from Charlestown as you come from the south.

Pinney's Beach anchorage puts the headland of Charlestown between you and the swell running from the south, while St Kitts and The Narrows still give some protection from swell from the north. The anchorage, which is easy to spot, lies in a long indentation in the coast rather than an obvious bay and is easy to sail into. Most yachts used to anchor south of the large, conspicuous beach hotel at Cades Point, between a beach restaurant and Lowland Point, where the holding in sand is good. However, mooring buoys have been laid here. Land on the beach and walk into town.

Pinney's Beach is not the classically beautiful anchorage it used to be when we first cruised here in the early 1990s, and certainly not the empty and remote place it was when I first sailed here in 1969. Not all development is for the better. The view of the beach from the sea suffered when a recent hotel development planted diseased palm trees from Florida. The hotel saved those in its own grounds but the local palms making up the several miles of iconic palm-fringed beach died. So, that must be something to do with the virulence of the disease and certainly nothing to do with the priorities of the hotel.

Still, Pinney's Beach anchorage has a wonderfully open aspect which I hope will never be taken away from it. Most secure anchorages in the Caribbean are in bays and can feel enclosed. This anchorage is on the long coast of Nevis, with a high volcanic peak to the east, the crags and hills of St Kitts and Statia to the north, and nothing but the wide expanse of Caribbean Sea to the west.

If you anchor due west of Nevis Peak you will get an extra hour of sleep before the rising sun prises you out of bed.

When a swell rolls in to Pinney's Beach the anchorage at Charlestown will be much worse and you will probably find the best shelter on St Kitts in Ballast Bay.

We like Nevis. Charlestown is still a fine traditional old Caribbean town, with a mixture of splendid old buildings in various states of disrepair although the old stone colonial style buildings are usually well maintained. The new architecture is more sensitive to the old styles than in many other islands. The place has a sense of development and prosperity which, if not quite arrived yet, is surely on the way. Local people are welcoming, proud of their island and happy to talk to you about it.

We liked the little local museum too. It reminded me that Alexander Hamilton, one of the architects of the American Constitution, was born here, and that Nelson married the widow Fanny Nisbit here in 1787.

The charm of Charlestown is that it meets the needs of the islanders, not visitors. Unfortunately, this means that the market and stores are not good for re-stocking. Even the fruit and vegetables were imported from the U.S. rather than neighboring islands. But there are good old fashioned hardware shops where good old fashioned sailors can find things like hurricane lamps that the rest of the world has largely forgotten. And the town has plenty of ATMs that take a range of credit and debit cards.

In spring 2001 we saw what looked like major sea defenses being laid along the Charlestown waterfront, of the sort we have seen on other islands after hurricanes. We assumed they were fixing damage after Lenny smashed the waterfront in 1999 because they looked designed to withstand another hurricane. Actually these works were planned earlier than Lenny as a new one-way road system and a broad promenade along this magnificent sea front. By 2007 they had turned into a road protected from the sea by massive defenses. The road and defense works were funded by a foreign investment organization. We have seen many new developments on other islands funded by Arab countries and Japan. Apparently the quid pro quo for such investment is the Caribbean states' votes on a committee of the United Nations. The Japanese and Taiwanese factory-fish throughout the islands, and perhaps the Japanese also wish to buy votes on the International Whaling Commission that sets moratoria on whaling.

Critics have claimed that Japan buys votes of some member nations. It is true that after a moratorium was agreed in 1986 St Lucia and St Vincent shifted to support Japan's pro-whaling policies and shortly after that received new Japanese fisheries aid grants, that Grenada and St. Kitts & Nevis have voted consistently with Japan since joining the IWC in the 1990s and that Antigua & Barbuda became pro-whaling after 1996, but this isn't proof that these small and often desperately poor island states sold their votes, is it?

Antigua

Pronounced *Anteegah*. The state of Antigua and Barbuda, which includes the uninhabited half-square mile island of Redonda, became independent from Britain in 1981. Antigua is by far the most important of these three islands for yachts, and one of the most important yachting centers in the Caribbean. Land-based tourism is also a major industry here. Geographically it is at the center of the island chain. Antigua and Barbuda are on their own shallow bank separated from the main chain of islands. Navigation round Antigua is made tricky by its low-lying, featureless northern coasts and the surrounding reefs. Remember, this is not one of the mountainous islands. Antigua was created during the earlier period of volcanic activity. After the volcanoes died and were flattened by erosion the island sank under the sea to re-emerge covered by limestone and sedimentary rocks. There are many remote bays to be explored here but only after you have arrived and have time for exploration. You will need to do much of this with a detailed chart and eyeball navigation.

The easiest points of arrival are on the south coast in either English or Falmouth Harbours. Since they are only about a mile apart the choice is yours, but my own preference is English Harbour with its historic Nelson's Dockyard. I mean, given the chance to sail into a common-or-garden modern super luxury marina or a slice of the 18th century, beautifully restored and a living legend for sailing boats, I'm with Nelson. Also, Falmouth Harbour is not a port of entry.

Coming from the south the entrance to English Harbour does not feel as obvious as the approach to other islands, where the main harbor usually has some feature conspicuous from well offshore, or involves a run up the coast which eventually leads past your entrance. The coast of Antigua itself seems to lack distinctive features. This is a low island and the hilly peaks of the relatively higher western end first appear like a series of small islands, not becoming obviously connected together until you bring

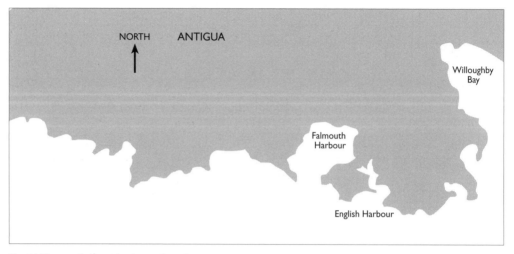

Fig 14 The south coast harbors of Antigua.

the island below the horizon. The western half remains clear long before you bring up the low-lying east, making the navigator nervous about why he/she is sailing past well to the east of the island. You are not, so hold your nerve, because the grave danger of heading for what you can see is that you will end up downwind and down-current of English Harbour.

English Harbour, which is on the dividing line between the higher west and the lower lying east of the island, is not easy to spot until you are within four or five miles of the coast, when the lava formations known locally as Hercules' Pillars become clear. These appear as a distinctive vertical slash of red rock just to the east of the entrance channel, and are well worth a closer look as you pass them. The entrance is usually easy although the current sets across it and waves and swell can be lumpy in the approach. The reef on the eastern headland is the only danger to be avoided, done by coming in close to the western shore or picking up the leading marks on the hillside above Galleon Beach.

Anchor off the beach just inside the entrance—Freeman Bay or Galleon Beach in sand—or go into the harbor and anchor wherever you can outside the fairway. I think of the harbor as having two parts: the entrance section between the chandlery/fuel dock and the Customs/harbor buildings; and the mangrove section behind these jetties. Holding can be poor in the entrance section because of a trough between Fort Berkeley and Antigua Slipway. I must have anchored on this trough on my first visit here. On the third day, having been secure till then and making visits inland, a tiny squall went by and we dragged immediately. How ironic, to drag so easily in one of the region's great hurricane holes. The section surrounded by mangroves has less boat traffic, less wind and is an easier row ashore if you persist in this form of locomotion.

English Harbour with its high surrounding hills is a great hurricane hole, especially because some of the worst storms of the last 30 years have missed Antigua. That's the best luck you can have in any hurricane hole. Antigua had two hits in the mid 1980s and a near miss from Hugo in 1989. Luis in 1995 showed Antigua's luck was running out and Lenny in 1999 could have been bad. When it got upgraded from a Category 1 to a Category 4 storm, yachts were given 48 hours' warning that it would hit somewhere between Antigua, St Martin and Tortola. By then Antigua was getting 40-knot winds with stronger gusts and torrential rain. These are not the conditions to be laying out storm gear. Then in 2008 Antigua felt a bigger swipe from Omar than did the other Leewards and had a hurricane alert for Earl in 2010. Antigua Slipway will put boats ashore from May to November on concrete hard standing and with hurricane ties.

History makes this a beautiful anchorage but also brings an unwanted legacy. A few hundred years ago the British Navy laid four hurricane chains across the bottom to catch their ships. They are still there. Best not to get your anchor under one of these. You can get advice from the harbormaster but till then you should know that the four chains run:

- across Freeman Bay from a large anchor on Galleon Beach to Fort Berkeley point
- from the Slipway roughly due west to an anchor on the beach
- from the Slipway mangrove northish for about eighty yards
- across Ordinance Bay from Clarence House jetty to the Powder Magazine dock.

Some other old customs survive here. During hurricanes a yachting committee supervises yachts tying up in the mangroves, so that they do it in the approved way. For myself, I would be grateful for such advice and for a hand to do it.

Anchoring in either English or Falmouth Bay is not free, but then neither is entry, National Parks Authority Harbor Fees, port dues elsewhere on the island or a cruising permit for Antiguan waters. Cost varies according to length of vessel. Welcome to the premier yachting center of the Caribbean.

The chandleries and shops of English and Falmouth Harbours are very good indeed and most services needed by yachts will be found there.

Antigua Slipway is one of the most comprehensive facilities in the island chain. Since renovation they can slip boats up to 200 metric tons and 150 feet as well as crane masts up to 80 feet long. Big, even if not the biggest in the region. I like their chandlery more than most, and I like most chandleries more than I like even an ice-cream shop. The charm of this one is that it feels like the old chandlers I remember from my early sailing days on the English east coast—lots of galvanized stuff, boxes of hard-to-find-anywhere-else nuts and bolts, pipes of all sizes and materials that they will cut to length—updated with modern electronics and mechanical equipment. The young man at the till actually knew his stock. I couldn't believe it.

Antigua also has one of my favorite bookshops, Lord Jim's Locker. The main branch is now in Falmouth Harbour but the pretty, original shop is still in English Harbour.

Nelson's Dockyard and the harbor continue to improve, and not just in adding modern facilities for today's visiting yachts. The dockyard dates back to about 1725 and its historical character is being carefully reconstructed thanks to funding from Britain, Canada, the European Union and the National Parks of Antigua.

Yachting facilities have recently expanded at Jolly Harbour on the west coast which is also a port of entry. A good, almost land-locked inner harbor long used by local workboats seeking protection from heavy weather and the occasional heavy swell that spoils anchorages here.

Recently developed as a gated holiday resort with beaches, golf and shore entertainment, Jolly Harbour now has a marina for more than 150 boats, a dedicated superyacht terminal for vessels up to 200 feet long and insurance approved hurricane storage.

St John's, the capital of the island and a port of entry, is worth visiting. It was my base when I worked as a deckhand on a local schooner in 1969. I prefer to go there by bus from a quieter harbor. The bay itself, of course, is deeply indented and well protected and there is good anchoring. Like all the bays on the windward side of Antigua you must beware of off-lying dangers in the approaches. St John's benefits from the buoyed channel and leading lights to be expected of a major commercial harbor. There are good anchorages here and, since 1998, rumors have circulated that a marina is to be constructed.

Antigua is not only a popular cruise ship destination but a major center for international air travel and a connection hub for inter-island flights. It is a good place for crews to change here or connect. I have learned the hard way that it is always better for crew to travel to the yacht than the yacht to travel to the crew. Almost any form of transport is quicker and more reliable than a sailing yacht and with modern telephony and the miracle of the Internet no new arrival need worry about where to find the boat.

Like most Caribbean islands there are two sides to Antigua: the sophisticated, cosmopolitan Antigua aimed at tourists and visiting yachts, from live-aboard cruisers to the owners of mega yachts; and the colorful but impoverished small communities of the island with their churches and backyard banana and breadfruit trees and tiny, half-stocked shops. In Antigua the wealth divide seems wider than elsewhere.

Antigua has a reputation for being a safe and secure tourist destination and there is very little evidence of crime against visiting yachts. I only know of one violent incident when in 2009 a skipper was fatally shot in Nelson's Dockyard.

The Antigua & Barbuda Marine Association website www.abma.ag has useful information about ports of entry and regulations on entering and leaving the country, including a PDF file of immigration forms 1 & 2. This is to be completed on screen and printed so you can hand it to officers when you arrive. Don't bother to fill in the form unless you are plugged in to your printer. You cannot save your entries to your computer and nor can you email the form back to the authorities.

The Antigua and Barbuda Marine Guide, published each year by Lightwave Publications and available free from yachting centers on the island, is a 90- to 100-page guide and directory of supplies, places to visit and things to do when visiting Antigua by sea.

Antigua Marine Trades Directory, published by the Antigua Marine Trades Association, is also free from yachting centers in the island. 72 useful pages.

Guadeloupe

Pronounced *Gwadaloop.* This large and beautiful island is actually, geologically speaking, two islands narrowly separated by about 30 million years. Guadeloupe has a high volcanic, heavily forested half called Basse-Terre to the west and a flattish, low limestone half called Grande-Terre to the east, the two being separated by La Rivière Salée, a navigable saltwater strait. The bridge over the strait opens once a day, at 05.30 if traffic is waiting, but check this before arrival. The west coast of Basse-Terre is the easier side for passagemaking north or south. The other coasts of Basse-Terre and Grande-Terre are more dangerous, having extensive reefs and less protection from prevailing winds and current.

In March 1496, Columbus tried to provision at Guadeloupe but his landing party was attacked by armed women. He learnt that the whole island was inhabited by women and that it was from this and their strength, courage and skills in martial arts that the story of the Amazon women might have originated. He and those with him found it a most beautiful island.

> "There was a great mountain mass which seemed to touch the sky and in the middle a peak higher than all the rest. From here streams flowed in all directions. A waterfall of considerable breadth fell from so high it seemed to come from the sky. It was the most beautiful thing in the world to see the height from which it fell."
>
> Letter by Dr Chancra, first voyage of Columbus, describing landfall on Guadeloupe

Guadeloupe went from being a colony of France to a full overseas department in 1947. It is the center of government for the small neighboring islands of Iles des Saintes (The Saintes), Marie-Galante and La Desirade, as well as for the more distant islands of St Barts and St Martin. Guadeloupe, with a population of about 400,000, is the biggest island in the chain after Trinidad. English is usually acceptable but you get a better response if you make an attempt at speaking French.

The west coast can present very flukey winds. I have sailed north on a dead run for the first 10 miles and then crossed a very clear demarcation line after which I had the wind on the nose. I have had good winds offshore that petered out when I got to within five miles only to return within two miles of the coast. I have, of course, had to motor the whole length of Guadeloupe in flat calm. But I have also managed delightful sails the whole length of the island, going both north and south.

The magnificent mountainous Basse-Terre has surprisingly few ports of call for the passagemaking yacht. Indeed, for boats on passage from the south the most convenient stopover if you are daysailing is The Saintes. The main town and southern-most harbor on the west coast, also called Basse-Terre, is an exposed roadstead anchorage. Just a mile or so south of the town is the Marina de Rivière Sens. This has a small, well protected basin and facilities to slip yachts. It has always been too full to let me in but there is an anchorage in four meters just outside the breakwater from which you can dinghy into the marina. The marina was badly damaged in 1979 by Hurricane David.

My preference is to make Deshaies in the north. This is a long haul for boats coming from the south, although of course a very convenient jumping off spot as they continue north; and a convenient landfall for boats coming south. An easy bay to enter and good holding.

Anse à la Barque is a picturesque bay just six miles or so north of Basse-Terre and less liable to swell than Deshaies. It is a useful overnight stop on this coast for boats coming from the south. The winds don't always let you break your journey at The Saintes, and the lack of anchorages on the west coast can leave you struggling to make the trip up to the north of the island to reach Deshaies. Though little used by visiting yachts, coming in here is often preferable to another few hours motoring up the leeside into increasing night.

The harbor has two lighthouses as landmarks, both of which are usually working but I don't find either of them easy to spot during the day. The entrance, though narrow, is clean. The harbor bottom is littered with debris such as old hurricane chains but if you anchor in no more than nine meters you clear all of this. The only obstacles to getting into a depth of nine meters are the little local fishing boats which have moorings here. Once you have found nine meters you will feel as though you are on the rocks but you should have ample swinging room.

Anchor as though the wind is from the mountains. It will be, soon enough, though you might swing around in the meanwhile.

This small harbor, set in a natural rocky cut, can appear crowded with local fishing boats and the occasional yacht but it seldom is. We went in one day when there were two charter cats already at anchor. There seemed so little room that we stopped much too far out. When one cat left later that afternoon we took their spot. We went in as close as we felt safe to the fleet of local boats and dropped anchor in about ten meters in sandy mud. We left room in case we swung inshore. Of course we only swung offshore and seemed miles away from the local boats. We should have gone in closer.

The palm tree fringe and high hills make this anchorage very attractive despite the busy main road. The benefit of this road is that the bus stop for Basse-Terre is right where you will bring your dinghy ashore on an old and rather sorry looking concrete pier, and at Basse-Terre, the other end of your bus ride, the stop is right in the market place. A shopping trip to town from here is much more convenient than getting into the marina at Basse-Terre or trying to find bottom in the very deep water close in to the breakwater at Basse-Terre. Traffic on the road seldom goes by at less than full throttle. The drivers have French *panache*. They come down one hill at full throttle to take the bend for the opposite hill, and pass any slower cars at full speed.

Deshaies (pronounced *Dey Hey*) is the best of the anchorages on this coast. It is surrounded by green hills, has a very pretty little village, and is tucked well enough into the bay to feel secure. It has an inner harbor along the banks of the small river, used only by local boats. The outer anchorage can take 40 or so boats without feeling overcrowded. We anchored close to the beach in 5 meters. There may be a ground swell

The main beach at Deshaies, Guadeloupe. *Photo: Courtesy of Ph Giraud, Tourist Office of Guadeloupe.*

but not a dangerous one. If swell is running here, it will be running everywhere in the area. Landing from the outer anchorage is at a well maintained jetty. The little town has good small shops and restaurants, and buses to other parts of the island.

A tourist information center in the middle of the town, where the road north divides, can give advice about the island and will also arrange things for you, such as car hire. Customs and Immigration are on the outskirts of the town. Walk south along the main road, climb the headland and look carefully for their sign when you reach the first major bend. They are hard to spot, although the new building (2001) may be graced by more noticeable signs. Hours were uncertain and variable but this too may change.

I gave up on clearing in at Deshaies. On my second visit up the hill I found the cage with the Customs Office sign had been dismantled. But it was there yesterday! The *gendarme* in town merely shrugged and said that the office was open, sometimes, who can say when. So I went to the Customs and Immigration in Pointe à Pitre when we went there to sightsee. They were not used to yachts wanting to clear in here. If it hadn't been for their fluent English I would have been lost. My French failed to make them understand that we had arrived and wanted clearance, although I thought the context of being *Anglais* and having *un bateau, trois crew et quatre passeports* should have got my main message across. Apparently the right man was not there but, *pas du tout, çà ne fait rien,* I was taken to a large private office, invited to have the best leather chair, had a form brought for me, given a pen and told to take my time. My three crew were engaged in such conversation as seemed polite while I did the writing, then we all shook hands, waved to every other person in the main office, and left feeling like royalty. Never ever have I experienced such respect and courtesy from officials. I wasn't even wearing clean shorts, and as for my T-shirt, *zut alors*. *Vive la France!*

Clearing out of the French islands can be a do-it-yourself job outside of office hours. Make sure you pick up some clearance forms while the office is open. You simply fill the form in as usual and post one of the copies into the Customs' mail box when you leave.

The entry to Deshaies Bay is between tall headlands. There are no natural dangers but beware fishing nets and pots. These are a problem off many bays, not just this one.

The wind can strengthen in the approach to Deshaies and gust heavily in the harbor. This is an effect of the high peaks of Basse-Terre accelerating the wind around the north end of the island. Once clear of the northwest corner of Guadeloupe you should be back in the honest ocean Trade Winds.

When traveling the west coast beware the twin rocks making up Pigeon Island. This is now an underwater nature reserve and Jacques Cousteau center. Anchoring is forbidden. Mooring buoys are available. Cousteau thought this was the best dive spot in the world. Who, unless Hans and Lottie Hass, could know better than Jacques?

Pointe à Pitre, the main city of Guadeloupe, is a great town to visit whether as a sightseer or to get work done on the yacht. The approach from the south requires that you avoid shoals and reefs but as a major commercial port the approaches are well buoyed. The town has a very protected and large marina and protected anchorages inside Ilet de Cochons. A good place to leave a boat if exploring the interior of the island. Mooring buoys are sometimes available.

Pont de la Gabarre opens to give access to La Rivière Salée.

We found the volcanic heights of Basse-Terre, with its rainforest and national park, more scenically interesting than the flat lands of Grande-Terre. We did some traveling by bus but in the end were pleased to have hired a car and gone sightseeing. The rainforest is magnificent although I wonder how it compares now with those days when Europeans first arrived. One of Columbus's captains and his shore party were lost for several days because the trees on Guadeloupe were so thick they couldn't see the stars to find their direction. Not even sailors could climb high enough to see the sky.

The highlight of our visit had to be the *Chute de Carbet* in the national park. Even in the dry season and with a cast of thousands bathing in the bottom pool, this 800-foot waterfall was stunning. The *Route de la Traversée* across Basse-Terre went through magnificent scenery. The island has many good hikes.

The traditions here are a mix of French and African, with elements of Carib Indian and East Indian. Local music includes zouk and local dance includes La Biguine, but the influence of new music from elsewhere in the Caribbean can be heard.

The Saintes, Iles des Saintes

The Iles des Saintes are administered by Guadeloupe and popular with French holidaymakers who trip over by boat from Guadeloupe. In the 17th century the islands were a colony of Breton and Norman fishermen. Fishing remains important to the local economy and the local pirogues, "les Saintois," are renowned as good sea boats. The biggest island, Terre-de-Haut, is the only one developed for tourism although this is probably the main economic activity here now. The Saintes is a quiet and relaxing place after the bustle of Guadeloupe or Martinique but remarkably sophisticated after rustic Dominica. Everything here is on a small scale. Terre-de-Haut can take as long as half a day to stroll round, if you go slowly enough. Day trippers from Guadeloupe seem to prefer to cover the five miles of road on Terre-de-Haut by bus.

The care given to maintaining the streets and houses suggests that the islanders have retained a sense of their own identity. Caribbean, of course, but unmistakably French. French food and clothing on sale. Good restaurants. Bread and croissants delivered daily to anchored boats by a man on a water bicycle. Internet facilities from a little computer office by the town harbor, close to the *gendarmerie* (police station).

Clearing in is done at the gendarmerie on Terre-de-Haut, if you can persuade any of the gendarmes to believe that you really want to do this, and even then they might advise you not to bother. They fax the forms to Pointe à Pitre and you get them back an hour later. If your next stop will not be one of the French islands you will now find yourself coming into one of the pernickety islands without a stamped clearance form. The answer is that you should have picked up a blank clearance form or two from Guadeloupe or any other of the French islands so that you can complete this before you arrive in your next port of call. Either that, or tell the officials there the truth.

Anchor off the main town of Le Bourg on Terre-de-Haut, in the sheltered and beautiful bay. Beware a rock in the middle of the passage from Terre-de-Haut to Islet

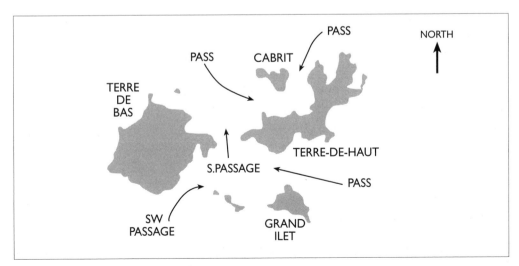

Fig 15 Islands and passages of The Saintes.

Looking down from Fort Napoleon onto the sheltered anchorage of Le Bourg on Terre-de-Haut. *Photo: Courtesy of Ph Giraud, Tourist Office of Guadeloupe.*

de Cabrit, marked by a buoy. The anchorage here can be gusty but holding is good. There are other anchorages on Terre-de-Haut, Islet de Cabrit and the prone to swell Terre-de-Bas, or wherever you see other yachts looking comfortable in the prevailing conditions. The views from the islands are stunning, especially the view from the fort at the northern tip of Terre-de-Haut. Terre-de-Bas has been less developed than Terre-de-Haut. You get a glimpse of what these islands were like 30 years ago.

Dominica

Pronounced *Domineeca*. This is not The Dominican Republic. Stress the "ee."

The nature island, Dominica is a high, green island with relatively little tourism. Its Morne Diabolin in the Northern Forest Reserve is the second highest peak in the Lesser Antilles. Dominica is well endowed for eco-tourism and Creole culture, being less physically and commercially developed than similar size islands in the chain and with a very natural and welcoming people. Creole applies to more than language. It probably derives from Spanish, meaning something created in the Caribbean but originating elsewhere. It refers to cooking, plants, building styles as well as people. French creoles were those people of French stock born in the Caribbean. In Trinidad French Creole has a different, more complex meaning, referring to people of a particular mix of race and probably dating back to the final period of Spanish rule when French planters were being encouraged to move onto the island. I am sure there is a whole book on this subject, just as there is a whole book on the Trinidad meaning of "Spanish." Don't try, you won't guess the answer.

The capital, Roseau, is one of the most charming and least spoilt Caribbean capitals. The island is one of the poorest in the region. The banana palms vital to its economy suffered damage from a succession of hurricanes since David in 1979.

The Commonwealth of Dominica is an independent country, previously a British colony. Though English-speaking, it has strong French influences. It was under French rule for much of the 17th and 18th century until the British took and held it after 1805. It lies between the large French islands of Guadeloupe and Martinique. The local Creole is very close to the Creole on those French islands. Dominica is probably the main home of the surviving Caribs in the region.

The majestic peaks, rugged interior, rainforests and friendly local people make Dominica very attractive to visiting yachts. The island has an area of bubbling pools and mudponds called the Valley of Desolation where nothing can grow, and its steaming crater lake, Boiling Lake, is the second largest of its kind in the world. Unfortunately for visiting yachts, there is virtually no shelf on the western side of the island and consequently no comfortable harbor.

Roseau has an anchorage but I have never found it comfortable. Prince Rupert Bay, at the north end of the island, is the more serviceable anchorage, and given Dominica's position in the island chain most yachts traveling in day-hops will want to put in here. Any yacht wanting to spend a few days on the island will use this bay. It is a large, wide-mouthed bay easy to identify and enter but subject to a rolling swell. From the north, the strange and distinctive double hill of Prince Rupert Bluff is a good landmark for the northern side of the bay; from the south, after passing the high headland of Rollo Head, the deep bay opens showing many more buildings than any of the previous bays, as well as the double hill of Prince Rupert Bluff away to the north.

Most yachts seem to anchor in the northern end of the bay, near to the little town of Portsmouth, but I have always found this the more uncomfortable location and prefer the southern end between the university buildings and a small hotel. I don't think yachts roll as much here, but this may be the victory of hope over experience. Anchor off the beach in about eight meters. The holding in sand is good. A few local yachts seem to have moorings around here. The main care needed is to keep an eye on the surf. If the surf starts to build, the surf line may move offshore and add to your discomfort. When the swell comes into the bay the rolling here can be as bad as any I care to experience. Skippers like me, sensitive to the finer feelings of their crew, then leave.

I've never been in Prince Rupert Bay when there have been any crimes against yachts but the mid-2000s were a time when many yachts reported incidents and the local marine associations were getting anxious. Security boats were organized by the associations to patrol Prince Rupert Bay and Roseau but in the meanwhile, since nothing official ever happens quickly, water taxis were commissioned by the Indian River Tour Guides in Rupert and various parties in Roseau to make evening patrols. So when *Petronella* came in to anchor in Prince Rupert Bay in those years I found it reassuring to know that the boat boys, who I rate especially highly on Dominica, were looking out for us.

I was only joking when I pointed to the yacht sailing to and fro off Prince Rupert Bluff and said they were trying to bump start their engine. Later I realized they might have been. Not long after we had anchored in the northern half of the bay a dinghy with three guys came up and explained they had a flat battery and a broken starter. Could they borrow a battery to get started for their night trip to Martinique. Ship's engineer Rb went off with them. He came back hours later, mission accomplished, carrying a bottle of rum for his trouble and to ease the worries of the skipper who thought (without doing anything about it) that Rb might have been kidnapped and held to ransom. They were a bunch of locals who had borrowed a yacht to trade food and drink with Martinique. Rb said they were rolling worse than us, which made handling our heavy battery difficult between the comatose bodies. When we went ashore the next day the boat boys at Indian River had clearly heard of our good deed and didn't hassle us at all.

Landing can be difficult in a swell. My dinghy and I have been up-ended and dumped up a small tree by a swell that had no right to start as far offshore as it did. When beach landing was too difficult I used to row in around a little stone breakwater off the hotel by the university, but this was removed by Lenny. Perhaps it will be reinstated eventually. When exploring the island we have anchored off the little commercial jetty used by local schooners and climbed ashore there. Even so you have to be nimble to get ashore between swells. There is a frequent bus service from Portsmouth to Roseau. Customs and Immigration can be dealt with in Portsmouth but any provisions are best bought in Roseau. The local attraction here for yachties is a dinghy trip up the mangroves of Indian River. Boat boys (almost certainly the most charming and courteous of boat boys in the islands) offering trips up the river will come to your boat often just as you are turning into Prince Rupert Bay. Yacht dinghies have been barred from this trip since the late 1970s. The trip upriver is sometimes done under outboard but the trip back with the current must be done under oars. The noise of an outboard will frighten away the huge pale frogs, the orange crabs and the flocks of birds and fish.

The high and massive mountains are covered in heavy cloud in the wet season and light cloud even in the dry season. The island seems to generate rain and squalls off either end during the wet season and in strong Trade Winds.

We last visited one April, late into the dry season. The land was scorched and suffering bush fires. There was morning mist over Morne au Diable and some rain at night, but nothing like our visit the previous February when there were strong squalls and heavy rain with the most stunning double rainbows. Unexpectedly the wind in the evening came in from the west but the rolling never amounted to much.

The economy of Dominica, still largely dependent on bananas but trying hard to diversify, was devastated by Hurricane David in 1979 and then hammered by Luis in 1995 and Lenny in 1999 and threatened by Dean in 2007. Some of the hurricane damage done to shipping can still be seen along the coast of Prince Rupert Bay. You can also see new building and other signs of investment.

Martinique

A sophisticated French island with a wonderful range of beaches, mountains and French culture. Martinique is a large island. It has the same size population as Guadeloupe although it's geographically slightly smaller. It has plenty of scope for sailing and a well developed sailing industry. Given the choices you have in starting a passage to Martinique, the island may be approached from the north, south or west. Fortunately, the island offers good anchorages for each of these contingencies. Anyone planning to spend time sailing round Martinique should buy the locally produced pilot for the area sold by Sea Services, a large and well stocked chandlery near the waterfront in Fort-de-France. This local pilot has excellent illustrations of how to approach anchorages. The English version was translated by Jacques, the charming and helpful French owner of the chandlery.

If you are coming from St Lucia you can head towards either of the two main centers of Fort-de-France or Le Marin. My preference is to take Marin first, since if you plan to visit both it is easier to sail from Marin to Fort-de-France than vice versa. For the 20-plus mile passage from Pigeon Island on St Lucia to Le Marin it is worth having the tide going with you. Even with the wind from the east you will need to sail tight, but with north in the wind you will be beating hard into it. The narrow channel between Martinique and St Lucia means you get a noticeable tidal effect.

Le Marin is a yachting center of international standard with a large charter yacht base. The main center is in the Cul de Sac du Marin. The entry to the Cul de Sac is well buoyed through a channel that twists and turns round rocks and reefs. The channel is well lit at night, but daylight gives more comfort since one shoal (Banc du Singe) requires you to approach the shore very close to the tip of Pointe Marin, and the channel later makes a dogleg between Banc Major and Banc du Milieu. Yachts can anchor in the Cul de Sac off the fishing jetty or around the marina, taking care to follow the buoyage. For a longer stay, berths on a pontoon or mooring buoys are available from the harbormaster. We once left *Petronella* here on a buoy for three months, and found her safe and sound on our return. Yachts can haul out and remain ashore at the Carenage yard to the west of the marina. Approach the Carenage along the mangroves taking care to stay in the narrow but dredged channel. Chandlers and services are available at this boatyard and the marina. Possibly a wider range of supplies than Fort-de-France.

An easy alternative to the Cul de Sac, and a good place to relax and recover after a passage, is the anchorage of Sainte Anne just outside Pointe Marin and before you enter the channel up to the Cul de Sac. Yachts tend to anchor off the fishing village of St Anne but I prefer the quieter anchorage about one mile further south, off the hotel beach but avoiding the seaplane mooring. The water is wonderfully clear; there is good holding in about 4 meters; and this is the start of one of our Top Ten Walks. This is an open bay but well protected from the Trade Winds by the high headland. The approach from seaward is straightforward, although we usually find ourselves having to beat along the southern coast from Diamond Rock. If doing this, take care not to tack too close into shore. A reef runs parallel to the shore at some distance off. The surface of the sea usually gives warning if you are coming in too close.

We were sailing hard to windward into the short choppy seas towards Diamond Rock because we had no alternative. I had foolishly forgotten to turn the diesel fuel back on after some engine jobs and now I had to sit in the engine compartment to bleed the system. G kindly called the tacks so I could shift my sensitive body parts across the hard protrusions of the engine as we went about. When she called to say two humpback whales had surfaced just ahead of us the best I could do was mutter whether one of them could hold the spanner for me.

The east coast of Martinique is rarely visited by yachts but if conditions are right it is a good place to explore from St Anne. You will need the local pilot book to find the several anchorages on this coast and how best to reach them. Eyeball navigation is essential.

From Le Marin to Fort-de-France a number of small bays with pretty villages lie on the west coast north of Diamond Rock. Anchoring here makes the journey to Fort-de-France more manageable. The journey from Marin to Fort-de-France is usually about half a day, with the wind in your favor most of the way, but time your leaving for early morning to avoid the usually strong wind out of Fort-de-France Bay in the afternoon. From Fort-de-France to Marin is a longer journey. The wind and current are against you once you come round the west coast. Allow a full day.

If sailing direct from St Lucia to Fort-de-France, the 26 or so miles will usually be a fast beam reach. You will get shelter from the waves as you close the southeast corner of Martinique but should still have a good sailing breeze, as the wind does its usual trick of following the coast.

Fort-de-France Bay is large, wide and buoyed for big ships. The main obstacle to yachts is the Banc du Fort St Louis reef off the headland of Fort St Louis, but this shouldn't bother you on a first arrival. The reef lies beyond the two main anchorages of Fort-de-France city and Anse Mitan. Around the headland of Fort St Louis in Baie des Tourelles are machine shops and haul out, cheap fuel and water from a jetty.

The wind usually funnels out of Fort-de-France Bay, often very strongly, but the fetch is too short for any unpleasant sea to develop. We have twice beat into the bay against what felt the top end of a Force Six. On both occasions we put into the anchorage off Fort-de-France city, where Fort St Louis headland provides a good lee. I might not do this now, having had some bad experiences anchoring here and having discovered the frequent ferry service from the easy, well protected anchorage on the other side of the bay at Anse Mitan.

The Force Six only dropped to Force Five as we came into the lee of Fort St Louis. We chose our spot in the line of anchored yachts and Rb let the anchor go on fifty meters of chain in eight meters of water. I motored astern to dig the anchor in and we kept going as though the anchor were on skids. Rb & G hauled up the anchor and reported that we had hooked a shopping cart. We dropped it beyond the channel used by ferries, where no one can anchor. In the belief that carts cannot strike twice we came back to the same spot. After five minutes my transits went haywire. Dragging again. We dragged another four times in different parts of the anchorage. Two other boats dragged onto their neighbors. All the yachts were rolling and pitching in the short chop. Even if we managed not to drag there was no way I was leaving the boat to go ashore. Being here suddenly lacked purpose. "Anse Mitan?" G asked. What a good idea. We anchored close to the beach, ate lunch in perfect calm and the boat behind us came no closer over the next two days.

The harbor at Fort-de-France has changed much in the last couple of decades.

Before the cruise ship terminal was built there was a much larger yacht anchorage and a dock where yachts could moor stern to and take on supplies. This dock has been in bad repair for the last few years, but dinghies could still come in to give sailors easy access to Customs and the shops in town. Work began in the early 2000s on new jetties, for a while making this an inconvenient place for dinghy landing and clearing in, but much is improved now. A great convenience is that the Sea Services chandlery is an agent for clearance. Remember, you can anchor across the bay at Anse Mitan and ferry across to clear Customs and re-provision.

Fort-de-France has a renowned (among French sailors) supplier of second-hand chandlery, Plus Nautique. Gear can be left here by sailors to be sold for them. Some is battered beyond use but you might be lucky. Plus Nautique opened a warehouse base out of town beyond the Customs HQ, at Baie des Tourelles. The chandler in Le Marin Carenage also stocks secondhand kit. I love places like that, even if they usually promise more than they deliver.

Fort-de-France is a city with a buzz. It has wonderful places to visit, with its meccano-type cathedral and the Schoëlcher Library. It also has wonderful fruit, vegetable and fish markets and the best spice market I have ever seen, not to mention good restaurants, laundries etc. Shops are excellent, especially food shops, with their mouth-watering stock of stuff containered in from France. Fort St Louis should be visited if for no other reason than to see the huge, old, blue iguanas.

Anse Mitan is a very useful little beach anchorage within Fort-de-France Bay and a short sail across from the city of Fort-de-France. The long spit of Pointe de Bout provides a lee from the winds blowing out of the bay. The anchorage is often quite crowded but we have always found room somewhere off the sandy beach between the ferry jetty and the fuel dock, recently rebuilt after being destroyed by a hurricane. Water and fuel is available. Water is cheap here. Fuel was more expensive than Trinidad.

The place has good facilities. The little resort town has a good range of shops including a small chandlery at the marina and two laundries. The marina in the little town is crowded with local boats, including tripper and charter boats. Live-aboards and visitors congregate in one corner of the marina.

From Fort-de-France going north round to St Pierre, the old capital destroyed by the eruption of Mont Pelée, the still active volcano, there are no recognized anchorages in the main pilot books except the little fishing village of Casse Pilote but the scenery is magnificent. High volcanic mountains with ridges and valleys running down to end at the sea as truncated cliffs. All along here are little fishing villages with brightly painted boats anchored close in or hauled up on the beach. It may be possible to anchor off many of these places but the chances are that they will be rolly. The last time we came down this coast we kept close in to the shore and noticed many more yachts at anchor than in previous years. It could have been the conditions. It could have been that they were catamarans, willing to run into the shallows and less susceptible to rolling. It could have been they had read the local pilot. Or it could just have been that this is a French island and the French will eventually sail their boats into any little bay just for the hell of it. Beware the occasional fish-farm rafts along this coast. Marked with buoys, but only just.

St Pierre is an open-roadstead, a wide bay sheltered by the high hills but subject to swell and near continuous but mild rolling. It is a convenient staging post for a passage to or from Dominica. The sea bed rises very rapidly from about 50 meters to a coastal shelf of about 12 meters and you need to come on to this shelf to anchor. Depths continue to shoal rapidly to the beach. There is usually plenty of space either side of the old jetty but the shore north of this is increasingly occupied by local fishing pirogues. Landing by dinghy is easy at the jetty. The little town of St Pierre has few shops but a very good market beginning at the usual Caribbean time for such things—dawn. No facilities for yachts. Pick up a free copy of "Ti'Ponton" the local guide for sailors. In English and French.

St Lucia

Pronounced *Saint Loushah*. A rugged, mountainous island popular with tourists and with some fine hotels and sights. It was once an island full of water-powered sugar mills, some of which are still working and can be visited. Ceded to Britain in 1814 St Lucia became an independent nation within the Commonwealth in 1979. It is the largest of the English-speaking Windward Islands but 150 years of swapping between France and Britain in the good old days has left it with French *patois* too.

St Lucia has magnificent volcanic peaks in the interior, but more rounded and gentler valleys in the geologically older northern part. The leeward coast is quite low-lying and this, combined with the angle St Lucia makes to the prevailing Trade Winds, may be why it is often possible to find a sailing breeze close inshore.

The volcanic headlands of the south make a series of low undulating cliffs about 100 feet high with small bays between them. Few of these are good anchorages but the island has two of the most historic and popular anchorages in the Caribbean—Rodney Bay and Marigot Bay. Both are often crowded. The island also has what is probably the most scenic and dramatic anchorage in the whole region—the Pitons, spectacular isolated volcanic plugs. This, however, is a deep water, palm-tree anchorage and a line must be taken ashore.

St Lucia is a major yachting center and still growing rapidly. It has five ports of entry—Rodney Bay, Castries, Marigot, Vieux Fort and Soufrière.

There have been a number of changes in regulations to make the island more friendly to visiting yachts, with the intention of using yacht tourism to stimulate economic development. One of these changes was that visiting yachties would be automatically granted a stay of six months. St Lucia is currently the destination for the popular annual Atlantic Rally for Cruisers (ARC). One reason for the yachting presence may be that St Lucia commands the wind between St Vincent and Martinique, at least in the sense of not being very far from either, and just a day-sail away with a good breeze. Also, unlike St Vincent, it has some easy and secure anchorages along its western coast. Beware the chop off the northern and southern ends of St Lucia where the waters are mainly shoal. Coming from the direction of St Vincent you might hope to escape the chop and the current when you reach close in to the Pitons, but if you are unlucky you will sail straight back into a short stopping sea when the north or northeast wind blows against the current down the leeside of the island.

Currents in the channel between St Lucia and Martinique run strong and can push you a long way west. Even coming out of Rodney Bay bound for Le Marin on Martinique, you will need to stay very tight on the wind.

We came out of Rodney Bay just after dawn and motor-sailed into the lumpy seas off the northern end of St Lucia until we felt the fresh northeasterly off the ocean. We stopped the engine and now sailed through lumpy seas, realizing we had been premature in stopping the engine. By the time we were out of the shoal area we were miles down to lee and struggling. A more modern rig would manage better I said wittily to G as one of them overtook us, but we beat on in comfort, a bad course but a good speed. By mid morning it was clear that the northeast wind was doing us no favors. We were pointing 020° but making no better than 300°. We weren't even going to make Diamond Rock. We weren't too bothered. We had a long day ahead still and good anchorages north of Diamond Rock if we decided to abort Le Marin. We made our first tack 200 yards off Diamond Rock, beat out a mile and found ourselves 50 yards off the precipitous Rock when we tacked back in, under some nasty looking overhangs. The next tack out was cautiously short to avoid the eight meter Diamond Shoal, which, when wondering about the turbulent water we were about to sail into, I had discovered from the chart lay half a mile southeast of the Rock. On the third tack we were clear of the Rock and its shoal, and free to get into the coast and short tack close in to avoid the wicked current. After gusty breezes and occasional black squalls we sailed serenely into a peaceful anchorage near St Anne with two hours of daylight to spare.

Rodney Bay and Anse la Raye make a good combination for passagemaking.

Rodney Bay is the easiest St Lucian anchorage to enter. It has the noise and bustle of a major beach resort during the day but most of this quietens down after dark. The lagoon and marina have a very comprehensive range of services for yachts. The marina and boatyard were upgraded in 2009 to have 232 yacht berths and space for 200-foot mega yachts, hard standing for 120 boats, a travel lift rated at 75 metric tons, and much shore-side entertainment. Rodney Bay was once one of the prime hurricane holes in the region and the marina owners claim to have learned from Grenada's devastation that there is no hurricane free zone in the islands but that more yachts will stay north if the facilities are right. I'm not sure that's the lesson I would draw. You can check the latest on the company's website www.igy-rodneybay.com.

The little bay at Anse la Raye, with its pretty fishing village, is easy to identify when sailing up the coast and is usually sheltered from the swell although a little rolly. Holding is good. We anchored in 3.5 meters on sand.

I have reservations about other anchorages on St Lucia. Marigot is one of the great anchorages of the region but is too crowded and too subject to change for me to enter except in daylight or unless I had been in and out in the last few days. In late 2002, the Marigot Business Association started a water patrol program to counter increasing fear of crime. St Lucia had been running a high number of incidents in the mid-2000s and security patrols were being tried in various anchorages. The model used in Rodney Bay was copied in Marigot. In Marigot security patrols were run from 19.00 to 02.00 each night, because no criminal likes to be out later than that. These patrols would also watch for dumping of garbage in the water and the mangroves so that the bay can come back to its old beautiful self. Check the status of patrols and crime incidents when you get to the area.

Castries, the main sea port, is a busy commercial harbor and the wind blows hard here. Put out plenty of scope if you anchor here.

Soufrière, the old French capital, is a town of charming old buildings, spectacular views of the Pitons, and a base for good hikes into the rainforest but the water is very deep and yachts need to take lines ashore. The Soufrière Marine Management Area (SMMA) founded in 1994 to protect the marine environment has improved the organization of facilities, designated anchorages and licensed water taxis and guides. The SMMA covers the area between Anse Cochon and Gros Piton. Anchoring is strictly controlled to preserve the reefs.

The Pitons are very deep anchorages too but also subject to bad squalls. Boats must be well anchored. You will need local help coming in here. The best advice I have heard is to let your anchor down on something like 90 feet of chain and when it catches the bottom, swing around to come in stern to the beach and put a long line ashore. When you are 30 feet off the beach take up slack on your anchor line.

Moorings have been laid in Anse Chastanet, just north of Soufrière Bay.

Vieux Fort is a commercial harbor on the leeside of the curious tail of land at the south of the island. Yachts can anchor here but I am not sure why they would. It has very limited facilities. Its location does not help much with any passage plan. To get there along the coast of St Lucia means motoring in the lee of the island dead into the Equatorial Current. The water in the harbor is well protected by the land but when we were there we found the wind was accelerated by the gap in the cliffs. Local dive boats moor up to the jetty and some posts but these are not available to visiting yachts and the most obvious visiting anchorage is, as we soon discovered, right in the swinging room needed by freighters.

Marigot Bay, St Lucia. *Photo: Courtesy of St Lucia Tourist Board.*

We were listening for hurricane warnings as we sailed south. The crew, G and Rb, were on full alert and unwilling to make even the day hop to St Vincent without a call to the met office. We foolishly beat our way along the southeast so-called leeside of St Lucia to put into Vieux Fort and make our call. The wind and chop were uncomfortable enough but when we put into the harbor it felt like a full gale was blowing. The wind howled through the rigging and chased us around our anchor cable. We spent an uneasy night checking for drag and called the met people so early that they weren't yet at work. We didn't believe the benign forecast they eventually gave us and left with two reefs in the main. A mile offshore we lolloped along at no speed at all until we had the courage to shake the reefs out. The true ocean wind that we met crossing to St Vincent was about half the strength of the wind in that damned harbor.

St Vincent & the Grenadines

This group of about one hundred small islands, islets and reefs between Grenada and St Vincent, most of which come under the jurisdiction of St Vincent, is a wonderful sailing ground with some of the best reef diving in the Caribbean. The islands range from those which are, in effect, dedicated to being a luxury hotel, such as Palm Island and Petit St Vincent (PSV), to being very poor, their old agricultural base long gone and tourism not yet developed.

The border between Grenada and St Vincent crosses between the little islands of PSV and Petite Martinique but the effective border is between Carriacou and Union

Island. Both of these have Customs and Immigration offices and make the most convenient location to check in and out of Grenada and St Vincent.

The Grenadines is famous for the trading schooners built and used here. Many were built on the beach at Carriacou or Petite Martinique.

St Vincent

St Vincent is the main island in the group making up the Grenadines, which includes Bequia, Mustique, Canouan, Tobago Cays, Union Island and Petit St Vincent. It became independent from Britain in 1979. St Vincent itself is a massive volcanic island with a high central mountain chain. Economically poor. Not yet heavily dependent on tourism but work to build a new international airport and expand its passenger numbers four-fold started in 2006 and will be completed in 2012. Developing policies to encourage yachting.

Nature hasn't been too kind to St Vincent. Not only has it suffered from lethal and destructive eruptions of La Soufrière volcano but also some bad hits by hurricanes. It hadn't even started to recover from the crop damage of the 1979 eruption when Hurricane Allen came through in 1980 and devastated the coconut and banana plantations. In 1987 Emily came through and destroyed 70% of the banana crop. In 2010 the island was damaged by Tomas.

St Vincent is green and intensely beautiful from the sea. Wonderful small bays along the leeside make for tempting anchorages, although in reality this coast has few easily accessible, convenient and calm anchorages. My usual policy is to miss St Vincent and use the anchorage on neighboring Bequia whether traveling north or south. On the rare occasions when Bequia is untenable, the lee coast bays of St Vincent will also be subject to heavy swell but the anchorage at Young Island should then be easy to make and secure.

Kingstown Bay where the capital is located is wide and easy to enter in most conditions but the anchorage off the town is in deep water, subject to swell, possible violent gusts from the high land during the day, and the disturbance of local fishing boats and ferries. There is supposed to be a tie-up for yachts but perhaps that is since my visit. I can't recommend it.

Log of 1998.

Sailing singlehanded south down the leeside of St Vincent in unusual weather. Looking to anchor in one of the small bays but the recent wind from the southwest makes them all untenable. Each, as I look in, have huge swells running up the beach. Kingstown Bay is huge. Locate what I hope is the part nearest to the town, its fish market and quay. Still in 50 feet of water when only 100 yards from the quay. Beginning to interfere with the turning circles of the local fishing boats so drop anchor—unwillingly. It'll kill me to winch it back.

I would like to tie up at the long jetty where the Bequia ferry lands but I can't see how to get ashore from there through the barbed wire. I dinghy to the fish dock. Half the population of St Vincent seems to be on it or jumping off it. When I reach the dockside fender I realize my mistake in coming here. The fender is a long fat tree trunk over which whole truck tires have been slid. The tree trunk is fastened two feet clear of the wall. The tires rotate freely. These rotating tires are my only hand holds before I reach the low wall of the dock. I jam the dinghy hard against the tires to act as a brake on them and put the painter in my mouth. I need all the hands and feet I have. Somehow I crawl across the rotating tires without spinning off into the sea. I clamber up the low wall on all fours and rise upright in the middle of the leggy throng, like a penguin coming ashore on a busy ice flow. I try not to consider my personal safety or, worse still, my dignity. This landing fails my "grandmother test." A little old lady with arthritis and bad knees could not manage this.

Had I known about it at the time I might have been tempted to put into Ottley Hall marina just to the northwest of Kingstown Bay. Reputed to be a new and ultra modern marina with a long list of facilities for yachts and ships including Customs and Immigration it has always looked a bit like a small shipyard when I've sailed passed. It is probably subject to swell and could have been untenable on the day when I needed it.

Young Island, a tropical garden just a few hundred meters off mainland St Vincent and a few miles east of Kingstown on the south coast, is a pleasant anchorage. I came in near the Aquatic Yacht Club jetty and was immediately given friendly advice about where and how to anchor. The current runs fast here and changes with the tide, so anchor with care or take a mooring. I used the yacht club as my landing and was most welcome. It can be hard to sail here from the west when the wind and waves are on the nose. The anchorage is only 10 minutes from the airport and a bus ride from Kingstown. Although not a port of entry a skipper is allowed off to clear Customs at the airport and go to Kingstown for Immigration. This is not inconvenient and while at Kingstown you can shop at the excellent market there. A great boon in St Vincent and its islands is that you can clear in and out simultaneously if you are not staying longer than 24 hours. There is no charge for clearance unless during overtime hours.

Also along this southern coast is the Sunsail 50 berth marina at the Blue Lagoon east of Young Island. It has a mini mart, fuel and water, laundry and shower facilities. One Customs glitch to be aware of for its obvious consequences if you are thinking of making your first landing at one of the west coast bays: a yacht has 24 hours to leave St Vincent after it has cleared out but, at the time of writing, you are not granted 24 hours to clear in. Officials haven't yet taken onboard the government policy that yachts are a valued part of tourism. The little practical problems the sea throws at us cut no ice with officialdom. If you don't clear in immediately you will be assumed to be avoiding the fee and you will be fined. Cumberland Bay is not a port of entry. Chateaubelair Bay is but many sailors won't overnight there, reducing its value as a place to clear in. Wallilabou Bay is also a port of entry but the Customs officers are reportedly rarely to be found, so again there is little point choosing it to clear in. Before you start your passage south to St Vincent with the intention of visiting the west coast bays check the latest on security and Customs. Remember: things change here; and there is always Bequia, my prime harbor, an easy place to clear in and with eight ferries a day to Kingstown if you don't fancy sailing across. Bequia is another reason why so many yachts sailing south pass the bays on the west coast without stopping.

Cumberland Bay is probably the best known of the "palm tree" anchorages up the leeside of the island. Heavily wooded and very pretty, unspoilt and lacking any tourism. The bay is wide and easy to enter. The water is too deep for an anchor until you reach the shelf just offshore. Here the depth shoals rapidly and the trick is to get your anchor into the shoal rather than the deep bottom or the narrow, shallow shelf. Then you take a long and stout stern line ashore to stop the boat swinging out to sea and pulling the anchor out downhill. Long before you get to shallow water, a local will come out to help. Take the help, but check the cost beforehand. Your local helper knows just where you should drop anchor, and this is really what you are paying for. I mean, it isn't too hard for you or anyone else to take a long line to and from the palm tree, but hitting the right spot for the anchor first time is probably beyond most new arrivals.

"Palm tree" anchoring is an experience to try if you have never done it before. Four things to note. First, your stern will be almost up the beach. That is how close you have to get to be out of the deep water. Just make sure you won't be bumping your rudder if a swell comes in. Second, beware chafe where the line runs round the tree. Even for just one night I would run the line twice round the trunk to spread the wear. If staying longer, put some anti-chafe on your line. Third, make sure of the knot. You don't want it to jam if you need to release the line in a hurry. Fourth, choose a helper from one of the people in the bay rather than someone who met you two miles offshore and wanted you to tow them back. The old hands in the bay are good but some of the newer ones may lack experience, and when relations go sour between locals and yachties it's often because the newer ones only have a very short term view of their business.

Being halfway along the leeside of St Vincent, Cumberland Bay is well placed for arriving or leaving from St Lucia, although not a port of entry. I would be happy to leave here in darkness if I had to but would certainly not come in with failing light.

Wallilabou is one mile south of Cumberland Bay and more developed. The restaurant and hotel have maintained visitor mooring buoys for some years now and if you plan to eat ashore you can take one of these and use their dinghy dock too. Good local walks. There is a history of trouble with the local boat vendors but this may now have been solved by the formation of a local association. Use vendors wearing membership badges.

Barrouallie is a place to explore only. It is protected from the north by the Bottle and Glass reef. You can anchor in about 25 feet if making a lunch stop or with your bow in shallow water and a stern anchor in the deeper water to hold you off the beach.

Security is an issue for St Vincent and some bays occasionally get a bad reputation for light fingeredness. The island has probably been damned since the knowledgeable and influential pilot author Don Street announced 50 years ago that the west coast of St Vincent was a trouble spot beyond the control of the local police. Chris Doyle also has cautioned against over-nighting on St Vincent although in his latest edition of *Guide to the Windward Islands* this warning is limited to Chateaubelair. I haven't experienced any problems on the west coast, and not even in Kingstown, though I took the hint from the police constable when I asked about getting back to my boat after dark and went on to Young Island.

I have looked at data from the Caribbean Safety and Security Net to see if I can get a feel for this. Back in 2006 a spate of robberies suddenly put Chateaubelair on the map. Since then, either because the problem has been addressed by the authorities or because no yachts were visiting, the number of crimes dropped off after 2008. The authorities have certainly seemed energetic. A rapid response unit began beach patrols in Chateaubelair and Cumberland. Pay phones were installed on the beaches. Police stations were equipped with VHF. At Chateaubelair dawn-till-dusk citizen patrols work with police and the rapid response unit to keep yachts secure. Best of all in deterring robbers, boat boys were re-branded as beach-front service providers and given best-practices training. Yachts are returning to these charming bays. Check with the local coast guard.

These are just some of the things I have heard of to improve yacht security on St Vincent. The effect, when I look through the Safety and Security data, seems to make St Vincent less of a crime center than Grenada or even St Lucia, though of course I would reckon Grenada and St Lucia have many, many more visitor yachts. We should give due weight to the numbers but anecdotes usually have greater immediacy and impact. When a skipper wrote to *Caribbean Compass* about being robbed in Chateaubelair in October 2009 the news ran through the cruising community like swine flu. For one thing it triggered another sailor to report how his boat had been boarded while in a marina in Le Marin, Martinique and then a few days later when at anchor in Le Marin. Now I have had my doubts about St Vincent, based on things I have heard rather than what has happened to me, but I never had fears of robbery in Martinique. Was I wrong?

The problem is probably to get your expectations right before you arrive. Crime happens everywhere. Most of us don't experience it at all or not very often. If we are concerned then we probably need to work out a more stringent code of practice. Check with other cruisers before going somewhere. Dinghy over to chat with other yachts in an anchorage. Keep an eye out for them. If there are yachty businesses, such as charter companies or restaurants, talk to them too and ask who best to contact if there is a problem. We can all be victims even if we stay at home, but why would you want to stay at home? Information for St Vincent and the Grenadines can be found on the port authority website: www.svgpa.com.

Bequia

Pronounced *Beckway*. Few island harbors have the grip on sailors that Admiralty Bay has. The first time I sailed in here I felt I had truly joined the sailing life. A wonderfully protected harbor unless the wind blows from the west. A wonderful mix of sailing boats from so many countries.

A pretty line of restaurants and bars along the front of Port Elizabeth but not pretentious. A long history of sailing and boatbuilding with some boats still being built on the beach in the old ways. The largest schooner built there, a three master 165 feet long, traded between South America, Cuba and the U.S. and was found drifting and abandoned in the Bermuda Triangle. Whaling was once a vital activity here and the island has aboriginal whaling rights to catch no more than two whales a year. By harpoon. The little town here truly faces the sea. No wonder sailors feel at home.

As I have grown more familiar with Bequia I have become a little blasé about the place. Perhaps too I have had time to suffer more unfortunate encounters with boat boys or problems with the laundry service, and these, though banal, are what takes the edge off the pleasure of a place. I can't quite see Bequia as I first did, but this shouldn't stop you from visiting it. It is, after all, the southern gateway to St Vincent and beyond, and the northern gateway to the Grenadines and places south.

> I nearly gave up on Bequia but the place reasserted its charm. I almost forgot that everything must change, especially in the Caribbean. I wasn't ready for the changes to this special anchorage. It wasn't just that buoys had been laid in all the best anchoring spots, bad though that is, but that there was no clear indication of who owned them, took responsibility for them, or if they were ever checked. Since no harbormaster is involved the fees do not go back into the public purse. The boat boys who guide you in don't own them and only receive a fee for one night regardless of how many nights you stay. The small amount of money that goes to the boys does not go far in the local economy. This year, though, coming down from the heavily commercial world to the north, the Bequia buoys didn't bother me half as much. It must be me who has changed.

Actually, that is only partly true. Since the buoys were laid over the last couple of years, more yachts now anchor off Princess Margaret Beach rather than pay the charge and this is what we did too. This is less convenient for town and my guess is that yachties are less likely to come into town to eat or drink in the evenings unless they are also using a water taxi. On our last visit there were plenty of empty buoys in the harbor but the anchorage was full, or at least it was for a while. This is the least protected part of the bay and when the wind got up all the boats started rolling. We had planned to stay a week, to revisit Hope Bay, one of our Top Ten Walks, and explore elsewhere, but we left after two days having done nothing more than the laundry and swim off the beach.

Holding off Princess Margaret Beach seems to be good, which cannot always be said of the main Port Elizabeth anchorage. The worst area of hard, dead reef off the Gingerbread restaurant now has "Danger" buoys marking it but it is always possible for a yacht here to drop its anchor on thin sand over hard reef.

> We were in my favorite spot just on the edge of the shallows where the old reef starts. With 50 feet of heavy chain out in 9 feet I was confident that we would hold in the gusts and not touch bottom in the swells. The 30-footer further out from us was in deeper water and, I assumed,

a good sandy bottom so when it started dragging it took me a minute to realize that it wasn't us on the move. Their crew had gone ashore. I rowed over and started to figure out how their anchor winch worked. No handles, no levers. No hope. I was struggling with locker lids and lines when a young boat boy came by and asked if I needed help. I explained the problem and between us, but mainly thanks to his muscle and outboard engine, we laid out the spare anchor on a long heavy warp. It held. When the skipper returned I suggested he radioed around till he found the boat boy and gave him some US$ as thanks. If we hadn't reanchored this yacht the next best thing for it would have been to snag one of the half dozen yachts anchored between it and the Caribbean Sea.

The problem of dragging isn't always that you drag out to sea but that a yacht ahead of you comes swinging down and rips out some stanchions and gouges your paintwork. Any yacht can do this but the ones to beware most are the bareboat charter yachts.

Sadly for me there is an added psychological trauma in anchoring off Princess Margaret Beach: chartered catamarans!! We once had one of these ram us while we were anchored in Martinique, even though the person on the helm was staring straight at me for the last 200 meters and the person on the foredeck woke up to my shouts and began screaming at the helm long before they whacked our stern. The skipper kindly gave me his name and phone number but these proved to be bogus. So I can only hope that the use of this anchorage by a fleet of French charter cats is a passing phase.

In keeping with the nautical feel of Bequia such services as fuel, water, laundry and engine repairs are brought to the yacht. Contact Daffodil Marine Services for most of these. Services are also available ashore. The Yacht Club at Bequia Marina offers dockside services and limited docking, fuel, two mooring buoys and club facilities. Several local shops specialize in yacht provisioning, so that the range and quality of foods here is unexpectedly wide for a small Grenadine island. Good fruit and vegetables at the Rastafarian market. Expect a good deal of friendly banter and high-pressure selling, but they take as good as they give.

Bequia Bookshop is a splendid little bookshop along the waterfront. It has a good range of sailing books as well as books on the islands and novels. They will order anything they don't have in stock.

The 20 year-old Bosun's Locker chandlery became part of Budget Marine in 2001. Their good stock of British and European chandlery will now be boosted by American chandlery, and anything they don't have when you visit can be quickly brought in from Budget Marine headquarters in St Martin. A sailor-friendly shop.

When on Bequia, go walking. The walk from Admiralty to Hope Bay is wonderful and the seascape when you arrive is breathtaking. There are many good walks and often some cruiser with local knowledge will organize a hike and save you from getting lost.

Bequia too is changing fast. Proposals have been made for a yacht yard in Spring Bay on the windward coast. This is a beautiful beach area but not, at first sight, an ideal location for yachting. The waves breaking on the protecting reef would put me off trying to enter this bay, and the proposal to dynamite the reef to open the access seems not only ecological vandalism but sure to make the yard more exposed to the power of the ocean. Perhaps the idea of the yacht yard is just to make it easier to get permission to build houses. Who knows. Not much has happened yet.

In the last few years Bequia has developed a bad reputation for petty thieving, especially from boats anchored in Princess Margaret Beach. Take care of your dinghy. Lock it or lose it. Recent visitors also report the boat boys to be aggressive. This may be something to do with those damned mooring buoys. I know I got a bit snappy the first time I had to take one, and the boat boy got a bit snappy back, making him seem noisy and aggressive, but it really wasn't his fault.

Canouan

Pronounced *Can-a-wan*. The first island south from Bequia, little Canouan is economically very poor but well worth visiting as one of the loneliest and most peaceful islands in the Grenadines. It is an easy 16-mile passage from Bequia. The walk to the northern headland is good and the views from there are magnificent. The main town of Charlestown is little more than a long, scattered row of old and new buildings in a mix of uses. No shops for a visiting yacht.

Charlestown Bay on the west coast is wide and easily approached from the north but take care to avoid some shoal patches across the entrance. These are marked with beacons. I usually anchor close in to the hotel, to the north of the beach and landing stage, rather than off the town. A swell usually makes any anchorage here rolly but not unbearable. The wind gusts off the high ridge down onto the anchorage but in the normal Trade Winds the holding is good. Strong Trades, such as the "Christmas winds" and blowing well over 30 knots, can make for gusts of up to 60 knots.

I like visiting Canouan and have not usually been put off by the rolling or katabatics but this time was different. After a comfortable lunchtime stop in Southwest Bay, we came round to Charlestown Bay planning to spend the night there and sail to Bequia the next day. I have never seen such a sight. An unprepossessing two-meter swell was rising to a dramatic three-meter breaking crest right across Charlestown Bay between White Rock and the two beacons. The dazzling white spray was rising to at least five meters and as we neared the wave we found ourselves looking through its prisms of spray to get sight of the land. Two boats were coming off the anchorage by the hotel. We watched them searching for a way round or through this breaking wave. We came up on the back of the wave twice to decide whether we would go through it and into the calmer water of the anchorage, but I was too cowardly and the anchorage looked too rolly. We skirted round to the anchorage inside White Rock but the one boat anchored there was rolling its decks under so despite the lateness of the hour we headed for Bequia. I hadn't realized this before, but Canouan is a place to visit when you still have time to make it to somewhere else.

THE GRENADINES

CANOUAN

NORTH

MAYREAU

TOBAGO CAYS   REEFS

Worlds End Reef

Chatham Bay

Clifton Harbour

PALM

UNION

PETIT ST VINCENT

PETIT MARTINIQUE

SANDY ISLE

Hillsborough

CARRIACOU

Tyrell Bay

Fig 16 The Grenadines from Canouan to Carriacou.

Mayreau

Tiny Mayreau is drier, and, if anything, poorer than Canouan. The days of cotton and cocoa and slavery are over but most of the island is still owned by heirs of the Marquis de L'Isle, an aristocratic family which fled France during the Revolutionary period and bought the island. Today its 250 residents may be prospering through cruise ship tourism.

> My English yachtie friends thought they were inconspicuous among the white skinned passengers from the cruise ship. On their third visit to top up food and drink at the beach barbecue one of the crew in smart whites and pretty shoulder buttons said quietly, "We don't mind you joining in you know, but we do know you are not with the cruise." My friends didn't go back for a fourth time but they speak very well of the discrete courtesy they were shown.

Its main role for yachts is that it is the nearest island to base a visit to Tobago Cays. If conditions are right you can also navigate inside Mayreau's reef on the east side of the island. Good holding in sand. Not Tobago Cays but you'll be the only boat there.

Tobago Cays anchorages

The Cays themselves provide good anchorages. With five islets within a huge curving reef, no wonder this is reputed to be one of the most beautiful sites in the Caribbean and in its natural state certainly would be. On the one visit I made I found it so overcrowded and overcommercialized that I never went back.

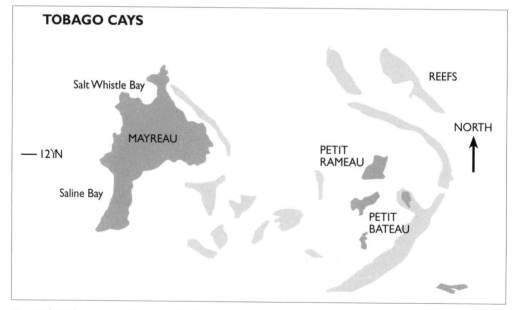

Fig 17 The Tobago Cays—Mayreau, Petit Rameau and Petit Bateau.

> Expectations were high as I turned between Petit Rameau and Petit Bateau islets. Tobago Cays and nothing but the breeze and a protecting reef between me and Africa. The mass of T-shirts hung out for sale on Petit Rameau were surely just an aberration and the three or four yachts anchored in the channel were surely all I was going to see. Coming through the channel I could see three yachts to the east of Petit Rameau so I turned away from such a crowd to go outside Petit Bateau. As the vista opened before me it was like the yachting equivalent of Grand Central Station. I sailed slowly between the lines of anchored yachts until I could find enough room for a three-point turn, then I headed back out of the channel and away. A couple of hours later, turning into Charlestown Bay on Canouan and finding it empty, I realized I had done the right thing.

Don't be put off. There are reasons to hope that recent change has been for the better and, anyway, any yacht visiting the Grenadines must make their own visit to the Cays. Even on busy days you may be able to find a secluded spot and, if not, you can still come away with a T-shirt.

The fragility and importance of the Tobago Cays ecosystems was recognized when they were designated a Conservation Area in 1987. In 1999 the government of St Vincent and the Grenadines acquired the Cays from their last private owner, the American Nicholas Fuller, at a price well below the market value because of the stipulation that the Cays would, in perpetuity, be "dedicated to use as a National Park . . . no buildings, structures, fixtures or construction of any form or any commercial activity whatsoever will be permitted save in pursuance of the objectives of and in furtherance of the maintenance of a National Park."

The Cays were already in urgent need of protection. A few years earlier, in 1995, NOAA and British scientists had observed the decline of the coral reefs here (as elsewhere in the Caribbean) and pointed to pollution, over-fishing and tourism as the primary causes. Not surprisingly the government decided to do something about the Cays and developed ideas and legislation for a marine park. Of particular concern right then was that fast boats made swimming dangerous, spearfishing was damaging the reef and goats were eating the vegetation. Implementation has not been simple or quick. The area was declared a marine park at the end of 2002 and administration came into life during 2003 with park rangers, codes of practice and mooring fees as well as continuing confusion about who would manage the park and how. You can find where things stand on www.tobagocays.org. Since the park became active there has been significant improvement. I don't know if a survey was done to see if the goats approve.

Transits are given in the pilots and should be used. Never sail here at night. The anchorage behind Horseshoe Reef is magnificent but open to the full force of the Trade Winds. Make sure your anchor is well dug in. Consider using two anchors if the current is running hard. If staying for a few days you will be able to get supplies from boat boys.

191

Union

Clifton Harbor on Union Island is one of the most secure and beautiful natural harbors in the Grenadines, and one of those rare anchorages on the windward side of its island, thanks to a long barrier reef. It is formed around an inner reef, Roundabout Reef, with two entrances. You'll know what I mean when you look at the chart. Of the two entrances the western one is marked with tall beacons, sometimes shown as buoys on the charts and pilots and sometimes shown with their colors the wrong way round. Take care to locate both markers before closing with the harbor. Reefs extend right up to them. I worry most about the reef on the western side of the entrance. It runs in an unbroken line all the way from the tall rock called Frigate Island and can only be seen from the changing color of the water when you are close to it. Coming from the south beware of Grand de Coi Reef, a shallow patch off Palm Island that should be marked by a buoy to the west. So keep to the west of this buoy, if it is there.

Once inside Clifton Harbor, you have a choice of anchoring in about 10 to 14 meters in the main part of the harbor on the western side, or picking up a buoy on the northern side of Roundabout Reef; or going through to the eastern part of the harbor further away from the town and landings. If you go to the eastern half, take care to avoid the shoal patch off the broken down jetty east of the Anchorage Yacht Club pontoons. You may feel the need to come too close inshore here to make sure of missing Roundabout Reef.

Clear Customs in town and Immigration at the airport.

The natural beauty of the main harbor was spoiled somewhat by the state of the town and the shoreline as well as by the mass of charter boats, but this was still a place I loved to visit and in recent years the main street has gained new businesses and really brightened itself up. The main harbor is now more organized than in the past. Boat boys will meet you on arrival and escort you to, and help you tie up to, mooring buoys and then will taxi you ashore. If you are only staying for a short while, or just to check in or out, you may prefer to anchor in the western arm of the main harbor, off the town. The wind blows strongly across the harbor but surrounding reefs keep the water flat. The holding in the main harbor has become doubtful in the last few years, judging from how often we and our neighbors dragged anchor, so the buoys give me a feeling of security when leaving the boat. During peak tourist season there are also police security patrols through the night here and at Saltwhistle Bay.

The marina and hotel (with its shark pool restaurant), the little airport and the road-train carrying passengers and their luggage all of the short mile from hotel to airport, are a world apart from the nearby town. Union Island's current economic poverty certainly goes back to the time when it was a cotton slave plantation under a single colonial family, but nor has it grown wealthy on the share-cropping and subsistence farming that followed the abolition of slavery. Being so far removed from the administrative capital of St Vincent, Union Island does not receive what it feels is its due support. Indeed, historically the island probably looked more to Martinique and Trinidad for the trade that kept it alive, than it did to St Vincent. The harborfront, much of which was created during the 1970s, was developed by a French businessman as an extension of the Martinique sailing scene.

But the truth is that St Vincent is not a rich island either and has little to put into the development of Union. However, the last time we visited there was a sense of change. The burnt out building that dominated the waterfront had gone and a new building was under construction. Bright stalls with a wider range of produce lined the main street that makes up most of the town. A tourist office had opened and the staff made us feel most welcome. This is an island I like to visit, despite the sense of grinding poverty. The people have always been open and friendly, and the island has stunning scenery and walks. I shall enjoy the place more when I feel that the affluence around the marina is rubbing off on the town.

Just to the west of Frigate Island are signs of marina development. Locals, who talk of money laundering, long ago ceased to expect the marina to be completed. The causeway to the mainland was built for the marina. You can anchor behind Frigate Island, usually in solitude.

Chatham Bay on the western side of Union is a fine big bay to anchor in, with a good beach, clear water and good holding in four meters. The gusts from the high hills may have kept yachts away in the past but on my last visit the anchorage reflected the increase in yachting everywhere in the region. Of course the anchorage wasn't exactly crowded but the eight other yachts and the three-masted schooner *Mandalay* was more than I had expected, and the arrival of a small cruise liner just further proved how things are changing. The bay is big enough to cope and the fishermen living on the beach remain as pleased to see visitors as ever.

> I wouldn't describe Chatham Bay as an undiscovered, remote jewel of an anchorage, but it's close. We groaned when the tripper boats arrived and even thought about moving on. But in the morning they were gone and we were back in serenity.

Chatham's sense of wild remoteness may be about to change. A new road has been built on the hill tops. Civilization may follow.

Grenada

Palm Island, Petit St Vincent and Petite Martinique

These are all little islands to explore. They range from super sophisticated and cosmopolitan to poor and welcoming.

Palm Island is a hotel island developed by the late John Caldwell and his wife Mary from a deserted island to a palm covered resort. John was called "Johnny Coconut" for his zeal in carrying and planting nuts on the islands he visited. Their story is one of the great sailing romances of the 20th century. John, as a sailing novice in Panama when World War II ended, decided to sail a little yacht to Australia, where the love of his life was stationed. His survival in mid Pacific after he had bailed out not just the wave that swamped him but most of his provisions too, is astonishing, gripping and a real inspiration. Buy a copy of *Desperate Voyage* which covers John's odyssey. Mary Caldwell wrote recently her own story, including the development of the island, in *Mary's Voyage*. It is a rolly anchorage with nothing ashore but the hotel. Visitors are welcome at the small yacht club. A day visit.

Petit St Vincent, generally known as PSV, is a more exclusive hotel island than Palm Island. Residents of the 22 cottages dotted around the tiny island use a system of flags to communicate to staff—red to remain undisturbed, yellow for room service. Visiting sailors are not encouraged to wander about the place—access only to the main building—but you can, as anywhere in the islands, stretch your legs by walking round the foreshore. Approach with care but there is a good anchorage near the landing stage. Fuel and water are available.

Petite Martinique a few miles away across the channel from PSV was originally settled by Bretons in the 17th century and is a world away from PSV. Economically poor and with little upon which to base a modern economy. There is a good local restaurant on the beach nearby the landing stage but beware of rocks and reefs in this bay. It is never comfortable. A less protected anchorage than PSV. A small local population usually very pleased to see visitors.

> The little dinghy bumped *Petronella*'s topsides and the lone fisherman held up a variety of seafood for me. I decided not to explain my allergy and dislike for most seafood so I just said no and asked how he was doing. We chatted for a while about PSV and Petite Martinique and after a while I offered him a plastic bottle to bail the half submerged dinghy. He wasn't making much impression with his cupped hands. It was a good bottle and I think he sensed I had been saving it for something special. Anyway, he thanked me nicely and sculled on his way with his single broken oar. Later that day, and within about 10 minutes of landing on Petite Martinique, I bumped into the same fisherman and was immediately and warmly introduced to some of his friends. From then on as I walked right round the little island, I was never far from a friendly smile or people wanting to stop and chat. The service in the little restaurant was double friendly. It was a good plastic bottle but I forget now why I wanted to keep it.

Carriacou

Carriacou—pronounced *carry-a-koo*—is the largest of the inhabited islands forming part of Grenada. It has a varied history of particular interest to sailors. The island became a major boatbuilding center in the 1830s when local landowners brought English and Scottish shipwrights out to build fishing and trading boats. The Scottish connection remains in some of the family names—McFarlane, McLaren, McLawrence, McKensie.

> I half expected to see red-haired, hairy-kneed, whisky-swilling men in kilts when I first visited the Grenadines but a casual conversation on Union Island brought me up to date on the

Scottish connection. A Scot with the unlikely surname of Mulzac leased Union Island in the 1850s, passed the lease on to his son Richard in 1893, whose own son Hugh was fêted when in 1940 he became the first black man to command a US navy ship. Did Hugh have hairy knees? My source didn't know.

Local timber was recognized as more durable in the conditions of the tropics. Guyana greenheart and other hard woods lasted better and were stronger than pitch pine. Native white cedar was better than European and American woods for making floors and frames.

Boatbuilding and seafaring were more lucrative than farming the poor land and became the staple for the population after emancipation. Between the two world wars the master shipwrights on the island built about 130 wooden trading sloops and schooners, some of them over 1,000 metric tons. Steel hulls and engines killed this commercial business but small wooden sailing fishing boats may be seen under construction in the village of Windward and the occasional bigger schooner in Tyrell Bay.

Clear Customs and Immigration in the main town of Hillsborough and re-stock with local fruit and eggs at the local market and supermarket, but don't expect to find much of anything you need. The bay is not a good anchorage in winter months when the northerly swell rolls in. The traditional anchorage off the jetty is busy with local traders and rolly and I usually prefer to come in north of the jetty and anchor in about five meters off the beach, just outside the buoys used by local pirogues. Holding is reasonable.

Carriacou is an enchanting island. Out in Hillsborough Bay is one of the most beautiful and secluded anchorages I know. I first came here when Sandy Isle was a thin spit of sand with palm trees in the middle and reefs at either end, almost a caricature of every one's idea of a Caribbean island. The deep water anchorage close to shore has a wonderfully constant wind and current that holds a yacht without rolling. The sea here is a soft, warm turquoise. This century old island began to divide during the 1990s and preservation measures were introduced. Then came Hurricane Lenny.

Sandy Isle is gone!! I visited a month or two after Lenny's storm surges in 1999. I could hardly believe the change. It was as though a bulldozer had raised a six-foot wall of dead coral along the windward edge. Palm trees were down. Part of the island's long sandy tail was gone. When I next visited in 2000 the island had shrunk further, probably because more palm trees had died and the sand was less stable. Another year after that it was even more changed, but at least someone had planted new palms. Two years later the baby palms were dead and I had none of the old landmarks for the anchorage. Fragile beauty. Much reduced but mending now.

Approach Sandy Isle from southeast or southwest to avoid the reefs.

Tyrell Bay, the best anchorage on Carriacou and one of the best in the Grenadines, is round the corner from Hillsborough. The pilot shows the entrance as a narrow, buoyed channel along the northern shore of the wide bay but like most boats coming and going here I usually come through the middle of the bay. That way I can avoid the reefs of the buoyed channel, whose buoys I have seldom seen, and still have plenty of room to avoid the shoal patch on the southern shore. Boat boys bring food and drink for sale and will take garbage.

I was only 20 yards from the jetty when a young man politely asked if we could trade a U.S. dollar for the garbage bag in my hand. The idea, when I grasped it, was for me to give him both and he would dispose of the rubbish. The garbage skip, he said when pressed, was too long a walk for me. Actually I was desperate for a long walk but not averse to supporting a local entrepreneur so I offered to give him the dollar and the garbage bag but said I would walk with him to see where the skip was. He wasn't keen on that, so neither of us managed to clinch a deal. He grumbled off into the bushes and as I headed for the skip it gradually dawned on me where he would have dumped my rubbish. Into the nearest bush, along with all the other garbage bags. 100 yards later I nearly walked past the garbage skip, not expecting it to be quite so close nor quite so unmissable in the middle of the road. I saved a dollar and there was one less bag of garbage dangling from a branch.

Things have been happening in Tyrell Bay. A new concrete seawall has been built and the old jetties off the beach are gone. The little harbor on the south shore now has the look of a small marina and repair facility. This, Tyrell Bay Marina, is still in its infancy but has the equipment to haul and store yachts. The new yard has attracted contractors such as welders, steel fabricators, engineers who work from their own bases (often afloat), and a shore-based canvas shop and sail maker next to one of the supermarkets in the bay. This marina will always be limited for space but its prices are reputed to be much lower than Grenada and the quality of work and honesty of service were all being highly praised. We certainly found the marina staff very helpful. The yard will surely benefit from any spin-off from the growth of yachting in Grenada.

Tyrell Bay is an increasingly popular anchorage and a good base from which to explore other anchorages in the archipelago. And there are now at least four Internet cafes in tiny Tyrell Bay.

The rocks and reefs off the southeast end of the island have some lonely and beautiful anchorages but some of this may be threatened by destruction. A Brazilian company is negotiating with the government of Grenada to put a free-port on the south east end of Carriacou. This will truly be gigantic, a complex twice the size of nearby PSV with a container port, a cruise ship port, a duty-free shopping center, warehouses for storing Brazilian goods, factories for assembling various products, hotels, tourist facilities, and even a school for the children of people employed in the complex. It will have deep ramifications for the whole island. The company's site suitability study dated June 2010 almost makes the case against this development with its wonderful photographs and descriptions of what will be destroyed to make way for the concrete and barbed wire of the port. In my earlier incarnation as an economist I used to work with small communities to plan their future and make suggestions about how their government could help bring it about. This development brings almost no benefits that I can see. It is almost as though the distant government on the big island of Grenada are going to tear down and rebuild the smaller Carriacou. See what you think: http://www.gov.gd/egov/docs/other/carriacou_free_port-ecoplan_report.pdf

Grenada

Pronounced *Grenaydah*. Lush, mountainous and the main island in the southern chain of the Grenadines. It is the center of government for Petite Martinique and Carriacou. Known as the Spice Island, and most famous for nutmeg and mace, although it also grows cinnamon, cloves, pimento and bay leaves among others, and cocoa. You can still visit a working nutmeg warehouse at the northern end of the island. The island has wonderful walking, fine beaches and lush volcanic interior. A national forest and reserve is located at the dormant volcanic crater of Grand Etang. The area between Prickly Bay and Secret Harbour reminds me of European or North American meadowlands.

The last of the island's Carib population died in 1651 by leaping off the 100 foot vertical cliff at Caribs'Leap or Morne des Sauteurs (Hill of the Jumpers), rather than be taken prisoner by the French. The British and French swapped ownership of the island several times until the British finally gained it through the Treaty of Versailles in 1783. French influence remains strong in the place names and Creole. Grenada became independent within the Commonwealth in 1973. Its last spot of political bother was a revolution in 1978 which upset some of its neighbors and led to an American invasion in 1983.

Grenada began to become a yachting center in the 1970s and some of today's players began to emerge in the 1980s; but it really started to take off as a major center for the southern Caribbean in the 1990s and continuing into the 2000s. Most facilities are located on the southern coast. Prickly Bay expanded its already very good facilities, then Clarkes Court Bay and St David's Bay. These are very attractive locations and a joy to be in on a boat. Some of the new marinas have laid moorings which visitors can use, yet there are still plenty of little secluded anchorages on this coast, but now with the added advantage of being in closer reach of services when they need them.

It is likely that the next few years will see more changes in the scale, nature and location of yacht facilities here or the consolidation of those already there. The opening of big regional chandlers such as Island Water World in St David's Harbor and now in The Lagoon brings Grenadian sailors access to the chandlery stock at St Martin.

The one doubt I have is the Camper & Nicholson's development of Port Louis at the capital, St George's, occupying most of the Lagoon. The peninsular will have luxury waterfront and hillside housing, hotel, clubs and the like and 25 acres of lagoon will be turned into a marina with 160 berths for superyachts. The number of mega yachts is increasing through the island chain and some of the tourism pundits argue that more mega-yacht facilities is a key trend in Caribbean yachting infrastructure, with new legislation needed to facilitate this. Until this state of bliss arrives superyachts which can't find a berth in the Port Louis Marina will probably be allowed to anchor or moor in the Carenage. You and I will be told to take our ordinary yachts to the south coast.

Admittedly the Lagoon had become semi-derelict and polluted and with a few too many abandoned boats but I still have fond memories of it as an anchorage and the historic and useful services, hardware and chandlery around the always welcoming Grenada Yacht Club. I don't really need the Lagoon to become the best marina in the southern Caribbean just as I don't want all the blasting of rock and dredging of channels to overcome the present difficulties of navigating into the Lagoon. I'll be moored or anchored on the south coast, passing the new marina by bus as I come to visit the capital of St George's along the noisy main road that fringed the old Lagoon and will fringe the new one too. It is easy to visit St George's by bus from the south coast and better than hoping to park your boat in the Lagoon.

Grenada must be commended for recent legislation to make the island generally more friendly to visiting yachts and with preferential duties for yachts importing equipment. This is clear recognition of the potential economic benefits from yachts and to be welcomed. I hope the political message filters down to the officials in their offices. It wasn't always thus. I remember all too clearly when Grenada shot itself in its foot with Cruising Permits, tripling the costs of entry. Officials were levying the new permits on top of the old port dues and clearance charges although the government's intention was to replace rather than add to the older fees. For a while yachts going to and from Trinidad were skipping Grenada altogether.

St George's is a must for any visitor to Grenada. This picturesque little town has all the style and energy of a real island capital. Built on the steep crater rim of an old volcano, the lowest edge being the bar to the harbor, the narrow streets wind round both sides of a high rocky hill. On one side is the fine old inner harbor, the Carenage, used by local trading craft and cruise ships; over the hill on the other side of town is the noisy fruit, vegetable and spice market and the stunning backdrop of the Caribbean Sea. The red brick of the buildings came as ballast in British sailing ships. St George's also has good hardware shops for skippers needing their regular maintenance fix.

If sailing back to Prickly Bay from St George's or otherwise about to turn east to sail along the south coast, beware the wind shift, wind strength, and current as you come out of the lee of the west coast at Saline Point. You might consider reefing just before the corner. The west coast is steep-to and we usually get close in to Saline Point before the start of our beat.

Grenada's best harbors all lie along the southern coast between Prickly Bay and St David's Harbor. Some require careful reef navigation. Wind and current run hard along this coast and going east is usually wet and bouncy. The prime harbor for passagemaking is Prickly Bay, both easy to enter and with a Customs and Immigration office. On the leeward coast the little anchorage of Halifax Harbor in a lovely little bay would be good for an overnight stop, if it were not next to a huge burning rubbish tip. The millions of flies living there met me just as I put the anchor down.

St George's, Grenada, remains an old fashioned island capital with a wonderful mish-mash of roofs looking out towards the unruffled Caribbean Sea. *Photo: G Jardine.*

Prickly Bay

Prickly Bay, known locally as L'Anse aux Epines (*Lans-apeen* as the locals say) is the classic Caribbean: breezy, safe and halfway to being secluded. I always feel happy coming in here. With high cloud and hot sun, the cooling breeze off the high land along the east of the bay is most welcome. Once the anchor is firmly set it will probably not drag, despite the gusts. Boats anchor close off one another's sterns and drop back, relying on the steady wind and lack of current to keep them in line and clear of neighbors. A southeast swell can enter the harbor and set boats rolling, though seldom severely. A west wind will clear all the boats out, but such winds are rare and often only come from the passing of hurricane feeder bands.

Spice Island's yacht facility used to be located on the eastern side of the bay but during 2003 the little marina and boatyard transferred to a larger haul-out and service facility on the other side of the bay, next to the coastguard and on the bus routes to Salinas Airport and St George's. Now called Spice Island Marine Services they have room to haul out and hold 200 boats ashore and run a 70 metric ton travel lift. They have a chandler, sail and rigging shop and most services, as well as a free dinghy dock. The location is handier for transport than it used to be, but perhaps a little too close to the busy main road. The old Spice Island Marina is under new ownership but continues to provide yacht services. This is where you will find Customs and Immigration. It isn't necessary to go to St George's to re-provision. At the windmill traffic roundabout on your way from Prickly Bay to St George's, where you would catch a bus into town if you wanted one, is a very well stocked and reasonably priced cash-and-carry. You can stock up there and ask them to telephone for a taxi to take you back to the marina. On the bus route, halfway to St George's, is a shopping mall with a large supermarket.

Prickly Bay is a good place to unwind or recover after a long sail but once you are done with Customs and Immigration and provisioning, you might prefer to move somewhere that isn't under the airport runway, has less party music on Friday and Saturday nights, and fewer visiting charter yachts. If so, head south to explore the bays along this coast, starting with Hog Island, an isolated anchorage just round the headland. There is usually a small community of long-stay yachts here and on Sundays a little bar opens with local food, a barbecue and steel band provided by nearby villagers.

Take care here, though. The entry to Hog Island and its neighbor, Secret Harbour, used to have helpful buoys to guide you round the reefs. These buoys can no longer be trusted. Some are missing. Some fine looking spherical red buoys are not the navigation markers they so closely resemble, but were laid as private moorings, and are where green buoys would be more appropriate anyway. Trust nothing you see except the reefs you are so carefully eyeballing. And beware. Reports say that the reef has grown in the last few years.

Then take advantage of the new marinas and mooring buoys as you head east to explore the rest of the south coast.

I like Grenada. I enjoy relaxing here after all our pre-launch work in Trinidad and before we set off to enjoy the isolation and remoteness of the Grenadines. Grenada has so many attractions for yachties. Good shops and the continuing charm of St George's, good transport, fine walks and historic places to visit, enough attractive bays to spend a couple of weeks exploring all round the island, and good swimming. Now add to this the new modern facilities. The fly in its ointment is that Grenada is in the hurricane zone and I cannot recommend trying to sit out a major storm here. I know that yards have adopted storage techniques in line with insurance company requirements, but I love my boat and respect my insurer's integrity and have no intention of using the former to test the willingness of the latter to pay up on a total loss claim. Full yards may mean that there is demand to be in Grenada, but there is no safety in numbers when crazy old Huracan is growling. The yards were pretty full when Ivan came through, and the damage done to boats in the yards was only the beginning of yachties' problems.

I don't think we should base our survival decisions on insurance policy small print. In 2010 as a late season hurricane was developing a skipper put to sea because his insurance didn't pay out if the boat was totalled by a named storm when at anchor, in a marina or in mangroves. But he would get full compensation if he was totalled at sea. Riding out a hurricane at sea is pretty much the last resort for a small yacht and possibly suicidal. If the boat had become a total loss I wonder how he and his crew would have got ashore to make their claim and whether the insurer would refuse payment anyway on the grounds that the boat didn't have a full hurricane crew.

To my mind the island's main plus factor during hurricane season is its proximity to Trinidad. If you are there in the summer be ready to head south when an advisory comes through. Doing that saved some friends in St Martin when Luis came through in 1995. I wish some of our friends had done the same when they were in Grenada in 2004.

Trinidad and Tobago

Although Trinidad and Tobago are now a single state, this is relatively recent in their respective histories and Tobago's political history is quite different from Trinidad's. Tobago's history is more like other plantation islands in the chain. Tobago went from French, Dutch, and British possession 22 times until being finally ceded to Britain in 1814. During these uncertain times the island was relatively undeveloped.

Trinidad and Tobago were joined under British control in 1889, became independent in 1962, a republic in 1976, but still remain within the Commonwealth. The first prime minister after independence, Eric Williams, wrote what I think is still the best history of social and economic development of the Caribbean, *History of the People of Trinidad and Tobago*, first published in 1964. This is a complex, sad story of greed, violence, repression, racial tensions and lost opportunities. All too believable. Dr Williams definitely ends his book with a light at the end of the tunnel. I think the tunnel may have got longer since he was around. Read it not just for Trinidad and Tobago but for a better understanding of the whole Caribbean. And while you are reading it, wonder whether your own head of government could write such an informed and erudite history. And if they could, could they have done it in just one month?

These are two very different islands, geologically and culturally. Tobago belongs to a different geological age to Trinidad, and in many ways is more like the other Caribbean paradises of the island chain, although it shows signs of volcanic activity from a geologically more distant period than them. Trinidad was connected to South America when sea levels were lower in the ice ages, only separating some 10,000 years ago. It lies on the edge of the great Orinoco River Delta. This, and the proximity of both islands to the South American continent (Venezuela is only about seven miles away from Trinidad), mean that their rainforests are fabulously complex with the same range of flora and fauna as the mainland. Rainforests on other Caribbean islands are local and more limited. Tobago has over 200 species of birds and Trinidad has over 400, compared to the 20 or so usually found on the other islands. There are 620 species of butterflies, 2,300 species of flowering plants and shrubs, 100 species of mammals and 70 of reptiles. The Trinidad and Tobago rainforests are more accessible than any in South America.

Both Trinidad and Tobago lie close to the fault line of the South American and Caribbean plates and are subject to earthquakes. Strange things lurk here, like the 14 acres of black treacle making up the inexhaustible Pitch Lake. A fracture in the sandstone some 250 feet below ground allows crude oil and bitumen to seep through, endlessly replenishing the lake. Sir Walter Raleigh used the stuff to re-caulk his ships.

I always look forward to coming here but I must admit to some grumbles with Customs and Immigration. True, I have seldom had the peaks of annoyance when clearing in and out of Trinidad & Tobago that I have experienced in the smaller islands in the chain, but nor have I experienced here the well-oiled speed typical of the French islands. Overall, cruisers seem exasperated by the time it takes to clear in and out, especially Immigration; by unreasonable and possibly unofficial requests for overtime charges when a skipper is at the office during normal hours but will be sailing at a time outside office hours; and the paper-filling obstacles in the way of moving between anchorages even on the same island. There are security reasons for this last niggle, since Trinidad is only a few miles from major Central American sources of drugs, but overall the rudeness, if it comes your way, is obnoxious and the triviality annoys. We might put up with it in the ramshackled office of a remote town on one of the small islands but it rankles when it happens here, yet again, after an hour or three in the queue at an over-staffed office of an experienced port of entry in the biggest island. Be prepared and hope things will have changed for the better by the time you get there. The wonderful Yacht Services Association of Trinidad and Tobago (YSATT) is, even as you read this, taking their cudgel to the Customs and Immigration fiends.

I've been told by some yachties that they have been put off coming here by the reputation of Customs and Immigration. Don't let this put you off.

There is no charge for clearing in or out in office hours. Customs will charge you $TT50 for the first 30 days of navigation dues, the balance to be collected when you clear out. Harbor fees are TT$50 for every 30 days in Trinidad up to a maximum of TT$500 in any one year.

American, British and European nationals do not need visas. Visiting sailors are given an initial three months' stay extendable by another three months on application. If leaving a boat here, the vessel must be hauled out (or for a short trip away from the country, moored at one of the marinas) so that there is no question of it being imported. Although Trinidad and Tobago are one country, let officials know if you sail from one to the other, so that they can pass over your file.

Trinidad

The larger island of the two-island state of Trinidad and Tobago. Columbus on his third voyage of discovery landed here in 1498 but Trinidad was not settled by the Spanish until a century later, and remained under Spanish rule until the British captured it in 1797. It has a heavy French influence from the Spanish period. The French largely managed and ran the plantations during the last days of Spanish rule until the British took the island.

Trinidad was a prosperous and organized place before the Europeans arrived.

> "There were houses and people and fine cultivated land, as green and lovely as the orchards of Valencia in March."
>
> Christopher Columbus, log of 1498, describing the south coast of Trinidad

You will soon find as you come south that Trinidad is a magnet for yachts. If you visit Trinidad you will almost certainly stay longer than you planned. You will find more here than you imagined.

Trinidad is the largest island in the Caribbean chain with a population of about 1.3 million. It is the most industrialized English-speaking island, having large oil and gas fields, with massive new reserves recently being discovered. With its technical sophistication Trinidad is bidding to become the financial center of the southern Caribbean. It was immensely prosperous during the oil boom of the 1970s, but slumped with the collapse in oil prices in 1984 and is still struggling—from oil to cocaine overnight, the locals cynically say. It remains heavily dependent on oil and gas, and wide open to international price fluctuations. The Trinidad and Tobago economy has shifted from state planning to a more liberal, free market approach and policies to enable more inward investment, with the possibly unexpected result that while some of its main sector of oil, gas, and petrochemicals is nationalized, a large chunk is now owned by U.S. multinationals.

It is a bustling, cosmopolitan island with much greater cultural, ethnic and religious diversity than any of the other islands. I believe it was calling itself the rainbow nation before Nelson Mandela applied this to South Africa. An unusually large proportion of its population originate from India compared to other Caribbean islands. Trinidad is the only English-speaking island with two majority races. East Indians, like the smaller ethnic groups such as the Portuguese from Madeira, Chinese and Syrian Lebanese, mainly arrived as indentured labor when slaving from Africa was abolished in the 1830s. The local culture also reflects the periods of Spanish rule and French occupation prior to the island finally coming under British control.

Perhaps it also reflects the culture of people from an earlier time. Trinidad has some survivors from the earlier Amerindian population. These Indians were probably not the Caribs of the smaller islands but a mainland people. Columbus described them as handsome, tall, with fine limbs and bodies, straight black hair, clothed in woven cloth and fairer than the other peoples he had seen in the islands to the north.

One of the wonderful things about modern Trinidad is how local culture combines this diversity to create a composite Trini identity, without losing the identities of those participating. Hindi, French and French Creole, though minority languages, are spoken as well as the main language of English. Perhaps Syrian, South American Spanish and Portuguese as well. Hindu prayer flags on houses are a common sight. Traditional celebrations include the Christian ones of Christmas and Easter, the Hindu ones of Phagwa and Diwali, and the Muslim ones of Hosay and Eid-al-Fitr. Calypso comes out of the rhythm and verbal mockery of Africa but with elements of Spanish, French, British and East Indian. Carnival, the major event of the year and on a scale to make Trinidad's Carnival one of the world's largest, has clear European, Roman Catholic roots but has flourished here as a black cultural development.

I love Trinidad. It is real, a grown up place, with more buzz and dimensions to it than the little islands in the chain. I love coming back to this life after the slow days on the little islands. People from the small islands find the buzz too much for them, much as some people must live in fear of the big city life of New York or London. They will tell you Trinidad is the crime capital of the world, and indeed it does seem to be going through a period of increasing and violent crime which the police seems unable to deal with. Since G and I spend more time in Trinidad & Tobago than on the other islands, seeing family and old friends, we see the effect of crime on the local community as well as the sailing community. My observation is that relatively little of this touches the sailing community although I find that fear of crime runs remarkably high among some of the visiting yachties in Chaguaramas.

Don't get this out of context. I have lived in big cities all my life and traveled from one end of the U.S. to the other and through most of Europe. G tells me I should worry more about crime when I'm out on the streets but actually it seems to me that I run a kind of continual and natural low-level attentiveness, although one day I may be proved wrong. In cities I know really well there are always places I won't ever walk around, and several I will not go to after dark. In Trinidad violence and crime are mainly gang related and occur in the inner city neighborhoods east of Port of Spain such as Laventille, Morvant and Barataria. I know these areas. They have their charm but frankly no foreign visitor should be in places like that without a score of local friends, and even then not after dark. So rising crime in those areas doesn't frighten me too much. I'm not often going to be there. More of a problem is when tourists are robbed at places like Fort George, the Pitch Lake and Las Cuevas beach as well as at car parks of supermarkets, shopping malls and restaurants, since these are the normal habitat of visitors. And that is why I find crime against tourists in Tobago, the holiday island of the twin island state, and the reported inability of the Tobago police especially worrying. In the last three years the incidents of serious and violent robberies in Tobago would have been unheard of in the 1990s. It isn't that there have been many incidents but their impact is out of all proportion to the number. Visitors come to Tobago to wander at will and feel unthreatened on the beach or in their hotel. Everyone on the island, other than the perpetrators, feels shock when this normality is broken.

Fear of crime is insidious. It threatens our sense of ourselves without ever making itself tangible for us to tackle. But like children wanting to play games that take them to the edge of fear, so we want to hear about crime. Novels and movies and other forms of fiction is one thing but what is it about TV and newspapers that they have to frighten people with their stories?

I had just arrived here and was getting frightened just reading the newspapers in Trinidad. There was a murder report on every page. Sometimes two or three. Some were full headlines; others just tiny reports. This, as well as the huge number of murders, manslaughters and terrible crimes of violence for such a small country, set me wondering. I read more carefully. The Trinidad papers were bulking out their own violence with reports from all over the U.S. All over, mark you. Not just New York or Baltimore or the Bay Area of San Francisco. That should keep their pages filled till hell freezes over.

Yachties have their own form of newspaper stories to frighten themselves and at times overstate the case. VHF, SSB and the Internet. Somehow information exchanged on these media lacks the self-restraint natural to a conversation in a bar or restaurant where you may be overheard and asked to develop your anecdote for the sake of others or be challenged on your facts, even if you have barely started to inflate them. In the last few years I have heard and read frightening tales of crimes to yachties in Chaguaramas and other parts of Trinidad. I have spoken with people who should know more than most about the yards and the island and whose opinions I rate as trustworthy and unvarnished, and they tell me the stories sometimes lack substance. I appreciate that. G and I have been in Chaguaramas when a bank was robbed by armed men. They escaped in a dinghy they stole by nearly shooting the owner. The robbery was real but note the "nearly" of the shooting. G and I had a bicycle stolen from under our boat. A bicycle! When I spoke to our favorite night security guard I made the mistake of saying one of the workers in the yard had probably taken it. "Can you see one of those guys riding around Carenage or Port of Spain on that scrappy little fold up thing of yours?" he asked. It was G's favorite bike but I could see his point. No, I couldnt. Some of the frightening tales just don't add up. Some of the claims are slanderous. Reality is bad enough without inventing more stuff to frighten us or put us all off. Good advice from Melodye Pompa of the Caribbean Safety and Security Net. Beware of getting bad advice from the Internet. These are unchecked facts and often get another lease of life by being picked up by TV and newspapers. Crimes from 20 years ago get peddled as this year's. There are too many rumors in the cruising community for all of them to be true.

Trinidad isn't heaven. At times it is a rough, tough place but none the worse for that. Sailors who spend time there say it has the kindest, most hospitable people. The warmth of the local people is genuine. No one stands on ceremony here. You will be invited to join in wherever you are, whatever is happening. But most Americans and British people lock their doors at home, and when they go traveling they would be foolish not to take the usual precautions against theft or break-ins.

I used to have this thing about Jamaica. About what a scary country it was. Murder capital of the Galaxy. Corruption on every corridor of Government. Too dangerous for any one to visit. Now the thing is: I've never been there. I have no first hand knowledge of the country. Did that stop me dishing the dirt about Jamaica? "Never been there" doesn't stop bad opinions being passed around. I hear sailors who have never been south of Grenada warning that the boatyards of Trinidad will rip you off. In the time we've sailed the Caribbean G and I have thoroughly renovated two boats in Chaguaramas, getting to know all the contractors and most of their workers. So we are always interested in hearing of the poor work by so-called craftsmen in Trinidad, whether this is woodwork, metal work, engine repairs, sail making or painting. We have heard terrible tales of people paying for work that ended up badly done, and then having to pay again to get it done right. We once had steel work made that didn't fit. It wasn't all the fault of the fabricator. We paid the bill one time only. They did the work twice. I have given up arguing with people who say these things without ever having been there. I grow tired of being told "Well, that's not what I've heard."

Here are a few things to bear in mind that apply in Trinidad but will also help you in other ports you visit:

- The Trinidad yachting industry has grown from nothing in the 1970s to be the unrivaled leader of the Caribbean. It has sucked in experts from Europe and the U.S., bought brand new gear to U.S. standards, and is training local workers not just in technical skills but customer relations. In such rapid growth, and when standards and attitudes have to change, there is plenty of scope for work to be badly done, but work can be done badly anywhere. I've seen bad work that could have been avoided if the yachtie had been as pro-active in specifying and supervising as he or she would have been back home. There is good reason for yachting in Trinidad to be booming, and for those involved to want to keep it growing. Take your problems straight back to the contractor or the yard managers or YSATT. There is plenty of scope to complain effectively and, as G tells me so often, what's the point of an ineffective complaint, however far you can make it travel.

- Trinidadians have different values from North Americans and Northern Europeans. Different but not any less valid. The Caribbean culture puts greater value on social time and is less driven by the clock. This isn't laziness. It is a different perspective on life. When you are inclined to complain that there is no "work ethic" try substituting the phrase "modern industrial conditioning" and ask yourself whether this is really something to wish on anyone.

- The Tropics is a hard environment to work in. You and I might be driven to work flat out for a day or two in a crisis but try this for a week and you'll realize that careful pacing is needed to keep going day after day. This isn't much different from work back home. All workers develop ways to save energy and keep going efficiently day after day.

- No matter how industrious the individual workers, the bane of most economies is usually management and motivation, and this is almost the key problem by definition in developing economies. Combine this with a newly developing industry largely driven by overseas professionals who rarely bother to understand the values of locals, and poor management is a big chunk of why you are tearing your hair out in the boatyard.

On top of this, try asking yourself whether a single-minded concern with varnishing, painting, refitting and the cost of things allows you the mental time and space to appreciate the world and culture around you. Beware of adopting the blinkered view appropriate to a charter yacht skipper who has the owner's refit timetable in his email box. You aren't here just for that. How do you want to live your new life, now that you've become a cruising yachtie?

There was a time when the government of Trinidad seemed to prefer yachts to go somewhere else but those days are over and much is done by government and local businesses to make sure that visiting yachts are made welcome. Chaguaramas, historically the anchorage for the tall ships of Britain, France and Spain during the centuries of imperial struggle, and a U.S. naval base from 1941 to 1967, has become a large yachting center almost in my time. When I first arrived in 1995 there were four boatyards where you could haul out and three of those had only just opened. Now there are at least seven (depending on what you call a boatyard) and several marinas where you can tie up alongside one way or another. One of the newer marinas which I think of as really being a hotel with a pretty view of yachts has now got itself a 200 metric ton travel lift. Go tell that to Grenada, Antigua or even St Martin. From now on I shall consider it a major modern boatyard.

The yards I use for my lesser needs also have new and top rate travel lifts and tractors able to handle big and small yachts. The men handling the gear are experienced and careful. The quality of the gear would shame most U.K. boatyards.

It isn't just the physical development that marks Trinidad as different from other Caribbean bases. It's the organization. I have not found anything to compare with YSATT, the Yacht Services Association of Trinidad and Tobago, for taking an overview of quality and being pro-active in meeting the needs of the boat population. We cruisers load YSATT up with our complaints and in return they smile and try to solve our problems. In December 2010 YSATT met ministers and government officials, senior police, Coast Guard and Customs and Immigration officials to lobby about the frustrations of yachties and the yachting businesses. Things were promised and things were done. Customs have extended the time yachts have from clearing out to actually leaving Trinidad. Overtime will not be charged to yachts arriving outside office hours. The Coast Guard will run night security patrols to augment the security patrol boat YSATT itself runs in Chaguaramas. The police are running regular patrols inside the marinas and boatyards, especially at night.

These are not trivial achievements. They address precisely the main concerns of yachties coming to Trinidad. They make our life better and our work easier. And do you have any idea how much pain is involved in getting disparate branches of government to meet and agree to act on anything? We cruisers don't see the amount of work that YSATT does for us, meeting after meeting after meeting. With luck YSATT will bring more collaboration between the yachting industry and government.

Trinidad has been getting a bashing over the last year, for reasons I cannot fathom. The complaints have been made in the sailing newspapers and rebuttals have been made, and I am none the wiser. I had thought of putting in my own pennyworth right here, but a Trini working in Chaguaramas did it for me in his letter to *Caribbean Compass*.

The "Trinidad bashing" letters as well as those in defense of the island are much better than any television soap opera. I cannot wait for the next issue of *Compass* to read the continuing saga . . . .

Will DS respond to RL's continued bashing? Will RL ever think that the people of Chaguaramas are trying to make life easier for cruisers? Will Immigration ever stop being discourteous and rude?

Tune in to the next issue, when . . . .

Fortunately for Trinidad there are many more sailors who appreciate what the island provides than those who decide never to return.

Chaguaramas has more flat open land for boatyards and hard standing than any other island in the southern Caribbean and it has always been possible to find a space ashore when we have wanted one. The busy months ashore are July to November, when around 700 boats may be on the hard and 300 to 400 visiting boats are on the water.

The popularity of Trinidad as a place to haul-out and refit increases as more sailors become fearful of hurricanes and aware of Carnival, so at some point booking will be necessary and prices may rise to the rates of other islands. However, I see the main competition for Trinidad, and the bench mark for their prices, as the marinas on the mainland of Venezuela. This should hold haul-out prices down below other Caribbean islands for a while yet.

Prices for work in Chaguaramas even now are caught in the gap between the low local wage rates to be expected here and elsewhere in the Caribbean, and the U.S. dollar expectations of the international entrepreneurs who have set up many of the specialist services. The minimum wage in Trinidad is TT$11 (about US $1.75 an hour) but a contractor in one of the yards might charge out his workers at anything from this up to TT$80 an hour. An expatriate specialist might be charging as much as TT$300 an hour. Local contractors working in the yards can hardly be blamed for pricing to the market and pocketing the excess profit when they see what the expats get away with. And yachties don't help themselves when they gloat to a local business about how cheap they are relative to back home. What is that if not both an insult and an invitation?

Yachts undertake most aspects of refit here but especially fiberglass osmosis repairs, hull painting and teak work. Odd perhaps, given the humidity and rain, but good painters are available and labor rates for the work are still much lower than on other islands. The specialist rigging shops in two of the main yards are very good, and can help take care of the fatigue caused to stainless rigging by the tropical climate. Elderly rigging, elderly skippers, both equally need respite from abuse by the climate.

Take care when maneuvering your boat in or out of the travel lift docks, the fuel dock at Power Boats (the only fuel dock in Chaguaramas) or the mooring boxes. The circular current is surprisingly strong for such an enclosed bay and will start to swing the yacht before you are half out, with entertaining results for onlookers.

Chaguaramas is a commercial harbor as well as the main yacht anchorage and the water here is not good for swimming. Quieter anchorages with clearer water exist to the west, in Scotland Bay and Chacachacare. Sail there when you need a break. Or if you are on the hard, take a ride round to the beautiful north coast beaches such as Macquaripe, Maracas and Las Cuevas.

Chacachacare—pronounced *cha-ka-cha-kari*—is the furthest island west from Chaguaramas, but only about five miles away. Inside the high, lush horseshoe shaped island is a fine bay protected on almost all sides from the Trades and with plenty of little coves to anchor in. The island is deserted now apart from the lighthouse keeper. The island was once settled by fishermen and small farmers but in 1921 these were relocated to allow the island to become a leper hospital. During World War II the island was also

Trinidad, Northern Range. Through the trees and over the hills. I know no better place to take time off ashore than the old house at Asa Wright, now a world-famous bird sanctuary. *Photo: G Jardine.*

used as a U.S. base, with about nine barracks and the roads to connect them. With the development of more effective drugs for Hansen's Disease and the switch to outpatient programs, the isolation of the colony was unnecessary. The number of admissions declined in the 1970s and the hospital was closed in 1984, treatment transferring to the mainland. The houses, hospitals, churches and other buildings remain, left as they were on the day the colony closed and partly now in decay and overgrown by vegetation.

East of Chaguaramas are the Five Islands, just beyond the famous prison island of Carrera. Peaceful, deserted, with water clean enough for swimming but beware the strong currents running here. Buildings on the islands are in various states of ruin but plans exist to restore them as a national heritage site. From 1802, Nelson Island was used by the British as an examination point for all vessels coming in to Trinidad. Indentured labor was processed through immigration here. Later, in World War II, the British housed Jewish refugees, mainly from Mediterranean countries. Lenagen Island had an isolation hospital. Caledonian Island, and its satellite Craig Island, were the resort islands for Trinidad's 19th century wealthy and are probably the main anchorages in the Five Islands for yachts now.

Carnival in Trinidad is like a hurricane. It is a great force of nature bringing yachts from all over the Caribbean to Trinidad. Yachts come crowding into Trinidad in the weeks immediately before Carnival but longer stay yachties will have already done as the locals

209

do and gone to many earlier events at mas' camps and calypso tents and pan yards in the regular annual timetable. Carnival is a local event, staged for locals by locals and making no concessions to visitor tourism, yet it is the most open of events. Everyone in the world is welcome and encouraged to join in. Carnival here has always been an open event, played out entirely on the streets.

Carnival began as a masked street celebration before the solemnities of Lent and now is a whole season celebrating music and art. It is probably less rooted in Roman Catholicism than Mardi Gras, and more rooted in Afro-Trinidadian rebellion and cries of freedom. Events start to build almost from Christmas and then reach a frenetic stage in the final last weeks before Carnival. The special things to catch are:

- Mas' bands and playing mas', a shortening of the word masquerade. This is not just an excuse to cavort in skimpy clothing in one of the huge costume bands that take to the streets on the last days of Carnival. It is also about themes, new and old, and many of the smaller bands relate distinctly to the older, formal traditions. Small bands might portray characters from Ol'Mas', the masquerades of long ago, such as Sailors (with firemen or stokers doing their poker dance) or Fancy Indians and the outlandish Midnight Robbers, Blue Devils, Red Devils and Jab Jabs, Guarahoon, Pierrot Grenades, Dame Lorraine and Minstrels, Moko Jumbies, Stickfighters, Bats, Imps and Dragons. All have the language or walks and dances of these characters. Each character has a role, relating back to spirits and gods or particular characters in the community, which they play out. Some are mimicking and mocking; others are bold and fierce.
- Steel bands, known as pan sides, whose practice place is known as a pan yard. Wander around pan yards with the local cognoscenti. The power, range and skill of a Trini pan side must be seen and heard to be believed.
- Calypso or its more up tempo version *kaiso*, earthy, witty, irreverent and sometimes scurrilous but never sycophantic; a social and political commentary heard in the calypso tents.
- Soca, a stirring, fast beat version of calypso fused with soul, rap and reggae, heard endlessly in the maxi taxis, and with an East Indian version called chutney soca.

Most if not all the islands in the chain have a carnival, although not always before Lent. Don't confuse carnival elsewhere with Carnival in Trinidad. These are no more than side shows to the main event.

Calypso is the musical force behind Carnival, even when it takes the form of soca. Calypsonians release their songs for this year's Carnival sometime around Christmas. In the weeks just before Carnival it will be clear which of the songs will be the main tunes for the mas' bands to chip along to. You will hear old-time rhymes, such as "bacchanal" with "carnival," and continuous calls to party, whine, jump-up and wave your rag. Hands in the air!! Hands in the air!!

Pan sides play in preliminaries to reach the final of the Panorama competition held in the week immediately before Carnival. Panorama is not just a musical event but high theater, from the drama of getting the band on and off the stage to the life-and-death energy of the players when it is their turn. These pan sides, with 100 or more players and racks of pans on wheels, are as different from the Friday night pan sides up the islands as an orchestra is to an ageing rock combo.

On the Monday and Tuesday before Lent the whole city is turned over to playing mas' as costume bands roadmarch through all the streets and over the stage at the Savannah, where the main judging takes place. Preceding this almost respectable display is the wild opening event of J'Ouvert (pronounced *joovay*). The start of J'Ouvert is officially announced at 4 am by the Mayor of Port of Spain. Steel bands and music trucks provide rhythm and drinks for the players. Players wear mud, oil and grease, cocoa and paint and brief, disposable costumes. Nothing clears the frustrations and suppressions of the preceding year like playing J'Ouvert.

Yachties can follow the excitement on the streets or join a band. Some Chaguaramas boatyards have their own section in a band and the long-stay yachties organize events over the VHF net.

Carnivals the world over are a great place to have your pocket picked. The Tourist Board have published guidelines for visitors to their Carnival which I think apply everywhere, anytime. Follow them and be safer.

- Dress simply. No jewelry.
- Don't carry more money in your wallet than you need.
- Don't carry anything there that you can't afford to lose.
- Don't carry your wallet in a side pocket.
- If you must carry important documents or large sums of money, use a neck or waist pouch carried under your shirt.
- Go with a group and have a fall back in case you get separated.

After the thrash of Carnival, you can retire for a quiet week on Tobago or up in the northern hills of Trinidad in a nature reserve like the world-famous Asa Wright, where birdwatchers come to hear the bell bird or see the sixteen varieties of hummingbird, and gourmets just enjoy the Creole cooking of home grown fruit and vegetables.

There is plenty of useful published information to get the most out of your stay on Trinidad:
- YSATT's website on www.ysatt.org gives information about contractors and services in the yards.
- *Discover Trinidad and Tobago*, a free tourist board publication available from Customs and Immigration or any boatyard. Useful about what to see and visit. There are more events and of a higher standard than on any of the other islands—cultural festivals; music; cricket, football, athletics, cycling, golf and other sports; flower and orchid shows.
- *Boater's Directory of Trinidad and Tobago*, published yearly by Boaters' Enterprise Ltd and available free at yachting centers in Trinidad and Tobago. More than 200

pages of information on visitor attractions, Carnival and cultural events. Very useful directory of services listed by type of service and firms alphabetically. Advertisements cover most things yachts need.

- *The Boca*, a monthly newspaper for yachties, published by Boaters' Enterprise Ltd, Crews Inn Marina. Email: boaters@Trinidad.net. It contains stories of interest to yachties, news of the local industry and useful classified ads and a timetable of events. A small newspaper but their own. The timetable of regular events for just one week gives a glimpse into the cruising life:

Every day	8 am	Cruisers VHF net on channel 68
Monday	7 pm	Alcoholics Anonymous
Tuesday	7 pm	Trivia night at TTSA
Wednesday	8. 5 am	Volunteers for learning support to Cocorite Community Center
	Noon	Writers' club meeting
	7 pm	Movie night and happy hour at TTSA
Thursday	2.30 pm	Bridge club
	7 pm	Movie night and happy hour at IMS
Friday	7 pm	Happy hour at IMS
Saturday	5 pm	Holy Mass, Gasparee island
Sunday	9.30 am	Church service, Westside community center
	Evening	BBQ in Tobago

Trinidad is the natural jumping off place for Venezuela and, indeed, the western rim of the Caribbean in an arc that will bring you round to Cuba and the Greater Antilles. Some visitors leave their boat in Trinidad and fly to Venezuela and other parts of Latin America. Those who sail to Los Testigos and Los Roques and want to get back to Trinidad face a long motor-sail against wind and current. One small encouragement is that the high land of the northeast coast of Venezuela makes for lighter winds close in.

Tobago

Pronounced *Toebaygo*. Tobago is still my favorite Caribbean island. Smaller, slower and more African than Trinidad. It has a population of around 50,000. Who would believe that sleepy little Tobago changed hands more times between Britain and France than any other Caribbean island. Tobago is the tourism island of Trinidad and Tobago. Commercial tourism concentrates in the southern half, most of it near the airport. Not yet heavily developed but changing fast.

Many Caribbean islands have high, green hills with the massive rainfall needed to support a tropical rainforest, and these are magnificent, often now designated nature reserves or protected lands, with hundreds of tree and bird species. Only Trinidad and Tobago, because of their geological history, have the full flora and fauna of a South American rainforest. Tobago's rainforest on the main ridge, rising to nearly 2,000 feet, has been protected since 1776, making it the oldest forest reserve in the western hemisphere. The forest was protected because scientists recognized the relationship be-tween rainfall and trees, and the concomitant danger of felling the forest. This was indeed a far-sighted eco-policy and yet 300 years earlier, when he discovered Jamaica during his second voyage of discovery, Columbus was making the same observations on how thick forest promoted thick cloud and regular heavy rain.

The massive rainfalls of the high islands and the associated weather may reach out and touch you as you close the land. They make for spectacularly beautiful landfalls. Sailing north up the leeside of Tobago you can watch rain clouds swirling round the high northern hills and still have time to pull on a jacket before the deluge hits you.

Relatively few yachts visit Tobago. Not just because it lies at the southern end of the island chain but because it is just that bit off a convenient route from nearby islands. I would rather not sail there from nearest neighbors Trinidad or Grenada.

We did it the classic way. We left Chaguaramas at night and motored along the north coast of Trinidad as close in as we dared. The big moon after midnight helped a lot. By early morning we were identifying every next headland as the end of the island, but disappointingly each one just revealed another one ahead of us. As I came up from sleep at about 8 am Rm pointed to Tobago still ahead of the beam. I cursed the bad angle. The wind was up to 15 knots or so but we were not getting waves that stopped us. The motor pushed us at less than four knots against the cur-rent and by mid morning we were hitting higher swells. There would have been no comfort in going faster. The scenery was unbelievably beautiful. We passed huge leather-back turtles, rest-ing after laying their eggs last night or preparing to swim ashore to lay them tonight. Finally we came to the unmistakable end of Trinidad, hoisted sail and turned off the engine after 18 hours of motoring. The four-hour reach across to Tobago was wonderful but a week later I was still thinking I wouldn't want to do that night again. Not for fun, anyway.

Tobago is more easily reached direct from Europe or Africa or, failing that as your start-ing point, somewhere as far north in the island chain as St Vincent. I regard Tobago as the best model to help understand sailing conditions around other Caribbean islands. Master sailing around this small island and you are set up for all the others.

The axis of Tobago is northeast to southwest, putting it across the stream of the Equatorial Current and down the line of the prevailing winds. The Equatorial Current hitting the Atlantic side of Tobago divides just to the north of the main town of Scar-borough, to run both ways along the windward side. The current runs fast around the southern end of the island as the Equatorial Current is squeezed through the 30 mile wide channel between Trinidad and Tobago. The current round the southern end is then pulled along the leeward side of the island and the influence of swell can be felt in all the bays almost all the way up the leeward coast.

Scarborough on the Atlantic coast is the main point of entry for yachts but is not a comfortable harbor. It has a headland, breakwater and off-lying reef to protect it from the ocean but this is not quite enough. Most yachts clear out after a couple of days and

The lookout post on the windward coast near Speyside, the center of Tobago's diving, with the wildlife sanctuary of Little Tobago in the background. And beyond Little Tobago? 3,000 miles of ocean and then Guinea-Bissau. *Photo: K Morgan.*

head south to go round the end of the island and north-about to Store Bay, Crown Point and Milford Bay, which is also where most boats coming from Trinidad or Venezuela would aim to arrive. This is a pretty little bay but subject to swell and wet landings on the beach. In bad swell, usually when the wind goes into the north and runs down the leeward coast over the north-going current, yachts can find more shelter in a reef gutway off Pigeon Point where the mass of Buccoo reef gives shelter.

A new facility here for visiting yachts is Store Bay Marine Services set up by Englishman John Stickland and with a mixed staff of locals and expats.

The best time to sail north up the leeward coast is early morning before the Trade Winds get up. After that, it can be a hard, wet beat. The little bays on the leeward side of Tobago are beautiful anchorages, but when the swell is up the rolling is uncomfortable and the beach landings may spill you out the dinghy. In these conditions the only place to go is Pirates' Bay, Charlotteville at the northern end of the island, hence my designation of it as the prime harbor on Tobago.

Englishman's Bay is still the most beautiful bay on the island and very quiet. No one lives here. People only come to visit it in the daytime and then only by car. The anchorage when I was last there in 2003 was still as deserted as on my first visit in 1995. Only us and another yacht rolling in the gentle swell as we both rested before sailing to Trinidad that evening. The noisy green parrots still flew overhead as the sun went down, the woods were still deep green with patches of bright orange where the immortelles bloom, and the million fireflies still flickered as the night grew dark. The only mark of progress was Beulah's little restaurant on the beach, opened in 1997 or so. I can't complain. Beulah's coconut ice-cream is homemade and delicious and perfect after a swim in the heavy surf.

Charlotteville is in a large bay open to the west but well protected from the Trade Winds. Pirates' Bay, the best anchorage, is just inside the northern headland, not off the town itself. This is also a good place to leave a boat while exploring the island by bus. Charlotteville is one of the prettiest villages on Tobago and has buses to the rest of the island. The town jetty allows a dry landing by dinghy.

Charlotteville is the anchorage most yachts coming from the north and even from the west would aim for, so the good news is that in mid 2000 Charlotteville became an official port of entry. In true Tobagonian style, this happened before Customs or Immigration opened an office there. Now, though, the little office is next to the Charlotteville police station.

When you leave Trinidad to go to Tobago and vice versa you must in effect sign in and out even though you will not be leaving the country. Get papers from Customs and Immigration and check what is required of you.

Another point of perspective—comparative costs of living

Our simple rule of thumb is that prices increase as you go north in the island chain. We reckon prices double between Trinidad and Grenada and then keep on rising. Within this general tendency you will find particular hot spots, especially now that many of the previously remote islands have developed extensive land tourism. One clue to these hot spots is that when prices are routinely quoted in U.S. dollars, rather than the local currency, you have arrived in a high price zone. This may be a whole island or just the place you are standing. The Eastern Caribbean dollar (EC) is pegged to the U.S. dollar and easily converted, but this doesn't mean that you are being offered a good rate on whatever transaction is underway or that the goods coming to you are at the price a local would pay.

One exception to our north/south rule has been that prices in the main French islands always seemed lower than their non-French neighbors. The more French the goods you are buying, the cheaper they seem. Wine, for example, is not a natural product of the tropics and is shockingly expensive in the English-speaking islands. Apart from loading up with duty free wine in Trinidad, we only buy wine in the French islands and prefer to get our coffee there too. French supermarkets are ahead of all others in the region in the range, quality and price of food.

One other exception is the Virgin Islands. We were surprised to see good prices for chandlery although the range is not such that I would rely on finding what I need here.

St Thomas may be different but I was not able to comb through the chandleries on this bigger island. Sometimes we were also surprised by the good prices of foodstuffs. Locals attribute the latter to an expansion in the size of some of the main supermarkets. Of course, good here is relative. It's still expensive by Trinidad standards. Also, costs go up if you want to use marinas in the Virgins. In brief, yachting here is geared to the charter fleets not to independent cruisers, and the services for cruisers is limited.

Our advice is still to stock the boat first in Trinidad, second in Martinique and third in St Martin.

10
Islands off the list

St Croix

Pronounced *St Croy*. Although politically part of the USVI, St Croix is isolated from the main cruising ground of the Virgins. It lies about 30 miles south of St Thomas and unlike the islands of the main group is open to the ocean swell. Most yachts coming to the Virgins from the north will not drop this far south initially, and most coming up from the south will initially not go so far east as this. Because of this, I regard St Croix as an "out of Virgins" experience.

St Croix is worth a visit. Getting there takes no great passage planning. It is a trip that can be done easily in half a day in the right weather, leaving plenty of time to arrive at one of the anchorages there. It is the largest of the three main USVI and has interesting architecture from its time under Danish rule. St Croix is a green island, still agricultural but with major oil and aluminum producing industries. Buck Island is the only underwater national monument in the U.S. and reputedly good for snorkeling. I would avoid the location of the Hess oil refinery on the south coast.

Anegada

The eastern-most of the BVI. The name Anegada means drowned, perhaps because the island is so low-lying that it can barely be seen on the horizon as you approach it. At about seven miles off, we saw disconnected peaks which could have been isolated rocks, that at five miles looked like worn-out toothbrushes, but later proved to be clumps of trees. This is the only coral island in the Virgins, less than 30 feet high in most places, surrounded by reefs, rocks and wrecks.

The only anchorage must be entered with great care and only when the weather is right. This is not an island for a passagemaker to approach after many days at sea, especially when the rest of the Virgins are so accessible. But Anegada is beautiful, remote, and relatively unfrequented.

We were surprised to see about eight yachts at anchor here. Visit Anegada as an exploration, in the right weather, when you are already established in the Virgins. A convenient jumping off point for yachts heading to the Azores.

Anguilla

Anguilla, from the Spanish word for eel, named after its long narrow shape, is one of the remaining British overseas territories forming part of the British West Indies. The others are Montserrat, British Virgins, Caymans, and Turks and Caicos. It is off the list for this book because it lacks good harbors for a passagemaker. Explore Anguilla when you have established yourself at St Martin.

Saba

Pronounced *Say-bah*. Saba is a tiny, Dutch, 5 square miles round, symmetrically steep pinnacle of high rock in rough seas and without a harbor. Few yachts visit. There are times when the seas are flat calm but beware, the seas can build quickly to make your stay untenable. Visiting Saba needs planning and crew. While some of the crew go ashore to see the island, others should stay with the boat to clear out if the swell becomes dangerous.

I visited Saba years ago when I was a deckhand on a two-masted schooner taking brave American holidaymakers around the islands on a kind of floating holiday camp. Even in the one place where an anchor will reputedly find bottom in this precipitous place our skipper refused to risk his ground tackle and one of us had to swim a line out to the single mooring buoy. I sneaked time ashore to see the wonderful meadows and pretty settlement inside the dead volcano. I never visited Hell's Gate, the tiny village on the lip of the crater, usually above the cloud, impossibly perched there like a mistake in rural development. Fine white sandy beaches and crystal clear water.

There are more mooring buoys now at Ladder Bay and I have come close to using one to break my passage from the north Leewards to the Virgins. But I never trusted the weather to stay calm for a whole night.

Montserrat—paradise postponed

I doubt there are many places in the world where five-year-old children are so well educated that they know the meaning of "pyroclastic." Montserrat is one of them.

Montserrat, one of the remaining British overseas territories, lies in the same geological chain as the small islands of Nevis through to Saba. It is called the emerald isle, in memory of the Irish who were the first Europeans to settle here, and for its lush green beauty. It would be a useful stop (swell permitting) for boats on the way between Nevis and Guadeloupe but I haven't yet visited Montserrat. Not many yachts have in the last decade. Montserrat has never had much of a harbor but this is less of a reason to avoid the island than the waking of the volcano on Soufrière Hills in the southern end of the island in July 1995.

This volcano, which first erupted about 100,000 years ago, had probably last erupted in the late 1500s. Since 1995, the volcano has remained active. The population of about 3,000 to 5,000 still living on the island have moved into the relative safety of the northern tip, putting the Central Hills between themselves and the volcano. Yachts are advised to pass only on the windward side and no closer than the two-mile exclusion zone.

Little Bay in the north is the temporary port of entry (call the port authority on VHF 16 on arrival) and is at a safe (so far) distance from the volcano. It is uncomfortable when swells come from the north and a stern anchor is needed. A new breakwater may help to change this.

The story of Montserrat is the story of many other Caribbean islands. The island chain sits on the subduction zone where the Caribbean tectonic plate meets the North and South American plates. All three of these plates are in motion. The North and South American plates, being denser than the Caribbean plate, are forced to push underneath it at a rate of a couple of centimeters a year. The action in this 50 million year old subduction zone has formed the islands of the chain. Rock at the edge of the subducting zone melts into magma which then rises in columns, not continuously over time, but in blips of activity. Thousands of years may pass between these blips of activity. The magma column rising to the surface of the earth creates magma chambers or domes against which later blips of magma must push. When the push is great enough surface rocks may slide out of the way, instantaneously exposing the fresh magma. The sudden exposure allows gases in the magma to expand rapidly and may lead to violent eruptions.

Montserrat's new Soufrière dome from the 1995 and subsequent eruptions sits over three older domes, the centers of previous, now inactive, eruptions, the last occurring about 400 years ago. The northern end of the island, where the much reduced population is now concentrated, has probably not been affected by volcanic activity for two million years. Montserratians must be hoping for no change in their lifetimes.

The re-activation of a volcano like Soufrière Hills takes time. In summer 1995, the hills began spewing out occasional clouds of grey ash and steam. This was followed by earthquakes and mud slides, then pyroclastic flows down the eastern side of the hills that turned ancient tropical forest into lunar landscape. Eruptions continued, with rock throws and ashfall dense enough to blanket the sunlight, until September 1996 when part of the dome collapsed. Rocks exploded from the side of the mountain, electrically charged ash particles sparked lightning and caused thunder. Rocks were flung as far as the boundary of the then safe zone, re-emphasizing the power and unpredictability of the volcano and the need for locals to retreat further north on the island. The old capital city of Plymouth, lying about three miles downwind of Soufrière Hills, is out of bounds, silted over by ash. A new delta has formed off the Tar River from the ash and debris running down to the sea. Blazing magma can still be seen glowing through the thin crust of the dome, an indication that volcanic eruptions could continue for decades (get the latest information from the Montserrat Volcano Observatory at www.mvo.ms). There is a chance for visitors to the Caribbean to get along to the Montserrat Volcano Observatory and some very different sightseeing.

The story of this eruption echoes that of earlier ones in the region, like Mont Pelée in Martinique. The 1902 eruption which destroyed the then capital of Martinique, came after much smoke and warning rumbles from the mountain were ignored. Nothing much remains. Along the island chain, other volcanoes show signs of activity, though none has yet erupted like Montserrat.

In 1998, on a flight from St Kitts to Antigua, I saw the clearly visible column of steam and dust from the 3,000 feet high volcano and the dense, high ash cloud drifting westwards out to sea. In 2001, looking out from the islands of Antigua and then Nevis, I could still see a high cloud over the volcano though less dense than three years earlier. At the end of July 2003, a couple of months after we had sailed by without seeing any signs of smoke, heavy rains caused the dome to collapse. Fine ash and dust was flung as far as Puerto Rico. In the years since then there has been a series of rockfalls, mudflows, pyroclastic flows and earthquakes from the continuous series of repeated formation and collapse of the volcanic domes. Business as usual for an active volcano.

Barbuda

Privately owned for 200 years until 1870, Barbuda is politically now part of Antigua and the two islands sit on the same underwater bank. In the great days of sail, Barbuda was reputed to be the greatest danger to shipping in the West Indies. The low island, mainly just a few feet above sea level, is surrounded by reefs. The island and its reefs account for at least 360 wrecks. Wrecks were once a major source of income for the people here.

Barbuda is off the main track of cruising through the island chain. It has many off-lying hazards, badly charted shoals, and many coral heads. It must be approached with great care.

Barbuda—the beautiful coast of this low-lying island. *Photo: Courtesy of Antigua and Barbuda Tourist Office.*

Marie-Galante and La Desirade

These two islands (and their neighbor Petite Terre) are best regarded as a side trip to be made from The Saintes. They are a definite beat into the wind and current but your reward will be to find few other yachts. You can anchor off the long white beach of Marie Galante, probably without another boat in sight. Desirade was seldom visited by sailing boats because its harbor was too shallow for them, but it now has an entrance channel dredged to nine feet and a reported depth of six feet in the harbor.

You don't have to come back to The Saintes from here. You can ride the wind and current to English Harbour, Antigua.

Barbados

Barbados is not really a Caribbean island since it is surrounded by the Atlantic ocean, sitting on its own small bank with deep water of 7,000 to 8,000 feet between it and the island chain. It is also geologically different from most islands in the chain. It is a flat limestone wedge of sediment being pushed upwards as the tectonic plates move together. Its surface rocks are the remains of old coral reefs which grew as the waters over them became shallower. Not having high hills, it is dry without rainforest or grand rivers. But the Trade Winds sweep over to give the most delightful cooling breeze over the pleasant rolling countryside. Beaches are of finest white sand. Coastal waters are a strange milky blue.

In culture and spirit Barbados is wholly part of the region and the only reason I don't include Barbados in this guide is because I haven't sailed there, and relatively few yachts cruising the island chain will call there. My best time to have landed in Barbados was at the end of my Atlantic crossing. Now I probably won't visit the island except by plane. This isn't because I have any reason to dislike the island. On the contrary, this "Little England of the Caribbean" seems to have many charms and the Bajans I have met are fine people. The problem is that its location so far to the east of the island chain makes for a hard sail against wind and current from almost anywhere in the Caribbean.

11

Staying in touch

VHF radio nets—a treasure from the bilge

Cruisers gathering for any length of time set up local VHF radio nets for social and sailing news. The two main VHF radio nets, those of Trinidad and St Martin, reflect two features: the long term stay of many yachts and the willingness of U.S. sailors in particular to set up and maintain networks. The nets introduce yachts to one another and cover social events, security matters, weather and tides. They manage some very useful services, such as the gas run to re-fill bottles, link those who have "treasures from the bilge" to buy, sell or give away, and provide a link into the local island community. This link can be a "what's on" catalog of cultural events which yachties might wish to attend, or a helpline through which yachts can provide equipment, clothing or expertise to the local community.

The Trinidad net goes out on channel 68 at 08.00 every day. The St Martin net goes out on channel 14 at 07.30. In the island chain the main calling channel is 68 and channel 16 is only for emergencies. Switch to a working channel as soon as contact is made.

The Trinidad net is run by yachties, a small nucleus managing it and a wider group taking part in the daily running. The St Martin net is run each day by Pastor Tom. The Trinidad net is more extensive, perhaps because the yachting community is so involved in it and perhaps too because Trinidad has such a tight concentration of yachts around Chaguaramas. This focus around the major yards in Chaguaramas enables a wide range of cultural, social and tourist activities to be promoted.

SSB—a fine net to be caught in

SSB is the best way of staying in touch with other yachts over the whole cruising area. It is a very imperfect form of communication but most live-aboards will get round to having an SSB transceiver eventually, as they become aware of how much social life they are missing by not being able to meet up with cruising friends.

One snag to SSB is that weather and astrological conditions affect the distance the signal can travel. This is random and unpredictable. On almost all SSB nets, some stations will be inaudible and on some nets on some days all stations will be inaudible. You have to hope that the main actors in the nets you depend on, such as George, Alex and

Eric for the weather, will come through. George and the Caribbean weather net usually send very strong signals, but at the worst the weather report is not usually a matter of life and death.

Weather nets are a bit like buses. There will be another one along soon. This is not the case for one-to-one arrangements between sailing boats. The unpredictable effect of astrological conditions on signals means that it can be chancy to set schedules to contact others without making allowance for the failure to get through. People get anxious if they don't hear from you at the pre-arranged time. Even other sailors can forget how yachts are subject to all sorts of unplanned events that can throw schedules off track. A few days of unexpected silence is sometimes enough to set in motion thoughts of a search and rescue operation.

Another snag to SSB is that it can also raise anxieties in other ways. It is a fine way to pick up and pass on opinions, good or bad, accurate or not. In this, of course, it is no different from the VHF nets except that it broadcasts these over a wider distance. With VHF nets your proximity to the matter being opinioned might encourage you to make your own judgements, whereas with SSB you might pass an off-the-top opinion just to have something to say. With SSB and VHF, even more than when you are sitting in a bar, you never know who is listening and who you might influence or offend. The word travels far. Best if it is a good word, and accurate.

Coffee and cookies—finger-licking email cafes

Things are changing fast with cell phones in the Caribbean and it may be that by the time you get there you will find an affordable network covering all the islands you want to visit. At the moment there are still glitches in the coverage and connectivity of the main players—Digicell and Cable & Wireless—although competition between them is heating up. If you only want to visit one island then you should get a local SIM card for your own cell phone. Till then, you have public call boxes and email.

Email is surely the now and future communication method of choice for cruising yachties. It is independent of geography and time zones, cheap, and readily available through Internet cafes. These cafes exist in the most unlikely places and if you can't find one in the boatyard, the marina, the beach or on the street, ask in a hotel. Hoary-headed old salts, who a decade ago might have regarded computers as instruments of the devil, have become email junkies since cruising into the Caribbean. Some even manage their finances this way.

The onboard way to go for cruising email must be the satellite mobile telephone but prices have yet to fall low enough to come within my budget or that of many of my cruising friends.

Surely this will happen soon, on the back of all the technological wizardry of land-based mobiles. Until then the best onboard alternative for most cruisers is a radio modem linked to an SSB transceiver and run through a computer. One popular modem, the Pactor, costs between U.S. $500 and U.S. $600. Different software exists with different access rules, usually depending on whether you have a full SSB license or not.

Probably the most used SSB email service provider in the Caribbean is Sailmail, a not-for profit organization based in the U.S. and run by yachtsmen. Sailmail has a global network of about 20 stations. Choose the nearest, but emails can be received and sent by any station. Sailmail uses the Airmail3 program developed specifically for the Pactor modem. If you link a GPS to Airmail3 the program will work out the best frequency to reach a Sailmail station from your current position. Sailmail, though, is not a web browser when used through SSB. It is limited to transmitting text.

The popularity of SSB email, not to mention the casual use of SSB and VHF, has led to requests for yachties to behave themselves—not to transmit Pactor email or have extended SSB conversations from 06.30 to 09.30 Caribbean time. High powered SSB transceivers can disrupt broadband reception on all HF and some VHF and MF frequencies throughout the region, and this period of the morning is the main time for government and weather services and local cruiser nets.

Sailing newspapers

Caribbean Compass is a monthly paper published in Bequia and distributed throughout the Caribbean with local and sailing news; regular columnists; features on places to visit in the region, local history or culture and characters in the yachting scene, often by sailors themselves; book and art reviews; calendar of coming events; readers' letters; technical reports on sailing equipment; classified advertisements and advertisements from a wide range of yachting and non-yachting but relevant businesses. Some of the best sailing authors in the region are contributors. A good read and a very good introduction to sailing, walking and site-seeing in the area and always useful when actually in the Caribbean. I have *Caribbean Compass* to thank for some of the photos in this edition. Subscriptions mailed anywhere in the world. Website on www. caribbeancompass.com

All at Sea, a monthly paper out of St Martin, Anguilla and Tortola, with distributors from the BVI to Curaçao, has a focus on the Virgins and northern islands in the chain although it has features on all the main islands. Good range of articles but greater emphasis on racing than cruising. Good technical reports on services and equipment and on newly opened yachting businesses. Classified advertisements and large scale advertisements from yachting businesses. After 10 years in the Caribbean *All at Sea* has started a U.K. version.

Security—lock it or lose it

I started cruising in the Caribbean long after the days when yachts were few and far between and locals lived on cash crops like cocoa and bananas rather than tourism, but even so life was much simpler then than now and I thought nothing of leaving my hatches open at night and the dinghy hanging off a painter from the stern. Those days are gone from here and probably from almost everywhere else in the world. The more we recognize this, the better we can cope with it and find enjoyment in our cruising.

If you come from a country where crime is a major concern, then wherever you go in the world the concern about crime and security will travel with you, locked into your mental maps. I don't think crime is prevalent in the islands, except those I have mentioned in the Island Guides, although many anchorages have started to run coast guard and police night patrols to counter crime and ease the minds of yachties. Security is certainly a major fear among yachties.

> We don't have good facts on crime in the region but the perception among visiting sailors is that yacht related crime here is on the rise. With cruisers, perception often becomes reality.

I can't imagine that crime is any worse here than back home in Europe or the U.S. Indeed, quite the opposite. I would stick my neck out and say that the islands are generally safe but subject to isolated and occasionally very nasty incidents like anywhere else. But people everywhere love to swap tales of crime and small boat sailors have the inclination and with VHF and SSB they have the technology to embellish and broadcast. I have heard many stories of robbery and attack. I have read them in local sailing newspapers and heard them on the SSB; and the following day I have heard "eye witnesses at the scene of the horrific and bloody crime" say that nothing at all occurred to the so-called victim. I only know a couple of cruisers who I can say for certain experienced it. Local newspapers, of course, are full of stories about violent crime. In this they are no different from newspapers the whole world over.

Yachts are vulnerable places of course and the great fear of most people must be a robbery while they are onboard. What to do? The options for fight and flight are less clearly available. What if the burglar is armed? What if the burglar is a psychopath? What if the burglar is eight feet tall and has red eyes that light up? What if your imagination is running out of control? What if you have seen too many Dennis Hopper movies?

Casual robbery is probably not the worst fear. Yachts have their own special problem: piracy. The individual may feel able to cope with the domesticity of a burglar but piracy is a quantum leap from this. The event is potentially deadly wherever it occurs but the extra twist is that it may occur in what till that moment has seemed like a welcoming paradise, and catches you all unawares. Most cases of piracy seem to be around the mainland of Venezuela and Colombia, where extreme poverty, drug trafficking and lack of policing combine. These pirates have usually stayed close to their coasts but in 2009 the sailing community was rocked to hear of Venezuelan pirates shooting at and boarding a yacht 40 miles north of Trinidad on its way to Grenada. This wasn't the first Venezuelan pirate attempt in this area but it was the first time a yacht was boarded and robbed. It sent a shiver down the spines of those of us who regularly come this way.

Piracy is a scary subject. It certainly scares me. Perhaps it is a sign of the times that Klaus Hympendahl has written *Pirates Aboard* based on interviews with 40 sailors who suffered pirate attack. The sub title is "What bluewater cruisers can do about it." Well, that's a good question. *Piracy Today* by John C. Payne, while covering general piracy in today's news, also looks at what yachts should do to protect themselves.

Of course most Venezuelan boats between Trinidad and Grenada are there for legitimate reasons. It's the others you have to worry about. The government of Trinidad & Tobago has equipped itself to improve our security in these waters. They have state of the art radar and the Coast Guard upgraded from 10 meter interceptor boats to 40 meter rig supply vessels equipped for military purposes. In 2010 they equipped themselves with six new 60 meter fast patrol vessels and in 2011 will take delivery of three 90 meter offshore patrol vessels capable of carrying an interceptor and a helicopter.

Drug trafficking is such a concern that, although you may never see them, the U.S. and Britain, to name but two maritime nations, put frigates and other warships on patrol here to intercept drug runners.

There is a more local form of drug-related obstacle that we sailors might stumble across. Most of us like to stretch our legs and see the countryside when we visit these islands. Beware the ganja farmer. Often the beautiful hillside walks share their space with ganja crops. It doesn't just happen in the Caribbean, but it certainly does happen here. In some islands where cocoa and coffee are now failed crops or the legitimate banana crop has been battered by hurricanes and squeezed out of markets by U.S. and European protection policies, or where poverty is endemic and made all the harder to bear by extreme income inequalities, ganja is one way to scratch a livelihood from the land. In my innocence I cheerfully took a long walk around the stunning high hills of the very poor island of Union, only to be told later that I might have walked into places where I wouldn't have been welcome. Actually, I had and I had greeted and chatted with the people I met there who were, admittedly, surprised to see me but whose natural Caribbean charm overcame any tendency to knock me on the head. You don't have to be as foolishly innocent as me but you don't have to forego a hill walk either. Find a local guide. You might even get a guided tour of a farm that no agricultural official has ever seen.

A Customs officer on St Vincent explained that after a ganja crop is sold it is three months before the next harvest. If the farmer is broke in that time he may need to steal a little to get by and yachts are a natural target. This is the classic tourism dilemma of locals with very little rubbing up against visitors of apparently unlimited wealth. And we yachties do appear to be stunningly wealthy. What happens may only turn out to be a minor and unprovoked crime, although no one likes to be the victim of crime. More serious crimes against yachties can happen when a sailor's drug deal ashore goes wrong, in which case it is best not to blame the locals.

Casual robberies usually involve the theft of outboard engines and dinghies. Of course, these have to be left in all sorts of public places with relatively inadequate locks and chains, and their value, the relative ease of stealing and disposing of them, must be a temptation to impoverished locals and yachties alike. In some anchorages all the time, and in other anchorages some of the time, dinghies should be hoisted out of the water for the night to discourage theft. In St Martin, for example, dinghy theft can become a major problem around carnival time. We heard that in one year 19 dinghies were stolen in a two-day period. Some thefts were a bit of a double whammy: the dinghies were actually stolen while their owners had gone aboard another yacht to help them recover their stolen dinghy.

G and I became thieves by accident. We found the RIB drifting a few miles west of St Barts as we were hurrying south to Trinidad for hurricane season and rescued it. We didn't know that a local coast guard had spotted us and called the owner, a charter company in the BVI whose name was stencilled in huge letters on the RIB, to say he had seen their dinghy being stolen. We couldn't sail hard enough to windward to make Antigua as planned so we diverted to St Kitts to find a pay phone. We were hoping to drop the RIB off rather than tow it hundreds of miles. We left a message on their answering machine and our next chance to call them was Dominica where we again diverted just to find a phone. I was annoyed when accused of theft and threatened to cast the RIB adrift but was persuaded to tow it to Grenada where their agent would collect it. We hung around Grenada and nearly missed our wind for Trinidad because their agent didn't show. In Trinidad, now booked on a plane home and with the clock ticking, we were assured that the man from the BVI himself would himself collect the RIB as part of a delivery he was making from Trinidad to Tortola. When we called the day before our flight we were told he was in Venezuela on urgent business. We hauled the RIB out, laid it under *Petronella* and put the outboard in storage. We didn't bother even tying the RIB with a line. We were fed up with it and hoped it would be gone, legitimately or otherwise, before we returned. Clearly the charter company had reported the loss as a theft and bought a new one with their claim money. Now here's the thing. It was still under *Petronella* when we came back. You can't rely on a dinghy thief when you want one.

Most yachties speak as though the thieves are inevitably locals. This is not the conclusion I naturally jump to. The people with most need of a good dinghy are other yachties and being a fellow sailor is no guarantee of honesty. A yacht with a stolen dinghy is invisible, but most locals running around with a yacht tender would stand out. Some "thefts" may not be about intent to permanently deprive. Callow youth on the way home and having missed the skipper's shore run may be tempted to borrow a handy dinghy. Some thefts may not involve another person at all. Even the most experienced old salt may tie a bad knot and blame theft rather than carelessness. It can happen.

The problem with crime when it is essentially random like this is that the experience of others and their advice are largely obsolete. Where there is a spate of robberies or attacks then action can be taken. Places can be avoided. But here, when spates occur in the smaller islands of the chain, they are often the work of a specific bunch of baddies, and sooner rather than later these people get caught or discouraged. In the meanwhile, listen out for warnings of these events and treat more random, individual events as remote and usually unrepeated.

What should we do ourselves about the possibility of being attacked or the fear of crime? A few years ago *Caribbean Compass* put together some responses from cruisers. The theme of "I'm not going there" was clear and came at three levels:

I'm not sailing south to Trinidad, clearly pinning the label Crime Center on that lovely island;

We're not sailing further than Guadeloupe or Martinique because of "the crime problem farther south," which is a bit like not sailing in the real Caribbean at all;

and

We've decided to abandon the whole Caribbean, not for the levels of crime themselves but because the governments and police are not protecting us cruisers. Which seems to be missing out on a lot just to make a gesture to some authorities whom you have no respect for anyway.

There was a fourth level, that of wondering whether it's time to give up cruising entirely if we have to lock ourselves behind bars at night, but that might just have been ironic.

It seems to me that every government in the island chain has embraced the need to make cruisers feel and be more secure. I can welcome that though at the same time it doesn't make me feel much better and I suggest that you don't grow over dependent on claims by officialdom or members of the industry whose agenda might only be to sweep a bad image under the carpet. Of course, some of the advice put out by officials is to the point, as is the advice frequently printed in *Caribbean Compass* and on the website of the Caribbean Safety and Security Net.

The Caribbean SSB Security Net takes place daily on frequency 8104 from 08.15 to 08.30. The net was begun by Frank Zachar on *Vagabond Tiger* in 1996, later taken on by Donald Kline on *Daisy S* and now by Melodyne Pompa on *Second Millennium*. Melodyne runs a tight net. First comes emergency and priority traffic, then such matters as missing vessels or people, crime and safety. Between topics she slots in some news of her own. When someone makes a report Melodyne reiterates the key facts, tells the person how to reach local associations for more details and, if appropriate, advises on a safer place to anchor. At the end of the net she signs off with the catchy "lock it or lose it." Well, perhaps you can't argue with that, but perhaps you don't want to let it build up to paranoia either. You can contact the net at www.caribcruisers.com.

Should the moment come when you need to call the police, their emergency number in the ex-British islands is 999, 12 for islands in the European Union, and in the Virgins you can use both 999 and 911. VHF channel 16 is usually monitored by officials and you would soon be in touch with the police. As well as your official report, let the local yachting association know of any incident too.

Wyatt Earp and Doc Holiday—not OK in this corral

Carrying firearms is not for the faint hearted. If you wave a gun at the wrong person you may find it doesn't protect you in the least, and that you are the one who gets shot. If you show the gun, you have to use it, and some say you have to aim to kill rather than to scare. This seems to me like a human tragedy in the making, with all the scope for one enormous and terminal error. Several sailors have been killed waving their guns at the bad guys and I doubt you could ever guarantee to be ahead in the arms race with pirates. Worse though, what if word got out that cruising yachts were a good source of weapons. Our boats might all be seeing much more of criminals in need of another gun. I think that sober, non-prejudicial and ad hoc judgement of the threat is likely to be a better way, on average, of dealing with events.

Firearms are not allowed ashore in any of the islands in the Caribbean. All islands require that guns must be declared, logged and locked up aboard, and some islands will impound them. This is not just an administrative nuisance but rather defeats the object of having a gun unless your main aim is to have a go against Kalashnikov-toting offshore pirates. As a result of this strictness most cruisers believe that U.S. sailors prefer not to formally trouble the authorities about their onboard arsenals. This isn't to say that European sailors are any less security minded, only that Americans and Europeans sometimes seem to have different attitudes to firearms.

12

Health and hazards

Sailing is a healthy life, in the main. Below are the health issues and hazards particularly relevant when sailing in the tropics. Sailors are all also likely to encounter the other health issues and hazards of the tropics but I shall leave those to other reference books.

Dehydration

Dehydration can hit us for many reasons in the tropics; just by sailing during the day or working in the boatyard, even if we haven't suffered sunstroke. And then there are all the little bugs that cause sickness and diarrhea and drain us of liquid. Take care and watch out for the symptoms.

The natural and best answer to dehydration is coconut water, available in most islands from nut sellers or in bottles. Ask for green water nuts for just water, soft jelly for water and a skim of coconut meat to eat afterwards, and hard jelly for an older nut with the sweetest milk.

Coconuts are a well recognized source of good liquid throughout the tropical regions. The milk is usually sterile and can be drunk copiously or even taken subcutaneously, intramuscularly, and intravenously. It has the correct electrolyte balance to rehydrate us. Local doctors recommended it to Caribbean mothers to rehydrate babies and children suffering gastroenteritis. This is especially helpful for those living in remote places or unable to afford expensive Pedialyte (the modern chemical solution available in pharmacies). It can replace glucose or artificial saline solutions.

Of special interest to sailors is the reference to Paul-Henri Petard's doctoral thesis on Polynesian plants in Bernard Moitessier's sailing masterpiece, *The Long Way*. On some Polynesian islands, coconut water takes the place of rain water when the cisterns run dry. It's also popular in the Caribbean when mixed with rum.

Sunburn

The tropical sun is immensely powerful and damaging. Don't trifle with it. Use high factor sun protection when your skin is exposed and cover up as much as you can when sailing. The glare from the sea and beaches is painful and the strong UV can cause permanent damage, especially to light colored eyes. G favors hats and glasses. I wear white cotton painter's overalls.

Mosquitoes and Dengue Fever

Mosquitoes cause illness in 97 million people each year and are the major cause of death in the Tropics, so the World Health Organization says. Malaria-carrying mosquitoes exist on the South American mainland and Hispaniola. They do not fly over to the island chain. Any malaria here is confined to travelers infected abroad. However, mosquitoes are always a nuisance wherever you find them and I personally cannot sleep after I have heard their penetrating whine. G and I use repellent, especially on ankles and wrists, and put in mosquito screens at dusk when ashore or close to land, and have net screens in all our deck vents. We also entertain ourselves with a battery-operated death-bat, somewhat like a tennis racket, that electrocutes the mosquito. Every so often if we have been bothered by mosquitoes we spray the boat, especially the dark and dank places like the engine room and bilges.

The worst mosquito-borne illness in the Caribbean is Dengue Fever. This is a viral disease causing a severe flu-like illness. Dengue Fever is unpleasant in all its four forms—wittily known to medical science as A, B, C and D. It starts suddenly with a high fever, rash, severe headache, pain behind the eyes, and muscle and joint pain. High temperature and severe body pain lasts one or two weeks, loss of appetite lasts about three weeks. There is no specific treatment—just painkillers and rest. G tells me you should avoid aspirin as a painkiller in case you have the most serious and unpleasant of the four types, the potentially lethal hemorrhagic type where blood vessels are leaking. Aspirin could cause massive problems and internal hemorrhaging resulting in death.

G had Dengue Fever in Trinidad at the time of the Jamaat-al-Muslimeen coup of 1990. They call it break-bone fever in Trinidad, because the pain in the bones is so bad. Other symptoms include severe headaches, acute pain in the eyes, fever and shivering. G couldn't bear light. As the fever leaves the body a fine rash may cover the torso. G had no treatment. The body has to get over the fever itself. Full recovery may be delayed by fatigue, loss of appetite and depression.

In the Caribbean Dengue Fever is transmitted by the *Aedes aegypti*, a small mosquito with distinctive black and white markings on its legs. This is a clever little devil. Not only does it have the random flight pattern of other hard-to-hit mosquitoes but evolution has made it a specialist at attacking in shadow, so that it comes at you from the rear, low down, to bite the unseen parts of your ankles and wrists. It also, unlike most other mosquitoes, bites during the day. As with malaria-infected mosquitoes, it is the female seeking blood to fuel her breeding which bites us and injects us with her saliva to stop our blood coagulating while she gets her meal. Dengue spreads rapidly, often occurring in epidemics. A mosquito bites an infected human, picks up infected blood and over the next 15 to 65 days of her life passes the fever on to the other people she bites. Dengue Fever is not transmitted directly from person-to-person.

Unlike most mosquitoes, which are happy to breed in dirty stagnant water, the Aedes aegypti needs clean, still water for its larvae. When you are in a boatyard for any length of time, take care not to let water stand in tarpaulins or tires or other potential receptacles, not even the barrel you laboriously filled to run fresh water through your outboard engine, since you will unwittingly be farming mosquitoes in general and Aedes aegypti in particular.

Having Dengue Fever once doesn't bestow immunity. One type confers no immunity from the three others, although of course you can have more than one type at the same time. Horrific. Also any immunity from the type you had wears off after about ten years. Repeat infections become more serious, even lethal. Best advice: don't get bitten.

Sand flies

Mosquito bites may carry a greater risk but they don't bother me half as much as those of sand flies. Called "no see' ums" in some places, sand flies are tiny creatures with a big and irritating bite.

They are most prevalent in the wet season. G says that a sand fly bite has the ability to reactivate its irritating itch 24 hours later for several days in a row. I don't know about that, but come 7 pm the itch starts up even though we are well out of range of sand flies. If they are around, wear socks and repellent in the evenings. Ointments from pharmacies can relieve the itch.

Snakes and other biters

If really unlucky you might get bitten by a poisonous snake, or a spider, centipede, scorpion or sea creature like a spined fish or sea urchin. Some books suggest you try—within limits, ha ha—to catch the beast for later identification. The intense pain from a fish spine can sometimes be lessened by immersion in very hot water, without scalding yourself of course. Don't try to dig out sea urchin spines. This only causes infection. The spines usually dissolve away when left but you can hurry matters along by soaking them in vinegar.

The reactions to poisonous snake bites are likely to be fright, local swelling and pain, sore lymph glands, vomiting and fever. If the bitten person has numbness, tingling of the face, muscular spasms, convulsions, shortness of breath and hemorrhage, get them to medical help immediately. Serums will be available at local hospitals. These usually need to be injected and this takes more practice than you or I may have. To stop the poison spreading keep the patient still and, if the bite is on a limb, immobilize the limb and put a tight bandage or tourniquet between the bite and the body. Release this for a minute or two every 15 minutes to allow blood flow. Death is very rare, so don't let the patient panic and don't do what Hollywood heroes do—cut the bite to suck out the venom. This usually does more harm than good.

Poisonous snakes are only found on a few islands. Pit vipers (the *fer de lance* on French islands and the *mapepire* in Trinidad, pronounced *mapa-pee*), are found on St Lucia, Martinique, and Trinidad. Trinidad has four species of venomous snakes, including the unpleasant coral snake. The largest of its mapepires is the bushmaster. Fortunately most snakes are shy of humans, but this won't help you if you stumble on one that isn't. Locals say that pit vipers don't like the smell of sulphur, so that anchorages like Soufrière on St Lucia should be free of them.

The majestic and non-poisonous boa constrictors, mostly found in Trinidad, are snakes of the mangroves and swamps. We saw a long rainbow boa hanging from a branch one day as we were taking a trip through Caroni Swamp in Trinidad. G tells me they can just drop down onto you. Well, there you go.

Don't bite the bad apple—manchineel trees

These dangerous trees are found along the beaches of the Caribbean. They are tempting shade trees, attractive, with a small greeny/yellow apple-type fruit but these apples and the sap are heavily toxic. Eating the apples can cause death. Avoid them. Only land crabs are immune to their poison.

Some of the men who sailed with Christopher Columbus on his second voyage were rash enough to try these apples while testing other strange fruits in these new worlds they were discovering.

> "No sooner did they taste them than their faces swelled, growing so inflamed and painful that they almost went out of their minds. They cured themselves with cold compresses."
>
> Letter by Dr Chanca, physician to the fleet of Christopher Columbus on his second voyage of discovery, writing to the city of Seville, 1494.

Sap in the eyes can cause acute pain and temporary blindness at least. Brushing against the leaves or just being dripped on while sheltering from the rain can cause burning and bad skin rashes. The Carib Indians poisoned their arrows by dipping the tips into holes in the trunks of the manchineel tree.

On some islands manchineel trees have a red stripe painted on their trunk. On the French islands it is not unusual for them to have notices with the international skull and crossbone warning for danger nailed to them.

So that's gravity—falling nuts

It may seem like stating the obvious but dry coconuts and those big palm fronds do fall to earth and it's best if your head isn't in the way.

Poisoned fish—don't smoke the ciguatera

Many sailors like fishing and eating fish. They should beware the local danger of ciguatera. In parts of the Caribbean, most commonly in the north, from Montserrat to the Virgins, a toxic single-celled, free-swimming organism called *Gambierdiscus toxicus microscopic* is eaten by reef fish and travels up the food chain through predatory fish and so to man, causing the bizarre and uncomfortable set of symptoms known as ciguatera. The fish, although host to the toxins, are not ill. In man, ciguatera's symptoms are painful and disabling. Common symptoms are extreme exhaustion accompanied by pain and difficulty in breathing. Some suffer a reversal of the sensations of hot and cold. Death can occur. Ciguatoxins accumulate, and individuals who have been previously exposed react at lower levels and experience more severe symptoms.

Conditions in some localities support a continuous population of these micro organisms and so produce more ciguatoxin-bearing fish than other areas. Storm surges, careless development or other disturbances to a reef can also cause the organisms to spread rapidly.

The worst places for contaminated fish are north of Martinique:
- near Redonda;
- between the Saba Bank and the Anguilla Bank.

Because the toxin accumulates in the body of the fish, large, potentially ciguatoxic fish such as barracuda may carry high concentrations of the toxin even in areas where ciguatera is rare.

Nearly 100 villagers from Owia near Georgetown, St Vincent needed hospital treatment in late 1985 after eating meat from the same 30lb barracuda. Numerous cats, dogs and chickens died after eating scraps. Cooking does not destroy the toxins.

Now you can find out in advance if the fish coming to your plate will poison you. Drop a sample of the fish into a Cigua-Check vial from Oceanic Test Systems of Hawaii and within the hour you'll get the answer. Better than using your pet cat or dog.

Fish are biting

Beware, it isn't just the bait that gets bitten. Fishing in the Caribbean is about trying to catch some pretty sizeable game fish, and sometimes these fish re-write the rules and bite the hand that is feeding them. Or, in our friend's case, the toe.

Ray is one of the keenest and most experienced game fishermen I have ever met. He does it for pleasure, not for a living, but he is off in his boat just about every weekend. He was obviously having a good day, hauling fish in one after the other, and didn't notice the big wahoo on deck was looking to get its own back on someone. Anyway, it bit Ray through his boot and took a chunk off one of Ray's toes. He said you don't realize how much you need toes till you lose part of one.

Jolly jelly fish

In the right season, jelly fish can take over a patch of sea. Beware of their stings, especially the Portuguese Man-o-War. They can give you a paralyzing shock. In the BVI, which is one of the few places to have a lifeboat service, many emergency calls are for people suffering jelly fish stings. Usually rubbing with vinegar neutralizes the sting and antihistamine cream does the rest. G tells me that if you haven't got this to hand, urinate on the sting.

Lionfish

Here is a fun little creature you may not have heard of. Native to the Pacific, new to the Caribbean but expanding their numbers rapidly, lionfish are voracious feeders on other fish, reproduce rapidly, and are very easy to spot. They can grow up to 55cm long and have long separated spines and are striped red, green, brown, orange, yellow, black, maroon, or white. They are not aggressive towards us but they have a very painful sting. It may be an exaggeration but some claim this could be the worst ecological disaster the world has ever experienced. You can do your bit to reduce the scale of this potential plague of fish by eating them.

The Reef Environmental Education Foundation have published *The Lionfish Cookbook*, a collection of 45 recipes to encourage the consumption of these invaders. Lionfish have a delicate, mild-flavored, white meat.

Coral scratches

Something in coral makes scratches become painfully infected. As soon as you are able, scrub with soap and fresh water. Fire coral (bright orange) is virulent and can leave a permanent scar.

Cockroaches and their friends

OK, so no one ever died from a cockroach bite, but I find cockroaches horrible, though not harmful and I don't want them on board. It is too difficult to get rid of them and too easy to turn into a roach farm. They say here that if you see one you have a hundred on board. We have been lucky. In eight years we have never been infested, and by magnificent vigilance always managed to eradicate the few who strayed on board.

As they are flying insects, it is always possible for a cockroach to find its way on board, but the ones most likely to fly in under their own power are the big ones, and therefore the most obvious to see and stand on. More of a problem are the little ones called German Roaches locally. They and their eggs can be brought aboard in cardboard, so we never allow any packaging to come aboard. When we leave the boat on the hard we cover all deck and hull outlets and vents. We use sprays and plastic traps known as "roach hotels." Boric acid powder can also be laid down to kill roaches and their nests.

> We have found roaches on board and don't like it. We think they are the German sort but so far
> we haven't seen them beyond the immature stage. We don't want them to get to breeding age.
> Every time we pass the galley at night we pick up a shoe and then flash a light at the counter. We
> know their habits now. They must be hard-wired to all behave in the same way. Hitting the spot
> just ahead of their run gets a better score than trying to hit the beast itself. The first blow usually
> slows them down and we whack them a second blow for sure.

Keep a clean boat and be fiercely diligent. It is always possible for a roach to board you. Don't leave it for a moment or you will certainly become infested.

Hospitals and health centers

Public and private health services are available on all the islands except perhaps the smaller ones in the Grenadines. Facilities range from local doctors' surgeries through clinics to fully blown modern hospitals. We have some direct experience of Trinidad hospitals and emergency facilities and they have been first rate. We were very impressed with the large and modern looking University Hospital Center we saw on Guadeloupe, but fortunately had no need of its facilities. When problems struck we were in a more remote spot.

> We were anchored in Bequia when Rm showed us the huge swelling on his elbow. He had
> bashed it a day or so earlier and now a great dome of water rose from the joint, in a painful sort
> of way. Get it sorted, we all groaned, and he went off to the little health center up the back of
> town. The treatment was agonizing but immediate, the conditions were clean and sterile, and
> Rm had nothing but praise for the skills of the doctor. Rather him than me.

You will find well stocked pharmacies in all but the smallest islands and these are good places to get advice on medication.

The only dentist I have had to visit in the Caribbean was in Trinidad, at the Seventh Day Adventist Community Hospital, where I was treated by an American-trained "missionary dentist." The treatment was excellent. Private dentists are, of course, everywhere in the Caribbean but you should check their certification before opening wide.

13

Stretching your legs—best walks

One of the great joys of arriving at an island is the chance to go walking. Sailing is a great sport but it can leave the legs underused. The Caribbean islands offer rugged and breathtaking exercise as well as gentle strolls or educational field trips. Most islands have large areas protected as forest reserves. Here you will see the most wonderful birds, iguanas, lizards and unusual mammals, like the agouti.

Some of our favorite walks of all time came when exploring the islands. Since this is not a land-based book I should point you in the direction of one that is. *The Outdoor Traveller's Guide to the Caribbean* by Kay Showker, now 20 years old and covering more of the Caribbean than just the island chain, has a wealth of good walks and good advice on how to approach them. It is, of course, of greatest value in islands where tourism and other guide books are less developed. You will also find good island walks in *Caribbean Compass*, written by sailors for sailors.

Take maps and in some places take guides. Carry water. Start early to avoid the worst of the sun. Avoid walking in open country in the middle of the day. Make sure you are back before dark.

On some islands cruisers will arrange walks. This happened once while we were in Bequia and is a regular thing in Trinidad where cruisers arrange group walks in the forest, with guides and snake-men (snake experts who will spot the snake before it spots you). You will need clothing to keep the sun and other hazards off. Grass can cut badly and in some forests little beasts called chiggers can brush onto you and lay their eggs in your flesh, so you might want to take a pair of trousers, strong shoes, and socks to tuck trousers into, as well as shorts and sandals.

In the high lands of some islands you may need to keep to well marked trails or if you are going across unmarked country to take a local guide so that you avoid accidentally visiting a marijuana farm. St Vincent in particular.

Look for these routes as walks to try:
- Peter Island, BVI—round the island along the high ridge in about 5 miles.
- St Barts—along the track from Anse du Colombier to Flamand.
- Martinique—the marked coastal trail southwards from St Anne.

- Bequia—across from Admiralty Bay to Hope Bay.
- Mayreau—head north from the anchorage to the end of the island.
- Union—around the Pinnacle, the main peak. Nearly 1,000 feet high. You may need local advice to find the track.
- Carriacou—from Tyrell Bay to the southern end of the island, to see tomorrow's anchorage off the little islets.
- Guadeloupe—to the waterfalls.
- Grenada—from Prickly Bay to Secret Harbour and, for the adventurous, to Hog Island.
- Trinidad—the rugged north coast walk from Blanchisseuse to Paria waterfall.

Diving

The Caribbean has some of the best diving in the world, and diving is probably a sailor's second favorite recreation. The volcanic islands combined with the Equatorial Current makes for thrilling wall dives and drop offs. The water, of course, is wonderfully clear, and nature has planted dense and colorful underwater gardens of coral and sponge just for you. Most islands also have plenty of wrecks to dive on. Plenty of dive shops to go with. You will find diving everywhere—from historic wreck sites in the Virgins to the world class drift dives off Tobago.

Don't break the bank—taking care of coral

Coral reefs are a major part of the sailing experience in the Caribbean. They are the key habitats and nurseries for fish and shellfish, the main source of the white sand for the beautiful beaches and the essential line of protection for some of the most beautiful anchorages.

Reefs here may look pristine but coral reefs the world over are dying. The United Nations atlas of reefs attributes this to global warming and quotes a remarkably high rate of loss. During the El Niño year of 1998 the UN estimates that 5% of reefs throughout the world were killed. The Caribbean is part of this global change although many also believe that local conditions, such as run off from the land, the deforestation of South America, over-fishing and careless diving and reef boats, are in part to blame and if changed could help turn round the collapsing reef ecology. Algae has been spreading fast in the last few years and many dive sites report a small fraction of their previous corals. The hard corals have been particularly hit.

Check on arrival in a new island to see what protection schemes are in place and how this will affect your sailing. In Antigua, for example, visiting yachts have been banned from fishing for the last decade and if fishing gear is not stowed in a prescribed manner the skipper faces a fine or even imprisonment. More recently the Antiguan Fisheries Division have begun to enforce restrictions on spear fishing and coral diving, and plan to designate areas as marine parks with restrictions on anchoring and mooring.

Marine parks are on the rise in the Caribbean. It goes with the rise in yachting here and the general rise in concern for marine ecology. Sometimes it means that anchoring is banned in remote or sensitive areas. Sometimes but not always moorings are laid as an alternative. Most yachties don't object to this but sometimes the designation of an area as a marine park is done as a kind of unthinking official reaction without having investigated the nature or cause of the problem. For many years yachts were accused of lowering sea water quality around Buccoo Reef off Tobago but the problem was later traced to run-off from the land and hotel sewage. The knee-jerk blaming of yachts and restricting them would have failed to deal with this real and significant problem. It was also a source of avoidable tension between locals and yachties. Laying moorings may seem like an obvious and simple solution to sea bed damage but moorings can be even more intrusive than anchors and come with their own set of problems. Marine parks don't usually have insurance for moorings they lay and nor do they always have a program for checking the ground tackle. Yachts have been reported as going adrift on broken moorings.

A recent project is to see whether fragments of living coral broken off by storms can be transplanted to help speed the recovery of other colonies. The Coral Preservation Project funded by the U.S. Geological Survey are looking into the benefits of transplants on existing communities. Applied Marine Technologies in Dominica is taking living coral from the reefs and breeding new populations in special tanks. The starter coral is attached to a fiberglass stand which, when the coral is established, will be screwed back into the ocean rock.

Whale of a time

We love seeing dolphin. But to see a whale is on a different scale. Humpback whales come into the island chain from January to June to breed, before returning north. We have seen them off Guadeloupe and Martinique and they go right down to Trinidad but the main area is reckoned to be in the north, from Anguilla to St Martin and into the Virgins. Don't chase after them. Watch them from a distance. You can't keep up with them even if you tried—they cruise at six to nine knots and can sprint at anything from 20 to 35 knots—but chasing may stress and tire the whales who often have calves with them.

Humpbacks are probably the whales you will see most but Bryde's whales are in these waters all year round, presumably because they can always find their food in warm tropical waters. They are like the sei or fin whales found in the northern Caribbean and the Gulf of Mexico, but smaller. They can grow to 50 feet and up to 30 metric tons. Grey, sometimes mottled with a prominent sickle-shaped dorsal fin. Usually seen in small family groups.

Turning turtle

The Caribbean is where the huge leather-back turtles come to lay their eggs. These are huge animals, traveling the Atlantic Ocean in a wide circuit until they come back to the Caribbean islands to lay eggs where they were born. The turtles need a particular sort of beach, one with coarse sand and which has been given a steep rise above sea level by the incessant surf. The females laboriously haul themselves up the rise, create a shallow indentation and lay their eggs. Weeks later, if dog and man haven't got there first, the baby turtles emerge and run to the sea. In this brief sprint they imprint the beach on their memory. Don't think of giving them a helping hand. It just makes them confused in later life.

The laying season runs from spring into summer and this is when you will most likely see these huge creatures out at sea. But you can also visit the laying beaches and watch for yourself. Only do this where there are locals to protect the turtles and show you how not to disturb them. Turtles navigate back to the sea by the moon and are confused by flashlights. Trinidad's north coast is one of the main turtle watching sites in the region.

14

In your own wake

Staying on

You will realize when you sail here that many yachts came for a season and stayed for many more. This is not only the best sailing you've probably ever had, it is also a region that takes time to discover fully. Also, you can't be in two places at once even if it would double your pleasures. One year in Trinidad for Carnival, another in The Saintes. One year in Antigua for Race Week, another somewhere else for a jazz festival.

You may, then, want to leave your boat in the region so that you can return to it for another season, without the hassle of sailing it a thousand miles or three in the meanwhile. Many of the islands provide services for boats being left in the area. Hard standing is probably your most basic need, although we once left *Petronella* on a mooring buoy in Le Marin for three months while we went home. It was cheaper and more convenient than hauling out and we carefully chose our spot to give us good shelter and proximity to the mangroves. Hard standing and haul-out facilities are available in almost all the primary anchorages identified in this book and the boatyards will provide other services, such as absentee management if you need this, repairs and supply of spare parts, secure dry storage for equipment.

Let us assume that you will find everything you need to leave your boat here, with or without you on board. You can plan, even before you leave home, the timing of how and where to take an extended cruise around the islands. It is time enough when you get here to start sorting out how to put this into practice. Visit islands, talk to sailors, and read *Caribbean Compass* and *All at Sea* to get right up to date with what is on offer.

Fitting out for the Tropics

Boats coming down from the U.S. seem to be larger and better equipped to handle the Tropics than boats from Europe. It is not uncommon to see European sailors changing up to a larger boat once they have reached the Caribbean. Boats that competently crossed the ocean are not necessarily comfortable in the Trade Winds and Tropics. Hulls need to be powerful to punch through or ride over the boisterous waves. Accommodation needs to be spacious and airy to cope with the heat below decks. The trick is to get these design features without adding to the complexity of the living systems. The paramount rule of living aboard also applies in the Tropics: keep it simple. Too many boats bolster their living systems with mechanical and electrical systems paralleling life ashore, and then spend more time fixing things than sailing. Fixing things gets harder the more remote and beautiful the cruising ground, in an exponential sort of way.

One fundamental redesign may be worth pursuing. It is a great regret to me that I have a boat with west-going tendencies. On any passage between islands, when the wind demands us to be close hauled she will put us down to the west whatever we do. I don't understand this, naturally, but I think a boat with east-going tendencies would be more convenient in the Caribbean. There must be some American boatyard with the secret of tuning a strong eastgoing tendency into hulls. Get your boat modified in whatever way will achieve this before coming down here.

Apart from that kind of major hi-tech only-possible-in-the-U.S. sort of work, assume that most things you need will be available here and that some of the really specialist gear you need for the tropics is best when designed and made in the tropics.

The designs I have seen in Trinidad for high-efficiency wind generators and low-energy refrigerator units seem more suited to the hot and windy tropics than the gear out of Europe and the U.S. Wait till you get here, if you can.

I am beginning to covet a watermaker because of my growing sense that a man of my age shouldn't be carrying water containers at all, but especially the ones I carried so effortlessly in my prime of only a few years ago. The problem is not only that they have become too heavy for me but that I feel embarrassed walking alongside G when she is carrying them for me. Watermakers are expensive and use lots of electricity but the ECH2O Tec design by Echo Marine in Trinidad has become almost a by-word for efficiency and reliability and is increasingly being seen at European boat shows. I have also seen a very different watermaker here which works by being towed off the back of a boat. Now there's an ideal way to slow the boat down in these over-boisterous Trade Winds.

Much of the innovation in these types of equipment comes from American or European sailors now basing themselves in the Caribbean. They have that great blend of hi-tech knowledge with years of sailing experience, and by being new businesses are more likely to be at the cutting edge of design.

For some sailors fitting out a boat from a catalog is too easy, and too extravagant. You will need many things for comfortable living in the Tropics, but you won't really know which till you have been here for a while. You will, of course, have all the usual gear on board and thought about lots of things you don't have. Here is my little list of things you might not have thought about before and some hints on how to get them.

Shopping and sailing

I am not one of nature's shoppers. A few minutes after entering a clothes store or even a French supermarket I become fractious and have to be sent out. But once inside a chandlery or hardware shop I become a shop limpet, only fractious when forced to leave. This bizarre aspect of an otherwise conventional disposition may be cause or effect of the boats I choose to own. My present yacht is a classic but elderly lady of mixed provenance—a 40 foot Joshua built in France, fitted out in Germany, endlessly repaired in the Caribbean. Very little about her or her equipment is modern as that word is understood by yacht chandlers. I have learned to take parts in rather than give part numbers or descriptions, but even so the usual response is "I've never seen one of those before." As a result of this and previous boats I have owned, when it comes to knowing where good spares are to be found, I'm your man.

St Martin and Trinidad are probably the best locations for spares and services in the island chain, though for different reasons.

St Martin is the longer established yachting center of the two. It has built up a major yachting industry over the last couple of decades. It has all the big name chandleries, such as Budget Marine, as well as many smaller ones, giving it both range and depth. Alongside that, it has excellent hardware stores and specialist auto-parts and electrical stockists where you can find alternatives at land based prices. St Martin is duty free, so if you are buying expensive gear this could be the place. However, St Martin is not a cheap island and the saving in duty may not make enough difference.

Trinidad has sprouted chandlers in the last three or four years. The area around Chaguaramas now has large scale chandlers and many small specialists. Like St Martin, almost all chandlery is imported, mainly from the U.S., so what isn't on the shelf can usually be brought in for you. The small specialist suppliers are usually quicker at getting equipment for you. The bigger general chandlers may have what you need "in the container" ie already in transit as part of their periodic restocking. Containers often take longer to arrive or unpack than you or I might think expedient; and their contents often differ from the original order or the Customs' manifest. Guess whose bit of kit won't be on board?

Trinidad also has excellent hardware and specialist wholesalers and stores, mainly in the Port of Spain area and out along the highway from Port of Spain to the airport. This range of useful stores is what you might expect simply because Trinidad has a larger population and a more industrialized economy than most other islands.

European yachts may find themselves becoming confusingly schizophrenic if they stay too long, swapping their metric nuts and bolts for U.S. standard threads. They may also dislike paying U.S. prices, with added shipping costs. For European equipment or less standardized gear, or the occasional bargain, you might strike it lucky in the other islands.

The French islands of Martinique and Guadeloupe both have large numbers of yachts and support good chandleries. Much of this is from the major French manufacturers but you will also find equipment from Britain, Germany, Spain, The Netherlands and other European countries. Prices and currencies are European and seem not to be inflated by transportation costs. I found spares for my Irish-made Gusher pumps more cheaply in Martinique than I could in England.

On Martinique the two main locations for chandleries are Fort-de-France and Le Marin. The main Fort-de-France chandlery is near the harbor, by the cruise-ship terminal. The owner of the chandlery and his staff speak very friendly English and are well informed about equipment and where you may find what they don't stock.

Just round the headland of Fort St Louis and close to the yacht club, in a not very salubrious area, are specialist engineers, welders, GRP fabricators and other serious trades. You can also haul out here for work to be done on the hull.

Le Marin not only has two good chandleries but good specialists. I bought a new aluminum French boom here at half the Trinidad price and little more than I would have paid in England, from a shop that specialized in rigging and stocked such major makes as Hood, Profurl and Harken. I also had a charge splitter for my electrical system fitted by a specialist shop. The kit was half the price of Trinidad and though the labor rates were more, the whole deal was cheaper and I had great confidence in the technical expertise of the staff.

Second-hand equipment is available through chandleries in Fort-de-France and Le Marin as well as through the notice board in Le Marin Marina. This usually has a wide range of gear advertised. Of the other islands I found good notice boards for used gear at Falmouth Harbour, Antigua and Rodney Bay, St Lucia but the best places for trade are St Martin and Trinidad. Both these places have a plethora of notice boards but better than that are the daily VHF radio nets which cover wanted and surplus gear. The St Martin net is good but the Trinidad one is better. Trinidad seems to have a more extensive yachting community now, with vessels coming and going to far-flung parts of the world and refitting accordingly. Sometimes the departure date comes before gear has been disposed of, and a little pile of "freebies" will be left on the hard. In St Martin the trade is relatively simple: you buy or sell. In Trinidad it is more complicated. Customs regulations forbid foreign vessels selling gear but allows "swap, barter or trade." If this involves a little bit of cash adjustment, that is a private matter between consenting yachties. As though to point to the ad hoc-ery of the rules concerning "swap, barter or trade," yachts will organize occasional boat jumbles in the yards when money very definitely changes hands. In all these places where yachts gather at anchor or ashore you will soon find people who are knowledgeable sources on what is being traded.

You may strike lucky and find the recently broken, vital part in whatever island you next land on, but most of the other islands can't be relied on to be systematically well stocked. The Virgins were quite good, but not as good as we would expect given the scale of their charter fleets. We were pleased to find that prices in the Virgins are not as high as elsewhere in the island chain.

Ventilation

In the tropics nothing trumps airconditoning. Units can be rented and installed when you are hooked up to the necessary shore power to run them. But once beyond the reach of a long wire, think of natural or low power ways to move air around.

One of the first things you might do to double your comfort is to double up on the number or size of the dorades on deck. If you do, remember to give them all protection bars. New dorade cowls are expensive anywhere but seem especially so in the islands.

Some boats also use a windscoop to funnel air down the forehatch. It works. We made one from a piece of light sailcloth and a broken sail batten.

We fitted small fans for added ventilation. We tried lots of types before we found the ones that made least noise or vibration and had two speeds. One small fan on double speed makes the aft cabin bearable quite quickly and even at the low speed would freeze us if left on through the night.

> G calls them bow-tie fans. The assistant in the shop had no idea what she meant but they really do look like a bow tie and you will know them when you see them.

In the saloon, where we needed to move more and hotter air, we positioned two fans opposing each other. The cross breeze makes all the difference.

Sun protection

The Caribbean has invented its own special sun cover—the bimini—to protect the cockpit while sailing. These can be designed and made locally, probably more cheaply than back home, and are not really wanted on a rough offshore passage across the ocean or down the eastern seaboard outside Cape Hatteras. If planning to stay in remote or dry locations build the covers to collect rainwater.

Sun protection for sails is essential here. This means covers or boom bags for standard mains and sacrificial u/v strips on roller sails. Make your covers easy to put on and off. You will be using them every time you reach an anchorage.

Varnish is something most boats learn to dispose of in the Tropics but if you have special brightwork or other finishes that will suffer from exposure to the sun, make covers for them too.

Personal care

I can think of three simple things to make your life here easier that might easily be overlooked.

- Bathing ladder—getting back on board must be easy. Make sure that you have the means of climbing back on board or lowering the ladder from the water, just in case you dive first and remember afterwards. Design it for elderly or out of condition non-sailors. Who else do you think will be visiting you next winter?
- Shower—it's an outdoor life. Shower on deck if you haven't got one below. Many boats use a pressure shower or sun shower on deck.
- Lee cloths—no one escapes sailing to windward and the distances and conditions mean that you might be doing the whole of a long passage on a single tack. The lee cloth is the only thing that will give you restful sleep.

Electricity generation

For most cruisers the quality of life afloat can probably best be measured by the availability of electrical equipment. Of course, what you need to generate depends on what amps you use, so you have to have some control over the big picture. You have the usual boaty needs of navigation and deck lights, GPS, sailing performance indicators, echo sounder and perhaps anchor winch, autohelm and radar. Below decks you will need to power internal lights, SSB, VHF and other radios, computer, television and video, refrigeration and freezer, water heater, water pumps, air-conditioning and watermaker. Then you may want to power or recharge a whole range of electric tools. This is not an exhaustive list, but it certainly far outstrips what we run.

The basic electrical generator on most yachts is the main engine, through its alternator or a belt drive. But the main engine is a large beast to run just to recover some amperes. Marine diesels are about 35% efficient. That is to say, they spend about 35% of their energy just keeping the engine cool and waste another 25% on noxious emissions. A 40hp or 60hp engine would be wasting kilowatts of power just to run a 90 ampere alternator. You may decide to install a second smaller diesel engine dedicated to running equipment and generating power. This gives you two diesel engines to look after instead of sailing, and you may not be putting either of them to work in a way which will prolong their lives.

Wind and solar generators produce much less power than a diesel motor but are quieter and cheaper to buy and run. Cruisers often have both. My preference is for solar. No moving parts and no sense of a jet plane landing on deck. See what electrical devices you can live without.

Clean diesel

Our boat had spent longer than us in the Caribbean and was suffering from years of bad diesel and fast breeding micro-organisms. The filters were covered in thick slimy, muddy stuff after only a few hours of running the engine and we were getting that dreadful "surge and death" syndrome that denotes clogged filters. We had the tanks cleaned in Trinidad and wondered at the varnish-like liquid that came out. It was better suited to sustaining strange life forms than igniting in our cylinders.

Dirty fuel is a major cause of engine problems after a year or two in the Caribbean. Clean fuel is essential and you should always buy from a good source and keep topped up. Finding a good source is not easy. We think we know that Trinidad and Martinique are good. We also run the diesel through a deck filter or Baja filter when filling tanks. It doesn't add much time to the filling and no one has yet objected.

Running fuel tanks low is a bad idea in these seas anyway, where downwind rolling or upwind slamming can shake up all the sediment in the tanks and suck it into the filters. We were lucky that after so many years of bad fuel our tanks were still shiny steel on the inside, and that all the muck could be sucked out.

We have thought about using additives but the feeling among those who have tried them, as well as among the local engineers, is that the additives can cause more problems than they solve and that their problems are more expensive to cure. Stick to the Baja filter, keep an eye on the water trap and change your filter elements frequently.

Outboards and dinghies

In the museum at Nelson's Dockyard, Antigua, is an early advertisement for the world renowned Seagull outboard engine captioned: "For sailors too weak to row ashore." No one rows ashore anymore, except us. The most common tender seen here is a RIB (rigid inflatable boat) with a big lump of outboard on its transom, whipping across the anchorage at six knots or more. Sometimes, for those of us who do have a rowing dinghy, the lost courtesy of those earlier days can cause uncharacteristic dinghy-rage.

I can recommend that you have a good dinghy with a powerful outboard. We don't. Yet. We still rely on a small inflatable with oars. This has many advantages. It takes up little deck space. It is so quick to inflate that we never travel with it either in tow or inflated on deck. It is a single handed job to launch or recover, without any need for mechanical aids. It is of so little interest to thieves that we could probably leave it at a bus stop and still find it waiting on our return. The snag is we miss a lot too. We don't dinghy around reefs for a spot of snorkeling. We usually have to anchor close to a jetty or beach to get ashore, when sometimes we'd rather be further off, in a quiet spot. On the very few occasions when we've had the use of a bigger dinghy and outboard we've felt very liberated, as well as more conventional.

The main drawback to the big dinghy and outboard is stowage. We briefly had a nine foot RIB and six horsepower outboard. Neither were easy to hoist on board and the RIB, even deflated, took up vital standing room under the boom. Make sure you have a good dinghy and outboard hoist. It needs to be quick and convenient enough so that you are willing to use it. In some anchorages it is the norm to hoist dinghy and engine out of the water each night for fear of theft. Often you will be hoisting as the hull is rolling badly to the swell or at speed to avoid the heavy wash of a boat coming by. This is no time to discover that the outboard is 10 pounds heavier than you can control.

Liferafts

I am of two minds about liferafts. I acknowledge that when the boat is sinking under me I hope to have one to hand; but I don't like the ones that just drift with the wind and current. This means all the ones sold to yachties. Here, in the Caribbean islands, you should probably arrange your sinking to take place on the windward side of an island, preferably close in. If you go down on the leeside, or even in one of the inter-island channels, the wind and current will whisk you westwards towards the American mainland before you've asked who packed the biscuits.

247

The aft gantry

The what? Before coming to the Caribbean you probably didn't know you needed an aft gantry. After you have sailed the length of the Caribbean and arrived in Trinidad you will know you do and what you want to put on it, and now you will be in just the right place to have one made. The stern of your yacht is not a source of aesthetic pleasure in its own right. It exists for the aft gantry.

- Aerials for SSB, VHF, telephone and television. Where did they all go before?
- Hoists for your dinghy and outboard.
- Solar panels where they don't get trodden on.
- Bimini or similar cover for sun protection.
- Steps for eyeballing your way through reefs.
- Radar radome for when you leave the Caribbean to go back to fog and mist.

Of course, our boat is a sweet sterned double ender with the added trauma of a mizzen boom. Built for beauty. We haven't figured out how to get an aft gantry up there.

Not hoist by your own petard

We don't have electrically driven running water nor powered sheet winches or hydraulically operated hatches. We don't even have a powered anchor winch. Not yet anyway. And there is something to be said for safety in this Luddite preference to do things by hand. We have heard too many stories of cruisers having to cut their way into their water tanks when their pumps or electrics fail.

Here is the dramatic story of the luxury motoryacht *Celestine*, sunk off Guadeloupe when on passage to Antigua early in 2003. One of *Celestine*'s engines caught fire and shut down. The fire spread rapidly and the skipper, not yet sure of the extent of the problem, decided to take his passengers and crew off in the RIB. This meant operating the hydraulic rams that launched the RIB. The AC generator was running but the breaker had tripped and *Celestine* lacked power. Fortunately the crew were able to manhandle the RIB over the side but the force they used damaged its steering so that it was impossible to drive. They were lucky, even so, because shortly after the RIB hit the water *Celestine* burst into flames. She sank only 25 minutes after the first engine shut itself off. With less muscle and determination the RIB might have still been sitting on its useless hydraulic rams when the ship burst into flames.

If it could happen to a luxury yacht it could certainly happen to us. That is why we have manual bilge pumps. We have a labor saving electric pump, too, of course, but we have it as first reserve.

Epilogue

Nightfall, and the warm air across the cockpit is soft and soothing. Somewhere ashore a pan side is playing. The music floats out gently to you, mingling with the sound of a long, low swell breaking on the beach. No lights from a hotel or village here. The moonlight reflects strangely white off the deserted beach.

Friends you last saw three islands ago are due to dinghy over for supper and the snapper you caught earlier today is grilling nicely on the Force Ten barbecue bolted to the aft guard rail.

You wonder if your friends are still planning to cross to Europe, as they were when you last saw them. Now there's an idea, you think, as the spirit of adventure mixes with the White Oak in your own recipe for rum punch. You raise your glass to the continuing dream of sailing, glad that you decided to go with its insistent message a few years ago. You have come a long way since then and seen a lot of places, made a lot of friends. The idea of buddy-boating across the Atlantic isn't such a bad one. After all, who was it who said that there isn't anything that two Americans can't do? Probably one of those damned Brits, being clever. Or ironic. You could do it now that you have so many off-shore miles under your keel.

You walk up to the foredeck. The anchor is where it should be. Three boats and you in this whole bay, and a million fireflies flickering in the trees. The deck barely moves to the gentle swell. Walking the deck seems more natural now than sitting at the wheel of a car. Your feet instinctively avoid the deck cleats and the lines. Your hand moves from rigging wire to guard rail. The old shipboard rules apply even at anchor, you tell yourself. One hand for the drink and one for yourself.

You hear the sound of oars. Your friends are too tuned to the peace here to disturb the night with a noisy outboard engine. Europe sounds a good trip to make. But not yet. There's a year or two exploring still to do here, in the bountiful Caribbean. You go back to the cockpit and add a little more rum to the punch.

Of course when Europe does seem to be coming closer you will need a good book to stir those dreams, help make those plans and finally decide when, where and how to leave for that trip to the Baltic or the Mediterranean or the wonderful drowned river valleys of northwest Spain. I can honestly say that the best book for you is *Atlantic Crossings: A Sailor's Guide to Europe and beyond*. I can honestly recommend it because I wrote it.

Appendix 1
Glossary of local terms

Aah rii all right? A common greeting as people pass you.

Chipping how Trinidadians road dance with their band at Carnival.

Carenage a common name for a coastal village or part of a harbor, presumably where old sailing ships could careen. In this near tideless sea where ships could not be left to dry out to have work done on their bottoms, they would be hauled over with lines from their masts.

J'Ouvert from the French *jour ouvert*, but pronounced *jouvay*. The opening day of Carnival. A particularly wild night, starting about 2 am and ending some time between dawn and mid morning. Participants wear rags or bags and cover themselves in oil, paint or mud.

Jump up any local dance.

Liming socializing; hanging out; just being in a group. How any Caribbean aspires to spend their time.

mas' from masquerade. To 'play mas' is to take part in a Carnival costume band.

mas' camp where the bands gather and you go to see them.

Ol' boys men of a certain age just hanging around talking.

Ol' talk sound and fury, signifying nothing. Just chatting by ol' boys when liming.

Pan a steel drum. Pan sides are steel bands. Pan yards are where they practice.

Pirogues a local launch. Some claim to still follow the style of the Carib Indians but now powered by outboard engine rather than sail or paddles. Look flimsy but beautiful and fast.

Slack rude, specifically as in the words of a rude calypso.

Whining "it how we dance" say the Trinis; "wow" say the visitors. A man moves his groin very closely onto his partner's buttocks in a dance more explicit than any scene from a Hollywood movie. Non-Trinis don't seem to have the pelvic flexibility nor the exuberance to manage good whining. "Where we've got joints and muscles, the Trinis must have wheels" (Mist McIntosh, published in *The Boca*).

Appendix 2

Measures of wind strength

The Beaufort scale of categorizing winds, developed to indicate appropriate sail setting in Britain's sailing warships, is still a very useful mind-set for sailors of modern yachts, even though today's onboard measuring instruments encourage the tendency to state exact wind speeds, and so push sailors and forecasters to work in knots. Quite often I am not interested in the exact speed of the wind but in its range. I'd rather know that it is a Force Five than that it is either 17 knots or 21 knots. If it's Force Five then it might rise to or gust up to a Force Six, and I know that I am comfortable with that. If it's 21–22 knots I don't know if it's at the top end of a Force Five or the bottom end of a Force Six. Force Six, in my experience, can rise to or gust up to Force Seven, and I'd like advance warning of that.

Frankly, I learn nothing from a forecast that tells me the wind will range from 15 to 20 knots, possibly 25. The sea state and the set of my sails will relate to the average wind speed rather than the top or bottom of the day's range.

The Beaufort scale

Force	Wind speed in knots	Name of wind force
0	< 1	Calm
1	1-3	Light air
2	4-6	Light breeze
3	7-10	Gentle breeze
4	11-16	Moderate breeze
5	17-21	Fresh breeze
6	22-27	Strong breeze
7	28-33	Near gale
8	34-40	Gale
9	41 -47	Strong gale
10	48-55	Storm
11	56-63	Violent storm
12	>64	Hurricane

The important thing to remember is that wind speed is less relevant than the wind pressure it produces, and the Beaufort scale deals with the significant steps in pressure changes for a sailing ship as the wind strength increases. The Beaufort scale also describes sea state, and this is often much more relevant than wind speed.

Beaufort took his scale up to Force Twelve and left it there. A practical man, why bother categorizing winds "which no canvas could withstand."

A scale dealing with the damage potential of hurricanes was developed in the 1970s by U.S. engineer Herbert Saffir, and the then director of the National Hurricane Center, Robert Simpson. I don't think Saffir and Simpson developed their scale for the benefit of those of us who go to sea in small yachts but to classify potential damage ashore. It relates wind speed, barometric pressure and storm surges.

Saffir-Simpson Scale

Name of feature	Wind strength in knots	Central barometric pressure	Tidal surge height
Tropical Depression	25—33		
Tropical Storms	34—63		
Category Hurricane—minimal	64—82	Above 980 mb	5 feet
Category 2 Hurricane—moderate	83—95	965 to 979 mb	8 feet
Category 3 Hurricane—extensive	96—112	945 to 964 mb	2 feet
Category 4 Hurricane—extreme	113—134	920 to 944 mb	8 feet
Category 5 Hurricane—catastrophic	>134	Below 920 mb	Over 18 feet

The Saffir-Simpson Scale rates tropical cyclones and hurricanes by maximum sustained wind. Gusts can bring much higher winds. Very few hurricanes reach the full ferocity of a catastrophic Category 5 but winds may gust at 50% more than the maximum for their category. Recently a new class of hurricane has been informally added. When Category 5 hurricanes blow at over 155 mph they are called super-hurricanes.

Index

Other titles of interest

Atlantic Crossings
A Sailor's Guide to Europe and Beyond

Les Weatheritt

"Reading *Atlantic Crossings* feels as though you have taken up with a seasoned captain who is taking care of all the details. Your only job is to follow his lead and cast off."
—*Ocean Navigator*

Desperate Voyage

John Caldwell

John Caldwell's harrowing account of finding himself stranded in Panama after World War II and setting out single-handed on a 9,000-mile journey aboard the 29-foot PAGAN to rejoin his wife in Sydney, Australia.
    "Could rank alongside the best thrillers for sheer irrepressibility of its hero . . . The book is utterly compelling."
—*Motor Boats Monthly*

Mary's Voyage
A Sequel to Desperate Voyage

Mary Caldwell
and *Matthew M. Douglas*

"Hard work, revolutions, and invasions do little to dampen Mary's zest for adventure and the couple's quest to build an island resort . . . a delightful tale and a home-spun glimpse into a Caribbean age gone by."
—*Cruising World*

Chance the Tide

Kenneth Mowbray

Taken from personal experience, Mowbray covers how to choose the right yacht, how to equip it properly, and provides valuable tips to make the trip down the Intracoastal Waterway and across the Gulf Stream to cruise the Bahamas all winter long.
    "A useful guide filled with sound advice for cruise lovers everywhere."
—*Midwest Book Review*

SHERIDAN HOUSE
America's Favorite Sailing Books
www.sheridanhouse.com

Other titles of interest

Piracy Today

John C. Payne

"Today, as in medieval times, travelers and businessmen are learning that after they set sail they'd better watch their back. *Piracy Today* will help them chart a safe course and remind them of what happens if they don't." —*The Wall Street Journal*

Doctor on Board

Dr. Jurgen Hauert

". . . a powerful survey for mariners who need a quick medical reference. From basic first aid to recognizing the symptoms of common and unusual illnesses and treating them aboard, as well as handling sailing-based injuries, this should be on board any sailing craft as a basic boater's reference while at sea." —*Bookwatch*

Yachtsman's Ten Language Dictionary
Third Edition

Barbara Webb & Cruising Association

Thoroughly revised and updated to cover all the subjects a boater might need, the third edition of this celebrated multilingual dictionary covers cruising terms in English, French, German, Dutch, Danish, Italian, Spanish, Portuguese, Turkish, and Greek. ". . . has kept pace with technology and cruising sailors' needs." —*SAIL*

Instant Weather Forecasting

Alan Watts

". . . has been a popular forecasting guide since its first printing in 1968. It features 24 color pictures of clouds (covering a variety of weather situations) and accompanying tables that can be analyzed to help determine potential weather events. The author is an avid sailor, and the book is intended to be particularly useful for the boating aficionado." —*Bulletin of the American Meteorological Society*

SHERIDAN HOUSE
America's Favorite Sailing Books
www.sheridanhouse.com

Other titles of interest

Essential Sailing Destinations

Adrian Morgan, Editor

Explores a wide range of sailing areas, including the Mediterranean, America's East Coast, Australasia and the Indian Ocean.

"The color photos are great and will definitely whet the appetite. But the text entries, which come from some of the world's best known boating writers, will make you even hungrier for adventure. . . . All you need is add water." *—Yachting*

Seasoned by Salt

A Voyage in Search of the Caribbean

Jerry L. Mashaw
and *Anne U. MacClintock*

"Read it for the story of a couple, deeply in love, who explore their relationship while cruising the Caribbean." *—Blue Water Sailing*

"Their adventures cover the highs and lows of what cruising is really like, combined with a lot of history on the areas they visit. Very entertaining."
—Latitudes & Attitudes

The Long Way

Bernard Moitessier

". . . there's no denying Moitessier's impact on bluewater sailing. This account of his most legendary exploit is a bible to ocean sailors with a metaphysical bent. His decision to quit the race and keep on sailing, in more ways than one, marks the point at which ocean racing and ocean cruising went their separate way." *—Cruising World*

SHERIDAN HOUSE
America's Favorite Sailing Books
www.sheridanhouse.com